PATHS CROSSED

Villains - Victims - Victors

Lessons Learned in the Line of Duty

by

Trooper

CLIF EDWARDS

PATHS CROSSED

Villains - Victims - Victors

Lessons Learned in the Line of Duty

by

Trooper

CLIF EDWARDS

Edited by Tyler Tichelaar

Published by
ShowMe Publishing, Michigan

Layout design and ebook creation by Stacey Willey
Globe Printing, Inc., Ishpeming, MI
www.globeprinting.net

ISBN No. 978-1481152419

Visit Clif at www.pathscrossed.info
for speaking engagements, email him at pathscrossed@ymail.com.

Dedicated

to the spouses and children of

police officers.

They did not choose the profession,

but loved the person who did,

and in doing so, bore an

untold burden.

Table of Content

FOREWORD

Michigan law requires troopers to be at least twenty-one years of age. By good fortune, I was sworn in as a state trooper on my twenty-first birthday. Few, if any, have celebrated this birthday in such a way. My training was extensive, experiences diverse, successes many, and I survived my mistakes.

Throughout my nearly twenty-seven year career, I kept notes and memories of my law enforcement journey. Since retirement, I have struggled with my "just the facts" police report style to craft an interesting book with meaning, absent the fluff and bluff.

Cop careers can be compared to fingerprints: none exactly the same, most pretty similar, and the majority lost to time. *Paths Crossed* is an accumulation of the villains, victims, and victors I encountered.

Occurring over the first half of my career, each chapter is a story that stands alone, but many are enriched by previous episodes. These accounts bring to light the reality, both personal and professional, of a police career. Embedded in these experiences are the many lessons learned during my evolution from rookie to veteran.

The Michigan State Police Academy instills immense pride in its troopers, undoubtedly reflected in this book. Even so, my mental list of the top ten police officers I proudly served with is comprised of many officers from other agencies.

My hope is that *Paths Crossed* will become a must read for persons considering law enforcement as a profession, be of immense interest to those curious about what a police career really entails, and offer endless moments of reflection for those who have experienced it.

These stories are true to the best of my recollection.

Clifton L. Edwards
February 1, 2013

Part A - The Calling
(Mid-1960s to August 1974)

1) Howie

Howard Stoker would never be eighteen. It was the first snow of autumn 1972 and "Howie," as friends called him, was home celebrating his eighteenth birthday a day early, with his mom and girlfriend. The Stoker family lived out in the country, and Howard's father was a truck driver, away on an overnight run.

Around 9 p.m., Howard noticed a car stuck in the ditch near his house and walked out to help. He found the steamy car occupied by a man and a woman. When the man rudely refused his assistance, Howard returned to his home and told his mother, who telephoned the information to the state police in Jackson.

The roads were slick with the season's first snow when Troopers William Connors and Barry Trombly began their twenty-eight minute drive. During that time, a nightmare was unfolding at the Stoker home.

A few minutes after his mother called the police, Howard answered a knock at the door. The woman he had seen in the car pleaded to be let in, saying that she was afraid of the man in the car, whom she said had a gun. Howard quickly motioned her in, then shut and locked the door. Assuming the protector role, he sent his mother, girlfriend, and the strange woman to the basement, assuming they would be safer there.

A second call was then placed to the police, pleading for them to hurry, only to be told that the snow slick roads prevented troopers from travelling faster than forty miles per hour.

Suddenly, the front door, which Howard thought he had locked, sprang open. Howard, a star football player, ran to push it shut, only to be shot dead by a bullet to his head.

Panicked or shocked by what he had done, the shooter turned and fled to the woods. Still hiding in the basement, the women waited, unsure of what they had heard until blood began dripping down the stairs. Howard's mother crept up the stairs. There she found her son's motionless body. She again called the state police. It was now an emergency.

Minutes passed slowly before the troopers finally reached the Stoker residence. They were met by Howard's mother, who sobbed, "My son is dead; my son is dead." Confirming her terror, troopers secured the scene and requested a tracking dog.

Trooper Richard Harms and his tracking dog, Thor II, responded. They tracked the killer in the darkness and well into the woods, and finally found him hiding under a fence crying, "Don't shoot; I give up." Finding no gun on the suspect, Trooper Harms had his dog conduct an article search of the area surrounding the arrest. In short order, Thor II located where the suspect had tossed the .38 special revolver, which was determined to be the murder weapon.

The murderer had been on parole when he killed Howard. He was eventually convicted of second-degree murder and returned to prison.

I never met Howard Stoker, but I like to say that I knew of him because he was a student and athlete at Grass Lake High, a rival school. On that dreadful night, December 1, 1972, both Howard and I were seventeen years old.

Until this tragedy, I had been intrigued with law enforcement as a career, but I believed it was too dangerous. This event caused me to realize that one's demise can come at any time and any place, which prompted me to consider law enforcement as my profession. I believed if something good could rise from something bad, not all that was lost was in vain. The murder of Howard Stoker served as my calling to a career in law enforcement, in which I would strive to do "something good."

Years later, I would work with Bill Connors, Barry Trombly, Richard Harms, and the detectives who handled this case. In fact, one of those detectives, Tim Ryan, selected me to serve as a district detective sergeant in 1989.

In 1992, I was the keynote speaker for the organization Parents of Murdered Children. I was invited to speak, because as a detective sergeant, I had recently solved a case involving the murder of a young man. I chose to use the murder of Howard Stoker, from twenty years earlier, to illustrate the disparity of our justice system.

When I had decided to check on the whereabouts of Howard's murderer, what I learned had turned my stomach. Having served his time in prison, Howard's murderer was free and living in Westland, MI.

The football field at Grass Lake High School is named in honor of Howard Stoker. As I prepared this book for publishing, I contacted his sister. An emotional telephone call ended with her expressing gratitude that her late brother was remembered.

My state police scrapbook begins with this article:

Athlete Shot in Home
Grass Lake
Youth Slain

BY FLOYD THOMS

Citizen ZPatriot Staff Writer

A Grass Lake High School football star, who would have been 18-years-old today, was shot and killed Friday night by a man who invaded the youth's home.

Dead is Howard R. Stoker Jr., 17, son of Mr. and Mrs. Howard R. Stoker St., 5751 Mt. Hope Rd., Waterloo Township.

Held in the Jackson County Jail on a charge of murder is James Leroy Jones, 42, of 1410 Atkinson, Detroit, a parolee from Southern Michigan Prison.

State police said the youth was shot once in the face with a handgun as he stood in the foyer of the home about 10 p.m. Police declined to say what caliber of gun was used.

Jones, who fled the scene on foot after the shooting, was tracked by the state police dog Thor II and was found lying under a barbedwire fence a mile and a half south of the Stoker home in

HOWARD R STOKER JR.

Compliments of *Jackson Citizen Patriot*

2) Influences

When I ponder my first impressions of law enforcement, I wrestle between my grandparents' next door neighbor, Sergeant Whan of the Missouri State Highway Patrol, and my father's criticisms of the police. As a young boy, I remember playing in the park across the street when Sergeant Whan parked his patrol car in front of his home. Probably like most boys, I was drawn to the patrol car and his uniform. Curiously, I approached him as he tidied up the car. Wearing his campaign style hat and smoking a pipe, he noticed me watching and knelt down and talked with me. He then showed me the inside of the cruiser, the police radio and how the shotgun was stowed. He spoke well of my grandparents and my dad, who had married their daughter. I was impressed.

When I told my dad of this meeting, he told me about Sergeant Whan catching him as a teenager riding a motorbike without a driver's license and another time writing him a ticket for having a loud exhaust. But the tone of these stories was not negative, unlike other comments he would have when we would pass a police car. It seemed apparent that he respected Sergeant Whan and felt that he had always dealt with him fairly. Perhaps these opposing perspectives made me neutral, so that later in life I would be unbiased in considering it as a career.

While police are often generational, I am the first of my clan to enter the profession. I was born in Missouri and my earliest memories originated there. My parents were born and reared there and my mother married my father at age seventeen, just ten days after graduating from high school. I was born sixteen months later, the first of three children.

Since I was born in early autumn, my parents enrolled me in school early rather than late. Slow to mature, I often found myself to be among the smallest and youngest in my class. My dad taught me to stand up to bullies and said if I did, they would leave me alone. Being little, and our moving frequently, allowed me to test his theory many times. I remember other boys being tormented by bullies, which would have been me had I not stood up to them. Standing up to them seldom meant a fight since they always seemed to take the path of least resistance. Woe met David Goodnight who did not stand up to Johnny Russell. Later in the book, I will again quote Eddie Rickenbacker who said "There can be no courage without fear." The anticipation of confronting the bully was fearful but Dad proved right. Of the many things my dad taught me, this was a valued lesson.

While my parents' beginning was poor, their hard work and frugal ways were advancing them to middle class. The move to Michigan when I was thirteen years old was tremendously exciting.

While cultured to be a home maker, my mother was not content to be a stay-at-home wife/mother, which seems to have been a sign of the times. But as my dad and her children struggled with her transition, she was obviously happier and fulfilled in the dual role of mother and professional. She eventually became very successful in real estate. Looking back, I realize my mother's modeling of self-discipline contributed significantly to the person I became.

During my influential preteen years, my father, while tucking my brother and me into bed, would instill values and principles with stories that reinforced honesty, responsibility, and pride in name. He told us that no Edwards had ever been in jail, so wherever we went, we could hold our heads high. To this day when I hear Jim Croce's song "I've Got a Name," I remember those bedtime talks. As I approached puberty, my father talked to me about girls and told me never to kiss and tell. He preached the use of condoms and made us promise God and self always to use them.

When I was fifteen years old, I remember a time when the local police officer stopped me as I pulled into our driveway riding a small dirt bike on the road without having a driver's license or a license plate. I suppose it was reminiscent of when Sergeant Whan had stopped my dad when he was a teenager. My dad came out and challenged Officer Burt Ostrander for his actions and the officer did not cite me. Thinking about it today, I am conflicted. I was in the wrong, the officer was right and my dad was disrespectful to him. Perhaps there was something else going on that I didn't know. Over the years, I have learned the importance of counseling a parent, absent a family audience.

My parents seemed to measure success financially and that may have been their biggest misgiving when I considered law enforcement as a career. While dad had always been critical of the work ethic of government employees and specifically of the police, he did not discourage me from pursuing it. Years later when I was a Michigan State Police Officer, I would be haunted by my father's police criticisms. It seemed he was always on my shoulder, judging my actions, and I wanted to make him proud. In a good way, it would motivate me to prove him wrong.

In the police academy, we were taught that officers live an average of two to four years after they retire. Bad hours, bad food, and a sedentary lifestyle sprinkled with adrenaline dumps were not advantageous for longevity. Sergeant Whan gave meaning to that. As a Missouri State Highway Patrolman, he had enjoyed a healthy life, but soon after he retired he fell dead.

In 1987, long after Sergeant Whan had died, I was attending sergeant training at the Michigan State Police Academy in Lansing. One evening, while browsing in the departmental library, I discovered a collection of yearbooks from various state agencies. Within the covers of the 1962 edition of the Missouri State Highway Patrol, I discovered a picture of Sergeant Whan. As I peered into his eyes beneath the Smoky Bear hat he was wearing, I realized he had first sparked my interest to be a police officer.

3) Rene

As a teenager, I got a job at Rene's Donut Shop in the Irish Hills of southeast Michigan. In the late 1960s and early 1970s, the Irish Hills was a popular tourist destination for people living in the Detroit metropolitan area. Attractions included a state park, numerous lakes, and the proverbial tourist traps, which created abundant summer jobs for the local high school kids.

Rene, the donut shop's owner, always paid about a dime more per hour than the going rate and seemed to hire pretty girls, which probably attracted more boy applicants. This formula produced a deep pool from which he selected his employees.

To keep his teenage workforce on task, Rene had the gals work days selling donuts while the guys worked nights making donuts. For a 12 x 60 foot trailer, Rene's Donut Shop did an amazing amount of business in the summer.

Because cops would stop for coffee and donuts, Rene became acquainted with troopers from the Clinton Post and got the notion that he wanted to pursue a career in the Michigan State Police (MSP). Back then, you couldn't be over thirty-two years old when you joined because of mandatory retirement at age fifty-seven, and it took twenty-five years of service to make retirement. Rene, who was nearing age thirty-two, appeared to be a good candidate except for a couple of minor traffic tickets, which he was able to get expunged from his driving record.

Rene succeeded in beating the age deadline by receiving a coveted invitation to the next recruit school. As if to strengthen his resolve, Rene told me there was no way he would drop out of the training. Back then, dropping out was a big concern since only about 50 percent of those who started recruit school graduated. Recruit school was often compared to Marine Corps boot camp, but was perhaps tougher because you could quit and the instructors were constantly encouraging you to do so—they only wanted candidates who were passionate about being troopers.

Prior to starting the academy, Rene confided to me his fear of the water, which stemmed from his sister's drowning. His concern was legitimate because recruit training included the infamous death swim. To my knowledge, the MSP was the only academy that required its recruits to complete water life-saving training, which often included the recruit sucking in pool water. For those who haven't experienced it, even a drop of water seems like a lot in the lungs. The department's justification for such training was that Michigan was the Great Lakes State so a person was never more than seven miles from a body of water.

However, I think the department's motives went beyond water survival and rescue. I think they used one of man's innate fears—water—as a venue to test things such as desire, perseverance, and commitment. Nevertheless, Rene went for it.

After a couple of weeks, Rene quit recruit school. He came home without excuses or bitterness and returned to his donut shop. But his failed quest increased my sense of intrigue with the Michigan State Police and the challenge of its training. This curiosity prompted me to pump Rene for information. He compared a man to a chain; every chain has its weakest link, and the MSP recruit school was designed to test each link and persecute the weakest. For Rene, swimming was the weakest link of his chain.

Rene told me not to be fooled by the physical fitness schedule, which posted only ten pushups daily during the first week of training. He explained that each pushup might take two minutes and often the physical training instructor would lose count at nine and have to start over. He advised me, that if I ever went to the academy, to sew a towel pad in the back of my gray sweats to prevent bleeding caused by abrasions from endless leg lifts and sit-ups in a gravel parking lot.

When my calling to the Michigan State Police came with the murder of Howard Stoker, Rene's advice would cause me to examine carefully my own chain, and strive to strengthen all its links.

4) Wayward

> *"What people are ashamed of usually makes a good story."*
> — F. Scott Fitzgerald

I am tempted not to tell of the stunts I pulled as a teenager. I'm not proud of them, and I've wondered how my life would have been different had I not gotten away with these antics.

My first car was a 1964 Pontiac Tempest station wagon, a six-cylinder with a manual three speed shifter on the column. I had been working since age thirteen and had saved the $200 to pay cash for it some three months before turning sixteen. That summer, I probably put a hundred miles on the car just going up and down our gravel driveway. Like most, getting my driver's license on my birthday was a huge step toward independence.

When deer season rolled around that November, I was headstrong about going hunting with friends in the Upper Peninsula (U.P.) of Michigan. I planned to go whether or not my dad gave me permission, but he consented. It was my car and I had paid every nickel for it.

I travelled to the U.P. with a good friend and two other guys who were merely acquaintances. Although we took my car, at sixteen years of age, I was the youngest of the group by a year or two. While all of us were underage, we had a lot of booze stowed to take with us.

I was stunned to discover that at every stop we made, these acquaintances were shoplifting. When we got to the U.P., we stayed in an old abandoned farmhouse owned by my friend's dad. The party was on! I'll never forget the eight-track audiotape of Derek and the Dominos playing "Layla" over and over again.

One day, my friend and I went hunting in the woods with our rifles. We had not been drinking. We split up, agreeing to meet back at the car at a specific time. While hunting, I walked by a brush pile where I saw a black pelted animal, perhaps a skunk, running down a log. I drew a bead on it and was beginning to squeeze the trigger when my friend stood up. He had long black hair.

Some years later, I told my dad that he shouldn't have allowed me to go on that trip. He said he knew that, but he had sensed that I would go with or without his permission. He was probably right, but his response surprised me since I had always perceived him as such a disciplinarian. I guess he had been choosing his battles. I have learned that rearing teenagers is challenging, but I never would have allowed either of my sons to take such a trip. Perhaps parents and society have become more protective, or maybe my career prompted me to be.

That spring, I sold my Pontiac and bought a Yamaha 250 Enduro motorcycle. In my eyes, you couldn't get much cooler than that. One evening in May, I had a big disagreement with my parents—over something I can't even remember—so I decided to move out. I packed my motorcycle with my tent and gear and moved to Hayes State Park, just a couple of miles away. It was early spring, and I was the only camper there.

Long after dark, I was awakened by a loud pickup truck idling through the campground. It stopped in front of my campsite, and as I heard its door open, I thought with a shiver, "This could be a problem!"

A few moments passed before I heard a low gruff voice say, "Hey, you in the tent, give me all your money!" I was scared to death and didn't want to see his face because I didn't want him to have a reason to kill me. So I held my billfold open, outside the tent door, and he took all of my money, a five-dollar bill.

After the pickup left and a few minutes had passed, I thought it was safe to leave. Under the influence of adrenaline, I quickly dressed, struggling with my tight blue jeans in the damp chilly night air. Abandoning camp, I kick-started the Yamaha and raced home to my dad. I rode that cycle right up beside the sliding glass door of his bedroom and yelled, "Dad, I've been robbed."

My dad and I got in my mom's 1965 red Volkswagen Beetle and spent the night driving around hunting for that loud pickup. That incident made me realize things weren't so bad at home so I decided to move back. Just before dawn, we reported the robbery to the state police, but they never solved it, or did they?

Some seventeen years later, I was a detective sergeant at the Jackson Post and worked a case where I arrested a man a couple of years older than me. It had been years since I had thought about being robbed, but the moment I heard his voice, it all came back.

This prompted me to look into his background. I learned that at the time I was robbed, he had lived in a nearby community and been involved in a lot of similar incidents. I thought, *even if he admitted to robbing me, the statute of limitations would preclude any legal action and even to mention it might enable his defense attorney to suggest bias in the case where I was prosecuting him,* so I said nothing and am left to wonder, *could it be?*

My next car would be a 1965 Plymouth Barracuda, a V-8 with red leather bucket seats. It would top out about 110 mph, not bad for a small V-8 engine. That fall, my parents went on a trip; they had an elderly woman, whom we called Grandma Russell, stay with us. One evening, some of my brother's friends stopped by and he left with them in their car. I suspected he was headed for trouble so I decided to play the role of dad.

They were headed for Onsted, and there were two likely ways to get there. I decided to head them off at the pass, M-50 and Onsted Highway, so I raced to that spot. When I steered the Barracuda out of what we called "Deadman's Curve," in what I later learned was a four-wheel drift, the speedometer showed 70 mph. Guess what? I met a Lenawee County Sheriff patrol. Lucky for me, back then the sheriff's patrol drove station wagons that served as both patrol vehicles and ambulances. As they passed me, I glanced in my rearview mirror to see their brake lights come on, so I pressed the accelerator to the floor. About a mile down the road, I made a quick left turn down Onsted Highway, went a short distance, extinguished the lights, and pulled down a private road into a residential area and parked among several cars.

As I lay down in the seat, the patrol car went roaring by. Somehow, I sensed they would be back so I held tight. Sure enough, a few minutes later, they came back, shining the spotlight here and there, but they didn't see me.

When they were out of sight, I continued to Onsted and hid my car in my girlfriend's garage. Her dad let me drive his car home since I figured the police would be looking for mine. Oh yeah—my brother didn't get in any trouble that night.

Close calls! Had the worm turned the other way, I'm sure my life would have been much different. I like to think I later gave back what I got away with.

5) Legion

Chuck Redding was a respected principal who influenced many lives. He helped to guide me, and later my sons, through high school. When I was in high school, he had a military type haircut and would make fun of my long curly hair, which resembled an Afro. Years later, when I would be checking on my boys at the high school and sporting my own military haircut, I would make fun of Chuck Redding's then long hair. I retired from the Michigan State Police before he retired from Onsted Community Schools. Neither of us had much hair when that time came.

In the spring of 1973, I learned that Principal Redding had asked Randy, a fellow student, whether he was interested in going to the week-long Student Trooper Program sponsored by the American Legion at the Michigan State Police Academy. Randy was athletic, a bully, and often in or on the edge of trouble. I was surprised that Randy had been asked and surmised that the principal probably hoped it might straighten Randy out. Fortunately for me, Randy declined and I made my interest known. By default, I was recommended by Principal Redding to the American Legion.

Getting to attend the American Legion Student Trooper Program proved to be a decision point. I applied, was accepted, and arrived to the program in my 1965 Plymouth Barracuda. At that time, the Michigan State Police headquarters and academy were located on the edge of Michigan State University in East Lansing. To make the week even more meaningful, there was a trooper recruit school in progress. The student troopers were housed in Mapes Hall, two students to a room, while the trooper recruits primarily existed in a small gymnasium where they did nearly everything: had class, slept in bunk beds, and practiced defensive tactics.

In the early morning light, we went to the parking lot for our physical training (PT) after the recruits had begun theirs. We ended our PT before the recruits were done. I vividly remember Sergeant Ken Casperson, the PT instructor, calling off, "1-1, 1-2, 1-3" and so on to the various calisthenics as recruits tried not to moan.

The week was filled with interesting classes on firearms, law, first aid, military drill, and defensive tactics while we got glimpses of the recruits going to and from class. I was awed by the intense discipline they displayed with their crew cut hair, spit-shined shoes, marching, and eyes locked straight ahead. My observations confirmed the stories Rene had told me about recruit school. That Tuesday night, I called home to tell my parents I would pursue my calling to law enforcement with the Michigan State Police.

During that week, Sergeant Casperson confronted me in the hallway and made a sarcastic remark about the length of my long curly hair, which I responded to in a smart aleck way. Luckily, I was a student trooper and not a recruit.

Years later, after I became a member of the state police, Ken Casperson would be my commanding officer and friend. And much later, I would be an instructor for his son when he was a recruit in the Michigan State Police Academy.

Mid-week, the instructors advised us to select a class orator who would present a three-minute speech at the dinner graduation on Friday. As when I had been elected sophomore class president, I was now surprised when my classmates elected me. When I was a boy, my dad had told me how powerful stage fright could be, but as class president, I had found public speaking to be invigorating so I gladly accepted the assignment. All of my spare time was then devoted to writing my speech, which had to be approved by our lead instructor, and then I had to practice, practice, and practice some more to foil any stage fright. I was proud of my presentation.

That week's experiences provided me insight that would better prepare me for the challenge of becoming a state trooper. During that time, I learned that the department was planning a Service Officer recruit school for the next year; applicants would have to be eighteen to twenty years old. I obtained a civil service application and mailed it when I turned eighteen that September.

6) College

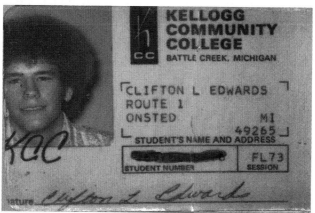

I did not apply myself in high school and my grades reflected it. While my participation in high school wrestling and cross-country would aid me with the physical challenges of recruit school, I needed to demonstrate my academic potential in college.

My high school sweetheart, Deb, and I wanted to stay close so we chose to go to the same school, Kellogg Community College in Battle Creek. She enrolled in a legal secretary curriculum and I in criminal justice. We broke up during that first year. At that time, the legal drinking age was eighteen, which I turned a month after classes started. Being allowed to drink, along with having my own car, apartment, and a part-time job made me feel pretty independent, and I liked it.

I qualified for a government grant called the Law Enforcement Education Program (LEEP), which was intended to increase the professionalism of law enforcement through education. So between the grant, my own money, and money loaned to me by my parents, I was financially solvent.

After moving into a one bedroom apartment, I went for a drive in my 1970 Dodge Duster in the big city of Battle Creek, cereal capital of the world. I hadn't gotten very far when I ran a stop sign and nearly got t-boned by a Battle Creek City Police car. I had my Michigan State Police shoulder patch, which we had been given at the American Legion Student Trooper School, sitting on the dashboard, but the officer didn't seem too impressed. Off to college to be a state trooper, I had earned my first traffic citation before classes had even started.

Remembering that Rene had dropped out of the academy because of swimming, I was not content with just having my American Red Cross Senior Life Saving Certificate, so I enrolled in Water Safety Instructor (W.S.I.) training. This class would better prepare me for the challenges that awaited me in the "training tank" of the state police academy.

While at college, I got a part-time job in loss-prevention (otherwise known as catching shoplifters) at Shopper's Fair, a chain store that would later go bankrupt. With my afro hair and army fatigue jacket, I did not look like someone designated to catch shoplifters. Sitting behind a two-way mirror or walking the floor surreptitiously, I began my study of human nature, aspiring to predict behavior.

Finally! The first bust came when I observed a male, about my age, conceal a pair of binoculars under his coat and head out the door. I followed him outside and announced my authority and intent to arrest him.

With that, he dropped the merchandise and my first real foot race was on!

Through the parking lot, I dodged cars across five lanes of busy traffic. Three blocks later, and feeling I could not suck in enough air after our chase, I caught him. As he tried to pull something from his pocket, I wrestled his arms behind his back and got him handcuffed. When I checked for what he had so frantically tried to get, I found a knife!

As I gasped to catch my breath before escorting the now handcuffed suspect back to the store, I vowed to myself never to be out of shape again. That lesson and promise would pay huge dividends in the years to come.

Another time, I recognized who I thought was the most beautiful girl at college shopping in the store. She did not know me, and the reason I watched her had nothing to do with her acting suspiciously. So, when she concealed two pair of panties in her mittens, I was shocked. When she left the store, I apprehended her. Sadly, she now knew who I was.

To my delight, it was the policy of Shopper's Fair to call troopers from the Battle Creek Post to handle our shoplifting arrests. This gave me an opportunity to meet many of them. One night, after troopers had departed with an arrest I had made, I received a telephone call from the sergeant at the Battle Creek Post. He told me the troopers had been impressed with my demeanor and wondered whether I had considered pursuing a career with the Michigan State Police. That comment was inspiring beyond words!

While at college, I took the civil service examination for the upcoming service officer school. A Battle Creek trooper named Newton Jerome was in a couple of my college classes, so I came to know him and shared with him my goal to be a trooper. He worked midnights and invited me to ride patrol with him some time. He told me he was breaking in a cub (probationary trooper) named Dave Haire. What I witnessed from the backseat of that patrol car was a real eye opener—the many skills, techniques, and tactics to a patrol, and how troopers were always looking beyond the driver's license and ticket for what I would later learn to be the lure of "the big arrest in the sky."

Years after college, when I was a trooper and dog handler at the Ypsilanti Post, Dave Haire was a trooper at the bordering Northville Post. It was a canine training day, and I was training with some other dog handlers in the Northville Post area. At lunchtime, we stopped at a restaurant sandwiched between the road and railroad tracks. As we dined, we observed a blue goose (MSP patrol car) scream north, red light flashing and siren blaring. After a set of railroad cars slowly rolled south, that same blue goose went screaming by the restaurant, now going south. Was the trooper crazy?

We later learned that some railroad cars had broken loose and were being pulled down the track by gravity. They collided with an automobile at a railroad crossing and were pushing it and its occupants down the tracks. Trooper Dave Haire was in that screaming blue goose, and he was too late in his first attempt to intercept the train. His second attempt got him in position to jump aboard the runaway train, set the brake, and avert a rolling catastrophe, undoubtedly saving lives. I don't know where he learned that skill, but it definitely wasn't taught in my academy. Trooper Dave Haire received a distinguished award for his actions and the incident was even reported in the *New York Times.* (Query "Michigan Trooper Takes On Runaway Train" on the Internet for article.)

I loved college and my grades showed it. I had goals and I recognized that these classes would help me achieve them. I learned to study, something I had never done before. I surprised my parents when my name appeared on the Dean's list with High Honors. I hoped it would demonstrate to the Michigan State Police that I could succeed in the academic portions of the academy.

7) Lifeguard

1974 image of author at Hayes State Park

My parents lived by Hayes State Park, a good place to look for "chicks" in the summer. Two summers prior to going to college, a friend and I met a couple of girls while working at Parkview Market, and they invited us to their campsite after work. The challenge was that the State Park did not allow visitors after 10:00 p.m., the time we got off work. I didn't think it would be a problem because I knew the back trail in and had a Yamaha 250 Enduro. It wasn't a problem until Ranger Kowalski jumped out from behind a tree and blinded us with his flashlight. That stunt earned me a ticket. What was I thinking?

After my first year of college, I applied for the position of lifeguard at Hayes State Park. Ranger Kowalski either had a poor memory, didn't hold grudges, or no one else applied, because I got the job. Ah, my first state paycheck.

While I did pull a few kids out of the water who got in over their heads, there were no heroic saves. I made a few citizen arrests for theft and provided first aid. One of my more vivid memories begins with my notice of a loose knit circle of men all peering over each other's shoulders at something. Just as when one person looks up, everyone has to look up to see what he is looking at, I had to look too. With a lot of looking going on, I observed a pretty young woman sunbathing topless. Duty called and I had to kneel down beside her to tell her such public exposure was prohibited. That wasn't a crowd pleaser, but it did provide me a closer look.

Another time, a visitor contacted me and pointed to a teenage male who was walking into a bathroom; the teenager had just stolen the visitor's billfold. I entered the bathroom and saw the young man rifling through the billfold. When he saw me, he took off running toward Wamplers Lake. I was in hot pursuit. He ran into the lake and took off swimming; then I was in wet pursuit. Didn't he know I was a lifeguard? In short order, he winded himself and surrendered. I held him in custody until Trooper Cliff Lambright of the Clinton Post came and arrested the scofflaw.

One of the seasonal rangers at the state park was a recently retired Detroit police detective. I volunteered my time to ride patrol with him at night to hear his war stories. I wondered why he would leave such an important job to work part-time as a park ranger, a question that would not be answered for me until some twenty-seven years later.

During the time I was a lifeguard, the state police were completing their review of me as an applicant. Having scored well on the civil service examination and passed the physical agility test, the next phase of the selection process for the upcoming service officer recruit school was a background investigation. Part of the background investigation is a home visit and interview, which was conducted by Trooper David Luhmann. When he asked whether I had ever used any illegal drugs, I must admit I thought about lying, but I didn't. I revealed that I had smoked marijuana once in high school and hoped that would not "cancel my ticket."

Once the background investigation was complete, the final phase of the selection process was conducted at departmental headquarters. There, a thorough physical examination was completed and a stressful interview before an oral board was conducted. The panel quizzed me on my past, present, and perceived future, and on biases and prejudices, while incorporating an array of hypothetical situations. While the physical was a pass-fail, the interview influenced my final score for selection.

Back then, you had to be at least 5'9" and weigh at least 150 pounds. I knew I was going to be close on the weight, so I practiced self-induced constipation. On the scheduled date, I traveled to East Lansing a couple of hours early where I went to an ice cream shop and downed three banana splits. Later that day at the physical examination, I weighed in at exactly 150 pounds.

I was told that I had passed everything but the hearing test. I couldn't believe it! I remember thinking about trying to bribe the civilian tester but thought better of it. I was told to go home and get an appointment with an ear specialist to see whether the problem was permanent or something temporary, like wax or water.

A few days later, before I would see the ear doctor, I received a telephone call from Lieutenant Ritchie informing me that the department hearing standard had been relaxed; it had been determined to be in excess of normal, and upon applying the new standard, I had passed. The days that followed found me anxiously checking the mail for the coveted invitation to the Service Officer Recruit School.

Part B – Service Trooper
(August 1974 to May 1976)

Badge issued to service officers

8) Hired

The department was never sure whether our title was Service Trooper, as appeared on our identification, or Service Officer, which appeared on our uniforms. So, as this story unfolds, do not let the difference confuse you as it did us.

The day the mailman brought my invitation to the Service Trooper Recruit School was a life-changing moment for me. The letter instructed me that I was to begin August 12, 1974, and it included a list of thirteen things to bring: a one-inch black belt, athletic supporter, white T-shirts, black paste shoe polish, white gym shoes, shower thongs, toiletries, black socks, two gray sweat-suits, three khaki pants, three khaki shirts, two white boxer-type gym shorts, and a black boxer-type swimsuit. The invitation warned me to bring little else because storage space was very limited, and it listed what the department would provide. Lastly, it directed me to have a short conservative haircut.

To be prepared, based on Rene's suggestions and my own observations at the American Legion Student Trooper School, I had been doing a lot of running and calisthenics. I celebrated the invitation by doing some hard slalom waterskiing on Sand Lake. Trying to make a personal record jump off the wake, I wiped out hard, hurting my ribs. This injury would pain me throughout training.

During this era, the Federal Government began applying affirmative action pressure to hire minorities, but not yet females. The Service Trooper Recruit School was the first and last of its kind, at least for the twentieth century. As I understood it, the school was designed to recruit qualified minorities and had been the brainchild of then Captain George Halverson, who would later become the director of the Michigan State Police. One day, Captain Halverson would give me one of my best gifts ever, trooper badge #854, when he administered my sworn oath of office on my twenty-first birthday. Years later, when my oldest son, Trevor, graduated from the American Legion Student Trooper Program, now retired Colonel George Halverson would be the keynote speaker. He died from cancer shortly thereafter. The Michigan State Police benefited greatly from his service.

Recruiters were only able to produce four minority candidates: two African Americans, one Native American, and one Hispanic American. But to make a recruit school worthwhile, about fifty candidates were needed, so they back-filled with guys like me, from the "unprotected" class otherwise known as white males. Of these four males from the protected classes, only two completed probation. So, by its objective to recruit minorities, the school was a failure. But for me, it got my foot in the door at age eighteen with only one-year of college under my belt.

The training was like a trooper recruit school, but abbreviated, being only four weeks long. It was very intense, but I had been preparing for some time and felt ready. I would attend the last recruit school held at the old academy, which was at departmental headquarters and across the street from Michigan State University.

When we reported that Sunday evening, the receptionist showed us to the gymnasium, above the "training tank"—state police speak for swimming pool. The gymnasium contained several bunk beds. Early arrivals usually chose the bottom bunk. The next day, bunks would be assigned in alphabetical order—no switching.

This old gym would be about 80 percent of our world for the next month. It was divided into half bunk beds and half student desks, with wrestling mats rolled up on the sides. When defensive tactics class started, we pushed desks and bunks together and rolled out the mats. There was a bathroom attached that consisted of a four-head shared shower, a toilet, two urinals, and two sinks with mirrors. In the morning after physical training (PT) and before inspection, fifty guys had about fifteen minutes to shower and shave. And while this environment built teamwork, when one recruit got sick, the rest usually followed.

That first Monday morning at orientation, our civilian life ended. We were told what would be expected tomorrow, starting at 5:45 a.m. We were issued belts, flat folding hats, pens, notebooks, and shoes. I was self-conscious about having only size 8½ feet so I told them to issue me size 9. I soon learned that oversized shoes become very uncomfortable during military drill!

Monday evening, about half us got a trip to the barbershop, which seemed to stay open late just for us. While I had cut my hair pretty short, I should have known better than to show up with any hair. It took me awhile to get used to feeling the wind blow over my ears and freshly bald head. Years later, I grew my hair long to work undercover and had to get used to not feeling the wind. My next tour of duty undercover would find me bald. Ah, the price of wisdom.

We did PT in the predawn darkness on a gravel-littered blacktop parking lot. I was glad I had taken Rene's advice and had my mom sew pads in the back of my gray sweats because while others bled through from endless sit-ups and leg lifts, I didn't. As we lay on our backs and did leg lifts, I tried to escape the pain by gazing at the stars and fantasizing about women. It didn't work!

All my swim training paid off in a way I had not anticipated. We were only in the second or third class when the ankle of a fellow classmate, Gary Cuperus, came between my left little toe and the toe next to it, nearly tearing the little toe off. I continued the class like nothing had happened. At the end of class, we all stood at attention on the wet deck to await dismissal when I caught hell for having my left foot in a pool of blood.

One of the instructors, Trooper Berry Beck, drove me to the hospital where it took several stitches to secure my little toe back to my foot. On the way there, he told me that the Recruit School Commander could send me home if I couldn't participate in fitness activities. The doctor's orders prohibited me from swimming until the stitches were out, but they didn't say anything about calisthenics and running. Fortunately, the notorious "death swim" was not part of the Service Officer training curriculum because I am sure they would not have allowed me to miss it. I suspect they would have sent me home had I not been a Lifeguard and Water Safety Instructor.

While I was being treated at Sparrow Hospital in Lansing, Trooper Beck introduced me to retired Major Daniel C. Myre, who was working there in security. Trooper Beck told me that when Major Myre retired, he was in charge of all the detectives in the State Police. One of the most famous investigations he had led was into a string of coed murders that occurred in the greater Ann Arbor area. That task force level investigation led to the arrest and conviction of John Norman Collins, a story told in Edward Keyes' book *The Michigan Murders*.

Again, I thought, *Why would a person with such an important job retire to provide hospital security?* I would not know that answer until I was forty-five years old. Years later when I prepared for the detective sergeant test, I read a training manual on death investigation that Major Daniel C. Myre had authored titled *Detectives vs. Death.*

During our predawn runs, the PT instructor would lead us as a group down the streets of Michigan State University. A blue goose (patrol car), with red light activated, would follow to prevent us from being run over from behind. The PT instructor would lead us in chants! We were told that the students in the dormitories had better complain about our noise or else we would have to run further the next day!

As the stress of the training wore on, fellow recruits quit. Most I never saw again. As the end neared, I was honored that my classmates voted me Class Orator for graduation, just like when I completed the American Legion Student Trooper program.

On the day of graduation, I decided not to shave until noon so I would look as fresh as possible at the afternoon graduation exercises. About 10:00 a.m., Sergeant William Parviainen called me out of class. I had no idea why. He led me to the departmental photographer and told me I was to be the model in the official orders for the proper wearing of the Service Officer uniform. I told him why I had not shaved. He said, "It better not show in the pictures."

UNIFORMS FOR SERVICE TROOPERS

Winter Uniform
(Jacket)

Winter Uniform
(Parka)

Winter Uniform
(Less Jacket or Parka)

Summer Uniform

The weekend before graduation, I arranged purchase of an almost new 1974 Chevrolet Camaro with a 350 V8, dual exhaust, and a 4 barrel carburetor. My brother gladly accepted delivery of it that week and drove it and my date, a girl of Swedish descent I had met while being a lifeguard, to graduation. I cannot put into words how I felt that afternoon after being class orator at graduation and then driving my new car with my girlfriend. My brother rode home with our parents. It was another day not to be forgotten.

Eight troopers cited

Eight local State Police officers have been cited for outstanding service.

They are among 30 state policemen and six civilians honored by the Board of Awards at East Lansing.

Unit citations went to: Stanley D. Black, John E. Behnke, Lyle R. Blanksvard, David W. Service, Douglas C. Lee and Barry A. Trombly, all of Jackson.

The six were honored for catching a disturbed youth without harm in a family trouble call last March. The youth had threatened his family, forced them from the house and shot at a relative and police officers.

Troopers John P. Fatchett and Gary J. McDonald, both of Jackson, received honorable mention. They apprehended without harm a suicide-inclined person who planned to shoot at a police officer, expecting that a companion officer would shoot him, police said.

Meanwhile, four men have been assigned as service troopers to the Jackson State Police Post.

Clifton L. Edwards of Onsted was class orator of the 46-member graduating class. He will be assigned to Jackson along with Richard B. Northrup, of Howell; Daniel G. Beckwith, Lansing; and Gary R. Hough, Grand Ledge.

Following satisfactory service, these officers, who range in age from 17 to 20 years, will become eligible for regular trooper training when they reach 21 years of age.

Their duties include clerical and other non-law enforcement-type duties at posts, districts or other department operations. Their uniforms are the same as those for regular troopers except for insignia and other emblem material.

The State Police service trooper position replaces the cadet position which started in 1968.

EDWARDS   NORTHRUP

BECKWITH

HOUGH

First Assignment September 9, 1974 - Compliments of *Jackson Citizen Patriot*

I was thrilled to be one of four Service Officers assigned to the Jackson Post since it was the closest post to my home that received Service Officers. We learned that when reporting for duty, officers briefed themselves by reviewing the complaint book, radio log, and current materials book.

Included in the current materials book were retirement postings that often included photographs of officers at the onset and conclusions of their careers. I was shocked by how much twenty-five years had aged them and was sure it wouldn't happen to me.

9) Vest

On December 5, 1974, Troopers Forreider and McMasters were working midnights out of the Alpena Post. They were doing what troopers do, hunting criminals. About 3:00 a.m., they spotted a car with three white males in the front seat and no license plate light, giving them a legal reason to make a patrol stop. One can only guess how much crime is thwarted by aggressive patrols of this nature.

Unknown to these troopers was that Michigan State Police Detectives suspected these guys of being burglars. Earlier that evening, they had terminated a surveillance of these same three men in the Houghton Lake area.

After pulling the car over, Forreider approached the driver's side while McMasters approached the passenger side. When the occupants opened the glove box, probably to retrieve the vehicle registration, they exposed a handgun. McMasters yelled, "Gun!" as he reached in and grabbed it from the glove box. The troopers then began ordering the occupants out. While McMasters was managing the two passengers, who were exiting through the passenger door, Forreider was dealing with the driver.

The driver did not respond to Forreider's orders. Trooper Forreider is believed to have then reached in to remove the driver physically, only to be shot in the upper chest. As Forreider fell back, he drew his weapon and began firing at the suspect who was fleeing on foot.

When the dust settled, McMasters had the two passengers in custody, Larry Forreider was dead, and his murderer had made good his escape.

Michigan State Police canine teams were summoned and a track initiated. During the manhunt, a car was stolen in the area, possibly by the murderer.

At that time, I had been at the Jackson Post for a couple of months and often volunteered to ride patrol with the troopers. I was riding with Trooper Richard Temelko when East Lansing Operations issued a statewide radio broadcast of the murder and to "Be On Lookout" (BOL) for the stolen car. We were assigned a point on southbound US-127 near Leslie to watch for the stolen car.

In our patrol car, we carried a 30 caliber M1 carbine, the patrol rifle of that era. Since Trooper Temelko was driving, he had me uncase the rifle and prepare it for service. He reviewed my role with me in the event that the stolen car came our way and the many "what ifs" that would be associated with it. Ironically, we were sitting very near the spot where Trooper Craig Scott would be killed in a shoot out some eight years later.

While we monitored southbound US-127, the canine team was running a track in the Alpena area that led to a grove of trees. As the team closed in, the murderer of Trooper Larry Forreider committed suicide.

At that time, Michigan State Police did not issue bullet resistant vests to troopers. As the story goes, Larry Forreider's wife had one under the Christmas tree for him. It is believed it would have saved his life. This tragic loss was the catalyst to the department providing vests.

Often, our first experiences are the most memorable. Unfortunately, Trooper Larry Forreider's death would not be my last experience with a fellow trooper's murder. He was the first of nineteen Michigan State Police officers who would die in the line of duty during my career, two of whom were personal friends of mine.

> *"For those who are in war and battle and on the fighting line, there is no triviality in shaking dice with death. It makes no difference whether a man gets his along with twenty thousand others, or falls on out-post duty all by himself. He is a hundred percent casualty to himself."*
> — Charles J. Post, The Little War of Private Post

10) Chase

The four service officers assigned to the Jackson Post, myself included, were primarily to assist Trooper Peter LaCroix and Trooper Richard Carstens in conducting Vehicle-Driver Check Lanes. Trooper LaCroix, a crusty trooper near retirement, had little tolerance for our youth and inexperience. He called us PiSOs, an acronym he derived from us being Probationary Service Officers. With Carstens utilizing praise and LaCroix criticism, they taught us much.

Allow me to describe what a check lane is. While some states require all vehicles registered to have annual safety inspections, at this time Michigan conducted check lanes instead. A check lane was strategically placed so the motorist would be trapped, hopefully preventing him from avoiding it. Trooper Carstens would stand in the road, stop traffic, and check driver's licenses. He would then direct some of the cars to the side of the road where Service Officers would conduct a check of the required equipment while Trooper LaCroix supervised, and when needed, issued tickets. This assignment provided an excellent learning environment for us; contacting drivers and checking their cars. A patrol car would be positioned at both ends of the check lane to enable troopers to chase down those motorists who would do a "U" turn in an attempt to avoid it.

During May of 1975, we had a Vehicle-Driver Check Lane set up on US-12 adjacent to the Michigan International Speedway. On this particular day, a middle-aged woman driving a Mustang was waved into the inspection lane and Service Officer Dick Northrup made contact with her to begin the inspection. She greeted Northrup by telling him that she had just received a ticket from the Michigan State Police and now that she was in Ohio (not), she supposed she was going to get another. She asked Northrup whether he was the one who had issued her the speeding ticket and had he called her attorney? Realizing the woman was confused, Northrup called Lacroix over to assist.

Suddenly, the woman put her car in drive and sped out of the check lane, running over Northrup's toes. Fortunately, the boots we were issued had steel toes. Carstens and LaCroix ran to the nearest patrol car but couldn't get it started, forgetting it had a rare option that required the seatbelt first to be fastened.

LaCroix yelled to me to get the other patrol car. I sprinted to the far vehicle, jumped in, and started it. As I drove it toward them, Carstens, remembering the seat belt anomaly, got their patrol car started and sped away in pursuit of the fleeing Mustang.

I wondered whether LaCroix meant for me only to bring them the patrol car or to assist in the chase. Service Officer training did include some training in precision driving, so what was I supposed to do? Not wanting a reputation of being timid and anxious to get in the fray, I decided that I would follow them, and if they didn't want me to assist, they would tell me via the radio. Until then, I guess I was in my first high-speed chase.

Carstens chased the Mustang at speeds in excess of 80 mph, while I, getting a late start, was trying to catch up to them. As the suspect vehicle approached the intersection of M-50, it suddenly darted into the Marathon Gas Station where Carstens pulled in front of the Mustang in an attempt to block it in. The suspect vehicle then took off again, nearly striking Carstens' patrol vehicle. The chase continued east on US-12 at a high rate of speed.

By now, I had caught up and was in the game. As we raced east, the Mustang drove left of center, nearly hitting a westbound car head on. Fortunately, that driver went onto the shoulder, dodging a catastrophe.

In a straightaway and with traffic clear, Carstens passed the Mustang and then swerved in front of it as he began braking. The Mustang pulled to the left and tried to pass. Carstens, using his rearview mirror, saw the pass coming and also moved to the left lane, continuing to block her. As she continued these maneuvers, Carstens, like a good dance partner, stayed in front of her. While they were both in the left lane, I pulled alongside the Mustang on the right. She was now boxed in, her escape blocked.

Carstens then resumed braking with me following his lead. When we were down to about 10 mph, she made a desperate attempt to break out of the box by ramming my patrol car. Since my Plymouth Fury outweighed her Ford Mustang, her attempt failed. We came to a screeching halt, the air fouled by the odor of burning rubber and scorched brake pads.

While Carstens and LaCroix leaped out of their patrol car and approached the Mustang, I had to crawl across the front seat and out the passenger door as my driver's door was metal to metal with her passenger door. The woman locked her doors in a futile effort to avoid arrest. Carstens, using his revolver like a hammer, struck her window in an unsuccessful attempt to break it. While the window did not break, it did prompt her to unlock the door. She was quickly handcuffed. Her behavior led us to believe she was suffering from a mental illness. She was turned over to another trooper and taken to court for arraignment on charges of attempted fleeing and eluding of a police officer and reckless driving.

The chase had ended on US-12, very near the intersection of Onsted Highway. This is a rural area and the same place where I had given the pursuing Lenawee County Sheriff patrol car the slip a few years earlier when I was in high school. It was also in front of Harold's Place, a popular local restaurant, where I had eaten many times. Some of the patrons of the restaurant witnessed the crash, one of whom was a family friend.

Trooper Peter LaCroix was furious that I had participated in the chase, especially since my patrol car had been wrecked. I would author my first "special" (an interoffice memorandum) to the Director of the State Police, explaining my actions. While Trooper LaCroix thought, maybe hoped, I would be fired, the Jackson Post Commander, First Lieutenant Floyd Garrison, viewed it differently. The crash was ruled "Legal Intervention" so there were no negative repercussions to me. Having a job was a good thing, especially since Deb, my high school sweetheart with whom I had started college, and I had rekindled our relationship, and we were planning to get married in two weeks.

Looking back, I realize it was my nature, like most of my colleagues, to charge ahead when in doubt, and over the years, I was fortunate to have mostly gotten away with it. Society needs "risk takers" to protect it and "risk takers" need wise leaders to direct, and sometimes restrain, them with sound policy. Sometimes, it is more prudent to terminate a chase than continue it.

11) Perseverance

In the summer of 1973, a year before I enlisted in the state police, Deborah Good was found murdered, having been shot twice in the head, and raped. I would be one year from retirement before the killer would be convicted. This investigation fell to the Michigan State Police at the Jackson Post.

The last person investigators could find to have seen Debbie alive was her boyfriend, who said they had parted ways at 2:00 a.m., some eight hours before her body was discovered. The boyfriend, whom I will call John Buck, was a person of interest, but detectives were unable either to eliminate or charge him with the crime.

When Deborah Good was murdered, DNA was unknown. But a far-sighted pathologist collected the ejaculate from the body of Deborah Good and turned it over to the state police for preservation.

Not long after the gruesome discovery, Detective John "Stubby" Southworth of the Jackson County Sheriff Department forwarded informant information to the state police that a Ronald Stanton might be responsible for this crime. It was among many leads, but try as they might, the detectives were unable to charge anyone in the crime.

There is no "statute of limitations" on the crime of murder, and the state police never close an unsolved one, but as leads are exhausted and new demands present themselves, such cases become inactive.

Two years passed and it was now 1975. At 5:30 a.m., a woman I will call Jane Doe, a girl I went to high school with, had just started work when she was kidnapped at gunpoint and driven several miles before the suspect turned the vehicle into a field surrounded by woods. The suspect then forced her from his truck with a knife and took her into the woods where he sexually assaulted her. Sensing that she was about to be killed, Jane ran for her life. In full flight, she ran over a mile to the lights of a farmhouse where she found refuge. Jane, in her courage, had lived the motto: "He who dares, wins," thereby living to be a future witness. The police were called and Jane was taken to the hospital for examination.

Most hospitals have what is called a "Sex Motivated Crime Kit" that awaits a day that one hopes never comes but always does. And when that day arrives, the medical professional unseals it to find directions and containers for the proper way, both forensically and legally, to collect potential evidence from the victim. This medical professional becomes the first person in the "chain of evidence," turning over the collected items to the investigator.

The lead investigator in this case would be Detective Southworth of the Jackson County Sheriff's Department who, noting the similarities of modus operandi to the Deborah Good murder, soon suspected Ronald Stanton. Southworth went to the hospital to show Jane a photographic line-up, which included a picture of Ronald Stanton, which he had assembled shortly after the Good murder and which had been patiently waiting in his briefcase.

When Jane came out of her medical examination, Detective Southworth took possession of the evidence and escorted Jane to an interview room. There, he developed a rapport with the victim and reviewed her statement. He explained that he had some photographs of some persons which might or might not include the person who had assaulted her. Having tried to prepare her for the viewing, he presented the line-up.

Detective Southworth would describe it as the most positive and definitive identification he ever witnessed. As her eyes fell on the picture of Ronald Lee Stanton, she first screamed and then sobbed as she identified him as her assailant.

While I have witnessed this situation, I have never known the emotions that Jane felt, and I hope I never do. I do have first-hand knowledge of Stubby's emotions, which in one word I would describe as "mixed"—where bad and good crash together. You are so sorry this crime happened and so thrilled that you have solved it.

This identification provided police "probable cause" to make a warrantless felony arrest of Ronald Stanton. That same day, Southworth arrested Stanton, recovering a knife and a .22 caliber pistol, but not a 9mm pistol like the one that had killed Deborah Good.

On March 3, 1976, after being convicted of this crime, Ronald Lee Stanton was sentenced to ten to fifteen years in prison. During this time, I was a service trooper at the Jackson Post; Stubby didn't know me, but after he solved this case, I knew of him. Having served his sentence, on June 30, 1984, Stanton was released from prison.

Christi and me outside our office in 1990

During the 1990s, Detective Sergeant Christi Palmer and I, then a detective sergeant, worked out of the same office, supporting Michigan State Police investigations for an eight county area known as the First District. Part of our duties included reactivating unsolved murder cases by applying a fresh look and new technology in hopes of solving them. DNA science had emerged and its forensic impact on crime would probably only be second to fingerprints.

In August 1996, Christi was tasked with reactivating the unsolved Deborah Good murder case. With the advent of DNA, she hoped the evidence that had been collected from the body of Deborah Good could be used to identify her murderer. In perusing the report, two suspects surfaced; John Buck, Good's boyfriend on the fateful night, and Ronald Stanton. She would first deal with John Buck.

In November of 1996, nearly a quarter century since Good's murder, John Buck opened a letter from Detective Sergeant Palmer, asking him to call her. Having been through the ringer before, he did not look forward to it again, but he hesitantly honored her request. In the telephone conversation, Christi invited him to the state police post to discuss the case. As he apprehensively sat down in her office, he asked, "Why should I trust and talk to you?" So, Christi explained her mission, and in doing so, gained his trust and cooperation. One does not have to talk with Christi long before you know she is a person of integrity. John Buck voluntarily provided a DNA sample, and when the results came back, he was relieved finally to be officially cleared of the murder.

Christi's attention then turned to Ronald Stanton, and in doing so, she consulted now retired Sergeant John (Stubby) Southworth concerning his knowledge and dealings with Stanton. Although retired, Stubby was excited that the investigation had been reactivated and advised and assisted Christi whenever asked. Christi located Stanton in a Texas Prison, where he was serving a term of forty years for another serious crime he had committed after being released from prison in Michigan. His projected parole date was May 30, 2001.

With Ronald Stanton being an inmate in Texas and the venue for the murder case being Michigan, the investigation was plagued with obstacles, but for the next three-plus years, Christi remained tenacious. Like a chess master, she considered every action she made several moves ahead to avoid creating a flawed or complex chain of evidence that would be undoubtedly tested in court for admissibility.

In March of 1998, Detective Sergeant Mark Siegel of the Michigan State Police would accompany Christi to the Texas prison near Huntsville for the purpose of an interview and to obtain a DNA sample of Ronald Stanton. As they began their interview, they offered Stanton a cup of coffee. He declined the coffee, saying, "I no longer have any vices, with the exception of one—lying."

In his smug way, Stanton denied any and all involvement with Good or the murder. They ended the interview by requesting a blood sample to be used for DNA comparison. With a blink and a gulp, he paled, refusing to provide a blood sample, knowing what the detectives could only hope.

Palmer and Siegel left the prison to appear before a judge in Hunstville, Texas where they obtained a search warrant for a blood sample of Ronald Lee Stanton. They then returned to the prison with search warrant in hand, a phlebotomist at their side, and a "Take Down" team of Texas prison guards on their rear, just in case the sample had to be taken by force. As they walked to Stanton's cell, he cut his losses by sticking his arm out through the bars, where the sample was taken and immediately mailed to the laboratory.

Then "Bingo!"…well, kind of. Eventually, a DNA match was made from the ejaculate preserved from Deborah Good to the suspect, Ronald Stanton. To those who have not done cold cases, it sounds like a slam-dunk. However, those who have done them know it never is. Locating witnesses and evidence from over a quarter of a century ago is never easy, and such a case is never too strong. While many obstacles awaited Christi, let me share but a few.

While the far-sighted pathologist, now deceased, had taken the future DNA sample from Good, he had neglected to sign the autopsy report. For a prosecution of murder, you needed to be able to present evidence to the court that it was a homicide, and it was unlikely an unsigned autopsy report would be admissible. Further, the sample taken from the body of Deborah Good, oh so long ago, was compromised and the statistical match was only 1 in 645, probably not good enough for a conviction. Most laymen believe a DNA match is absolute and positive, but it never is. It is a science thing that I cannot understand but have learned to accept. But, some statistical matches are pretty convincing.

To overcome these obstacles, Christi would do an exhumation of the body of Deborah Good. The instrument to such a procedure is a Court Order for Disinterment and Postmortem Examination.

On July 8, 1998, light would once again fall on Deborah Good. As if there were not enough to worry about, the sister of Deborah Good told Christi she was concerned the funeral home might have mixed up grave sites and bodies. The sister described the clothing her sister had been buried in so Christi would know. And when they opened the casket…the clothing matched.

Twenty-five years after her murder, a second autopsy was performed on Deborah Good and a pure DNA sample taken. Christi's efforts produced a pathologist who could testify to Good being a victim of a homicide and a DNA sample that allowed scientists to make the old sample more specific.

And with this pure DNA sample, a new comparison was completed. The new results gave a probability of Ronald Stanton being the donor of the foreign DNA found on Deborah Good's body to be 1 in 5.5 billion. Now that is pretty convincing.

Stanton was extradited from Texas and arraigned in Jackson on the charges of Open Murder, Felony Murder, and Felony Firearm in August 1999.

As Christi prepared the murder case for trial, she was reminded of the kidnapping rape case of Jane Doe which actually happened after the murder of Deborah Good. Both crimes had happened in the same county, with similar modus operandi, and Ronald Stanton had been convicted of one and was now charged with the other. It was legally possible for Christi to have Jane Doe testify against Stanton in the murder trial of Deborah Good under the "Similar Acts Clause" (Michigan Rules of Evidence 404B) if she were willing and able. Remembering that I was past friends with Jane Doe, Christi contacted me at the Jonesville Post, where I had since transferred as a detective sergeant. She asked me to meet with Jane Doe to see whether she would be willing to testify in the trial of Ronald Stanton for the murder of Deborah Good.

Jane, now married and a mother of four, by all outward appearances had put her nightmare behind her and was getting on with her life. When I met with her at her home to explain the situation and request, she, without pause, said she was willing to testify.

Stanton's attorney objected to allowing "Similar Acts" testimony, and Judge Charles Nelson ruled in Stanton's favor, preventing Jane from testifying. Nevertheless, Jane had again demonstrated her personal courage, exemplifying a victim turned victor.

Through perseverance, Christi was able to keep this case glued together through a four-day jury trial. On June 23, 2000, the jury found Stanton guilty of first-degree murder and felony murder, which carries a mandatory life sentence with no possibility of parole. Delayed by more than a quarter of a century, justice had been served for the friends and family of Deborah Good.

> *"Perseverance is more prevailing than violence; and many things which cannot be overcome when they are together, yield themselves up when taken little by little."*
> — Plutarch

Later in my career when I was a detective sergeant, it would be my privilege to work some cases with Stubby, now a sergeant with the Jackson County Sheriff's Office; we got to know each other well. Stubby was always willing to help, had a can-do attitude, and a seemingly never-ending list of informants.

After I retired from the Michigan State Police, I continued to teach classes to police officers. As I drafted a new lesson plan for a class titled "Investigative Probes," I reached out to retired Sergeant John "Stubby" Southworth for ideas. In true Stubby style, he sent me a detailed letter of suggestions that ended with a message for my students: *No cop working by him or herself will ever be a great cop.*

Christi and Stubby are on my top ten list of best officers I ever served with.

Go to **www.michigan.gov/otis** *and enter offender number MDOC# 119607 to view Ronald Stanton's photograph.*

12) Wrap-up

Looking back, the twenty months I served as a Service Officer were both influential and eventful. When my service came to an end, I totaled up the hours I had volunteered riding with troopers and was surprised that it equaled three months of full-time work. I had learned much, but I was anxious for the independence of being a trooper.

In May 1975, Deb and I married. I continued my college education, going part-time to Jackson Community College and slowly working toward my degree. Service Officers were guaranteed a position in the next trooper school after their twenty-first birthday. If they declined or were unable to complete the training, they were terminated from the MSP.

During this time, Fred Gibson, a white man, applied to the Michigan State Police 90th Recruit School but was not accepted; apparently, he did not score high enough. Through his attorney, he filed a reverse discrimination suit. That lawsuit triggered an injunction that blocked the hiring of new employees to fill the 90th Recruit School until the lawsuit was resolved.

While the lawsuit was playing out, MSP was near a record low of troopers. With Colonel George Halverson at the helm, command did some out-of-the box thinking. Since they had forty-seven or so service officers already hired and partially trained, how about sending them through training labeled the 89.5 Recruit School? They wouldn't be hiring new personnel, and they wouldn't call it the 90th Recruit School. It was a way around the injunction that would yield some sorely needed troopers.

Command didn't stop there; it considered those Service Officers who weren't quite twenty-one years old but would be within six months of graduating from the academy. I was one of nine who fell into that category. Remember, Michigan law requires a trooper to be at least twenty-one years old, but you are not a trooper until after completing training and then being sworn in. To include us in this recruit school would require another court ruling, which my colleagues and I anxiously awaited. Court rulings are often like a birthing—they occur when they occur. The days ticked by and the 89.5 recruit school began as scheduled on the first Monday of May 1976 with only those service officers already twenty-one years old.

Ironically, it was the same day that the long awaited ruling came down, permitting us to attend training that had already started. With the department now having the ruling in hand, the question was whether they would allow us to start training late?

These developments were unknown to me until that Monday evening when I was enjoying a family picnic at my parents' house and Sergeant Floyd Milliken hunted me down by telephone. Back then, if you were away from home, you were supposed to check-out on the log at the post so if you were needed, the desk sergeant could easily find you. While my parents' telephone number was listed on my emergency contact card, I had neglected to check out on the log. After scolding me for not checking out, Sergeant Milliken read to me the following:

ATTENTION DISTRICT AND
POST COMMANDERS:

Recent developments in the negotiations between the attorneys representing this department, the United States Department of Justice and plaintiff, Fred Gibson, has resulted in agreement between these parties to allow the following nine service troopers to attend the third basic police academy currently in session.

The following service troopers must be immediately advised that they are To report to the training academy at 8 o'clock AM May 5, 1976, to participate in this third basic police academy:

ROBIN D. SEXTON – DETROIT POST (21)

THOMAS R. MYNSBERGE – FLINT POST (35)

CLIFTON L. EDWARDS – JACKSON POST (41)

ROBERT C. BROWN – PAW PAW POST (51)

JOHN J. CORBIT – PAW PAW POST (51)

DAVID H. KOETSIER – BENTON HARBOR POST (57)

THOMAS W. BRUNET – ROCKFORD POST (61)

PAUL B. UERLING – TRAVERSE CITY POST (71)

DENNIS H. GIRARD – NEGAUNEE POST (81)

Questions should be directed to the Personnel Division.

AUTHORITY;   Col. George L. Halverson, Director

I was exalted. Sergeant Milliken told me to get my affairs in order and report to the academy Wednesday morning. Some might have been upset with the short notice and time to prepare, but I simply said, "Yes, Sir!"

Part C – Troop Training
(May 1976 to May 1977)

> *"You must be deadly serious in training. When I say that, I do not mean that you should be reasonably diligent or moderately in earnest. I mean that your opponent must always be present in your mind, whether you sit or stand or walk or raise your arms."*
>
> — Gichin Funakoshi

13) Academy

While our previous training had been in the old academy at departmental headquarters, our trooper training would be in the nearly new academy located west of Lansing. It consisted of a seven floor dormitory (two persons per room with centered bathroom/shower facilities for the entire floor), gym, training tank (couldn't call it a swimming pool or the legislature wouldn't approve its funding), indoor shooting range, lecture hall, cafeteria, and several classrooms. Not only was it plush compared to where we had completed service trooper training, but it was undoubtedly more conducive to learning. It remains an impressive training facility.

The training would be in the same format as Service Officer School, only three times longer and much more in-depth. Each week would begin on Sunday evening when we reported back to the academy. If the week ended well, we would be dismissed for the weekend late Friday afternoon. It was a live-in academy so you did not leave during the week.

The days often began at 4:00 a.m., and it was go, go, go until lights out at 10:00 p.m. The links in the recruit's chain were being hardened, and not all who started would complete trooper training.

Every day we had a new class commander, who was a fellow recruit. His job was to make sure the class was in the right place at the right time in the right way. For example, at precisely 5:45 a.m., the whole class, in formation, had to run into the gymnasium and line up at attention at their assigned spots. At that moment, the class commander would address the Physical Training (PT) Instructor with "Sir, Recruit _____ reporting, Sir. Forty-four recruits (or however many there were; if any were absent because of illness, he had to report that also) present and accounted for, Sir." If we did not line up correctly, we did it again, stealing time away from breakfast. It was Leadership 101.

You never knew until it was over whether it was going to be long calisthenics and a short run or short calisthenics and a long run. During PT, one instructor would lead while others circulated through the recruits, identifying cheaters with loud criticisms and consequences, often paid by the entire class.

During the runs, the class was led by the PT instructor, whom no recruit dared to pass or get close to. The stronger runners, who were not just watching out for themselves, would hang to the rear and encourage and assist the weaker runners. But, as the strong runners anticipated the end of the run, most (me included) would abandon the struggling runners and sprint to the front half of the class for the finish. The reason being, the second half often had to continue for another lap. Sometimes, the PT instructor teased the class by running by the door to the academy, causing the strong runners to fall back and again sprint forward in the formation as they neared the possible end. Not knowing where or when the end is paralleled the physical challenges that awaited us on the street and would be more psychologically trying.

Recruit Thomas Brunet, a Yooper, (someone from the Upper Peninsula—U.P.—of Michigan) had immense pride but was not a runner. As he fell back, we would try to assist him. We learned not to grab his arms or push from behind because his pride would not allow it. We learned to give our words of encouragement from outside his strike zone. Determination got him through the runs.

It would be a long time before I would understand the benefit of doing push-ups in tall weeds on a hot humid morning, other than being a smorgasbord for the mosquitoes. But when I would later be truly tested, chasing and fighting criminals, it was never in a ring, gym, or on a track. The real world always seemed to be in an unfavorable environment, just like the outdoors where we did our push-ups. Chants sung during long predawn runs still ring in my head:

Birdie, birdie in the sky, drop some white wash in my eye.
I'm not a deputy; I won't cry. I'm just glad that cows don't fly.
Sound Off.

After PT, the recruits ran up the stairs to their floor where they showered and dressed in preparation for the march to breakfast. In my opinion, the cooks provided us with great chow. Breakfast was the one meal you could "hog down" on, if you had time, as morning classes never included physical activities. One had to be cautious not to eat too much lunch or dinner because afternoon classes often included physical activities and the "demerits" you might be dealt during the day had to be run off immediately following the evening meal. Strenuous activity on a full stomach can be productive in a bad way.

After breakfast, we rushed to our rooms to prepare for inspection at 7:30 a.m. Rooms, bathroom, and self had to be spit-shined. We would stand at attention beside our room door as we were inspected. You quickly learned to lock your eyes on a spot on the wall across the hall, not on a fellow recruit. Questions asked, answers given, and things found by the instructors were often hilarious, but you learned to maintain your composure. To be caught just cracking a smile earned you a demerit. A demerit meant additional laps or chores to be performed after the evening meal.

For example, one day during inspection, Recruit Newton was standing at attention across from me when the instructor asked him what Newton's law was. Newton responded, "Sir, the Law of Gravity, Sir." The instructor had him demonstrate Newton's law by having him bear hug another recruit and hold him off the ground for the remainder of inspection. Witnessing this in my peripheral vision surely tested my ability to keep a "straight face." It still brings a smile today.

While at the time we didn't realize it, everything had a meaning. The ability to maintain your composure would pay dividends. In the field, you often witnessed events that would otherwise prompt a display of emotion that others might view as inappropriate.

We would go to the classroom for instruction on a wide variety of topics. Some instructors were great and some were boring. Woe to the student caught nodding off. As a recruit, you were required to take notes in class.

During the evening, you had to type those notes out in a prescribed format and then index them in a three-ring notebook for review by an instructor. If not done right, you did it over. It certainly inspired the acquisition of typing skills, a necessary ability for all the reports a trooper had to type. On Wednesday, you were tested on last week's lectures. Drop below 70 percent and you got a retest. Fail again and you were terminated, with a red X being placed across your face on the class picture taken the first day and hanging on display in the lobby.

Every afternoon for a month, we were divided into four groups that rotated through an hour of swimming, an hour of defensive tactics, an hour of firearms, and an hour of first aid. Each of the subjects would climax with a stressful event, i.e. death swim for swimming, boxing for defensive tactics, qualification with firearms, and an emergency medical scenario. These physical challenges were in addition to our morning PT and the running of demerits in the evening.

I vividly remember the first day of swimming when we stood at attention alongside the training tank, awaiting orders. Having been service officers, we knew the "death swim" awaited us in the end. The instructors seemed low keyed and said, "How about we just play water polo?" They divided us into teams and into the water we went—the deep end that is. We started playing hard, and as we tired, we went to the side to catch our breath. Wrong! If you touched the sides, the instructors stepped on your hands!

The intensity of the game mellowed as we paced ourselves for the remaining hour. We were spent at the end of day one of swimming.

Knowing that the death swim awaited us would cause stress for some and nightmares for others. We dreaded the final day of swim training, but I found solace in my preparation and skills. The death swim consisted of entering the pool from the shallow end for the purpose of saving an instructor playing the role of a drowning victim in the deep end. As you swam toward this victim, two other instructors actively interfered with your progress.

This made the sterile pool environment more tiring, like a lake or river might be. The process became one of evade and escape the first two instructors to approach the drowning victim. As you neared him, you would surface dive; then from underwater, grasp the victim's hips and turn him away; surface behind victim, place him in a cross-chest carry, and pull him back to the shallow end. While you towed him, you just knew he was going to spin and pull you to the bottom.

When my time came, I had to remember what I had said to myself a thousand times, "I can hold my breath as long as he can." Fortunately, I was right. When we both came to the surface gasping, I was able to complete the task with a more passive victim.

During defensive tactics training, Instructor Trooper Lenny Anthos used a recruit to demonstrate the infamous carotid chokehold. When the recruit recovered his sense of balance, he complained to Trooper Anthos that he had nearly been choked unconscious. With a bellow, Anthos grabbed him by the sweatshirt and dragged him across the gym floor. When he got to the door, Anthos kicked it open and threw him out. I never saw that recruit again! No one in the class ever dared complain.

Boxing would be the final component of defensive tactics. As our squad anxiously awaited our final boxing class, the instructors dragged out a fellow recruit, Tommy Tucker, who was in the squad ahead of us, which had just finished its boxing test. He was unconscious, his bloody nose moved to the side of his face. The ambulance quickly arrived to rush him to the hospital.

It was now my squad's turn in the ring. With our hands wrapped for support and boxing gloves on, we were matched with an opponent for a full go three-minute boxing match. I had learned in high school wrestling that a two-minute period can take forever and boxing was no different. The instructor's objective was that each recruit would get his "bell rung" (a phrase used to describe when a punch temporarily stuns you) so he could evaluate your will to prevail.

We had an odd number in our squad, which meant someone had to go in the ring twice, and that someone turned out to be me. My first opponent was a shorter, stockier guy, and the second one was a taller, thinner guy. We made it through without injuring each other.

The next day, Tommy Tucker returned to the academy with some raccoon eyes and bandages in and on his nose. Fortunately, that had been the last day of boxing and Tucker was able to continue trooper school.

> *"I watched you, Nic San. You fought well. So do not expect us to pander to your weaknesses. We would be very bad senpai if we did that....We are like soldiers. When a soldier puts on his uniform, carries a weapon, and goes to war, he is obviously willing to fight and kill his enemies. If he is willing to kill, then he must be prepared to die. It is only right. We must cultivate spirit."*
> — C.W. Nicol, Moving Zen

This intense schedule would be the catalyst to what we would call "Black Wednesday," because it culminated on that day. On that day, the mental and physical stressors of the academy peak, causing the class as a whole to be in despair. You realize you can't make it as an individual, only as a team, and that the whole is greater than the sum of its parts. Team spirit is born and collectively, the recruits "reach down and get a handful" (a phrase instructors were constantly telling recruits to do) and start their climb back. This psychological group experience is undoubtedly programmed into every recruit school, but on the inside looking out, you don't realize it. It validates the saying, "That which you survive will only serve to make you stronger."

My preparation was serving me well, but sometimes, luck goes bad. Our nation was celebrating its bicentennial birthday, July 4, 1976, and I was home for the weekend. I had been married to my high school sweetheart, Deb, for fourteen months. Deb and I were out riding our motorcycle when a car made a left turn in front of us without signaling. I laid the cycle down and we began sliding across the pavement with Deb on top of me. Fortunately, I had on a leather motorcycle jacket, but Deb wore only a tee-shirt. When the sliding finally stopped, I suffered some serious road rash but no fractures. Luckily, my wife was fine, having ridden out the slide on my back.

Like my foot injury in service officer training, these injuries were going to prevent me from participating in physical training for a few days. I was worried that I might get kicked out of the academy, but I didn't. As much as we all dreaded the daily early morning PT, I yearned to be with my comrades during the week my medical excuse placed me on the sideline....I guess we are all herd animals.

The week long precision driving school was intense fun with never-ending pressure placed upon us by the instructors. During the week, the training cars developed orange stripes from the traffic cones we scuffed as we maneuvered through them.

The final exercise of the week was night driving off the track. After class Thursday, we were dismissed for an evening meal and nap, to report back at 10:00 p.m. We were divided into squads consisting of ten recruits and two instructors divided amongst three cars. Each squad went a different direction for the night. One car would play the role of the suspect vehicle with an instructor aboard. The second was the police car, also with an instructor aboard. The third car tagged along, on deck for its turn in the fray. All night, the instructors presented us with a variety of high-speed driving and traffic stop scenarios. Being in an uncontrolled environment in the dark and being dependent on artificial light complicated our previous drills. At just predawn, we got back to the academy dragging tail. While all training is artificial, much had been learned.

This was the era when law enforcement was just beginning to prioritize drunk driving arrests. Our training would include a week of P.A.T. (Police Alcohol Training). During my career, I witnessed this initiative make a difference, reducing car crashes.

When I went into the academy, Deb and I knew we could be transferred to any post upon graduation, but we hoped to be reassigned back to Jackson. I wrote a memorandum requesting this reassignment, which was endorsed by the Post Commander.

MICHIGAN STATE POLICE
Inter-Office Correspondence

UNIFORM DIVISION

Date : April 23, 1976

Subject: Request for re-assignment to the Jackson Post after promotion to the rank of Trooper

To : Colonel George L. Halverson - Director

This correspondence is in reference to my post assignment upon promotion from Service Trooper to Trooper.

I would greatly appreciate your consideration of my request of re-assignment to the Jackson Post after attainment of the rank of Trooper. I feel that my re-assignment to the Jackson Post would be beneficial both to the department and myself. Please consider the following as my reasons for this request:

1. Since being assigned to the Jackson Post, I have become familiar with the post area.

2. My experience at the Jackson Post has included becoming familiar with the operation of Jackson Central Dispatch.

3. Re-assignment would be conducive to my attainment of a degree in law enforcement, as I am attending classes at Jackson Community College.

4. My wife and I own a mobile home in Jackson.

5. Re-assignment to the Jackson Post would be economical to the department as they would not be burdened with the expense of the move.

6. My wife has a successful job as a real estate salesperson with my parents' real estate agency.

Thank you so much for your time and consideration in this matter. My home town is Onstead, Michigan.

Respectfully Submitted,

S/O Clifton L. Edwards
Jackson Post

MICHIGAN STATE POLICE
Interoffice Correspondence

Date   :   4/23/76

Subject: Re-assignment of Service Officer Edwards

To   :   Col. George Halverson

From   :   Lieut. Floyd Garrison, Commanding Officer, Jackson Post

Service Officer Edwards has to be one of the better Service Officers. He continually works 10 to 16 hours a day (on a volunteer basis). He has an intense interest in policework and is dedicated to becomming the best Trooper possible. He has earned the respect of the Troopers at this post, as well as the Command Officers. He loves to work, and is anxious and eager to please. He would have no trouble making the transition from Service Officer to Trooper at this post.

He has married recently and has established residence in the Post area. If at all possible , consideration should be given to re-assigning him at Jackson.

He will conplete the Trooper school in July, but will not be 21 yrs old until Sept.

I approve the request.

Lieut. Floyd Garrison
Commanding Officer
Jackson Post

APPROVED

DISTRICT COMMANDER

Four weeks prior to graduation, wives and girlfriends were invited to the academy for a tour and a presentation on what they could expect from being married to a state trooper, assuming we graduated. In the rather extravagant evening meal in the academy cafeteria, we were given our post assignments.

At the end of the meal, your name was called along with your post of assignment. We held our breath only to hear—Romeo Post. Deb did not know where that was. So much for letter writing!

Deb and I were sitting with Doug Halleck and his wife, a couple we had taken motorcycle trips with during our Service Officer era. Doug was being transferred to the Alpena Post upon graduation. When Deb asked Doug's wife how she felt about Alpena, she replied, "Any post is fine."

What we later learned was that during the many weeks we were in the academy, Doug's wife had met someone else and had no intention of accompanying Doug to Alpena. I wouldn't see her for some sixteen years, when I would arrest her and her then husband in what was probably the most complex white collar crime investigation of my career.

Again, I was nominated to be class orator at graduation, but I declined, feeling someone else should have the honor. Academically, I had placed sixth in the class. When it came time for the class to be sworn-in, the nine of us under age were told not to raise our right hands because the law requires a Michigan State Trooper to be at least twenty-one years old. Those graduates of age received their badges and side-arms, and all of us got orders to report to our new posts the following Tuesday.

In our final gathering before dismissal, Sergeant William Parviainen closed by saying "Everybody complains about our training, but nobody complains about our product. Remember who you are and what you represent. Dismissed."

"Graduation is only a concept. In real life everyday you graduate. Graduation is a process that goes on until the last day of your life. If you grasp that, you'll make a difference."
— Arie Pencovici

New Troopers Assigned
Romeo State Police Post

Three Michigan state police probationary troopers sworn in by Col. George L. Halverson, department director, in brief ceremonies Friday afternoon, July 23, at the training academy southwest of Lansing, have been assigned to the Romeo post.

These officers completed four weeks of special trooper training at the academy. Prior to that instruction, they had completed an eight-week basic police training program at the academy with other law enforcement personnel.

The new probationary troopers first joined the department as service troopers (formerly called cadets) after four weeks of training in August and September, 1974.

The troopers are Charles J. Kleinhuizen, II, Dennis E. Woizeschke and Clifton Edwards.

DENNIS E. WOIZESCHKE

CLIFTON EDWARDS

CHARLES J. KLEINHUIZEN

Compliments of *Romeo Observer* Newspaper

14) Probation

When I reported to the Romeo Post I had completed trooper training, but because I was only twenty, looking eighteen, I would remain a service officer until my twenty-first birthday. The hazing would not end for some time.

Whenever I saw a Romeo trooper I had not yet met, I would introduce myself. I will never forget the day I introduced myself to Trooper Tom Garvale. He just stared at me for what seemed like a full minute, me with my hand extended but not met. He then said one sentence, "Now that you feel like an ass, why don't you empty some trash cans?" and walked away. Romeo was known for being tough on recruits, and three of us had been assigned there. After all that we had been through, we still had one more filter to survive. Of the three assigned to the Romeo Post, one would not complete probation.

During those six weeks, I provided support functions, like working desk and riding second person on day patrol. I remember experiences with Trooper Ron Lapp, a most charismatic trooper. At that time, the television series *CHiPs* (California Highway Patrol) was popular. Ron could have given the series star, Erik Estrada ("Ponch"), a run for his money.

Shortly after reporting for duty, Lapp and I had to relay a patrol car to the dealership in Sterling Heights for service. I followed him. As we got on the freeway, he radioed me with two words "Keep Up," and we were off. I had mixed feelings about driving at speeds in excess of 100 mph to deliver a car for servicing, but I guess I'll chalk it up to training. When the need for speed would come, there would be more things to keep track of than just driving, so honing those skills did have meaning.

When I rode patrol with Trooper Lapp, he had me carry his pocket gun, which allows an officer to discreetly have his gun in hand. We commonly referred to our handguns as one for show (the holstered revolver) and one for go (the pocket revolver). One hot summer day, we attempted to stop a car and a short chase ensued with the driver jumping out and running into the tall, late August corn. Lapp let me out for foot pursuit and sped around the field to block off the driver. When I got across the fence and into the cornfield, my visibility was reduced to about twelve inches. I ran hard for about twenty rows and then slowed and checked one row at a time, looking left and right.

A few rows later, I spied the suspect lying prone and panting. Having

Trooper Lapp's pocket gun, I held the suspect at gunpoint while shouting my position. Lapp came crashing through the corn and handcuffed him. It turned out the suspect was driving on a suspended driver's license that, at that time, carried a three-day minimal jail sentence he apparently hoped to avoid.

My first MSP foot pursuit had ended in success. Many would follow with none ever being lost. Although, I must confess, I think one would have gotten away had not another officer headed him off at the pass.

Attending my first autopsy was disturbing. Most people have a similar reaction. It is a mutilation of the human body with a legal and medical purpose. The face is just like a mask that is peeled off and then pulled back on. While they say the only things guaranteed in life are death and taxes, it can be hard to die without being gifted an autopsy. I have learned not to think about it. Putting a gob of Vicks under your nose can help cover the odor of death.

The death that provided me the opportunity to satisfy this field training requirement did not occur during my shift, yet I still have memories of the crash site, probably from the scene photographs. When the autopsy was scheduled, the sergeant called me at home so I could attend. While the driver, a young mother, had been killed, her baby had ended up on the right front floor board uninjured, but now an orphan.

While autopsies are performed by pathologists, in criminal investigations, they are hopefully completed by a forensic pathologist. The reason an investigator attends an autopsy is to understand better what happened to the victim and to take custody of any evidence removed from on *or in* the victim. The pathologist determines cause of death and type of death, which falls in one of four categories; natural, accidental, homicide, or suicide. You may also see "undetermined" listed in the type of death section of a death certificate.

The legendary forensic pathologist Doctor Werner Spitz provided the service at my first autopsy. With his German accent, he gave me a real anatomy lesson, inside and out.

One reason why Doctor Spitz is a legend is that he served on the Warren Commission that investigated President Kennedy's assassination. Some twenty years later, when I was a detective sergeant, I would complete a seminar titled "Medicolegal Investigation of Death" that he taught.

During the course of my career, I would attend more autopsies than I care to remember. If you're considering law enforcement as a profession, know that they are a vivid part of it.

On my twenty-first birthday, the Romeo Post Commander, my wife, and I drove to Michigan State Police Headquarters in East Lansing. We met with then Colonel George Halverson in his office, where he swore me in as a Michigan State Police Trooper and issued me trooper badge #854. I then went down to the quartermaster and was issued the rest of my gear, two Smith & Wesson revolvers, a Model 10 and Model 38. The quartermaster didn't issue ammunition, but he located twenty-five bullets, so I didn't drive that patrol car home with empty weapons. Another monumental birthday.

Trooper Les Hasler was assigned as my first senior officer, now known as a Field Training Officer. A dedicated weightlifter and a member of the Emergency Services Team (commonly known as SWAT), he had a dry sense of humor that would keep me in stitches. His two-week vacation started just as I was sworn in, so I was stuck on midnight desk with Sergeant Richard Campbell.

A few nights into the shift, I thought I should clean the used revolvers I had been issued. About 4:00 a.m., when things had quieted down, Sergeant Campbell went upstairs to work on paperwork and I disassembled and cleaned both weapons. I then reassembled them and was preparing to dry fire when the telephone rang. Interrupted and in the fog of a midnight shift, I forgot I had reloaded the model 10. I then resumed my activities by taking very careful aim at the logo atop the community relations policy that hung on the wall in the adjacent room. Nice slow steady trigger pressure, BANG, and the plaque shattered.

Sergeant Campbell came running down the stairs, yelling, "Tell me it was a firecracker!" My immediate concern was that the round had fired through the exterior wall of the post, and gone loose into the small village of Romeo. Fortunately, the brick construction prevented that. It was time to author the second letter of my career that started, "Dear Colonel...," in which I would try to explain my stupidity. Such letters are known as specials. I was fortunate only to receive a Warning/Counseling Notice.

Michigan Department of State Police
WARNING/COUNSELING NOTICE FORM

☐ WRITTEN WARNING NOTICE   ☒ COUNSELING MEMO

Employee	Social Security Number	Date
Clifton Edwards		5-12-77

Job Title	Work Station	Date of Employment
Trooper	Romeo	9-18-76

If Written Warning, state:

Date of Violation: _____ Time: _____ Location: _____

Describe below:

If Counseling Notice, check one of the following and describe below:

On _____ May 5, 1977 _____ I counseled ☒ Warned ☐ the above employee as follows:

This counseling concerns the accidental discharge of a weapon in the Romeo Post. The incident resulted from carelessness on the part of the Officer when he dry fired the weapon without first opening the cylinder for inspection.

The Officer has been thoroughly counseled as to the possible consequences of such incidents, and hpoefully it will not occur again.

A repetition of the above violation or occurrence of any other may result in disciplinary action.

Signature and Title of Supervisor	Date Given to Employee
Russell Beamish, Lt.	5-31-77

Shortly after Trooper Les Hasler returned from vacation, district approved me for working second person on night patrol. Our shift then began at midnight and Les hit the road running. Les was an ace at patrol and we were making stop after stop. About 4:00 a.m., when traffic was thinning, Les pulled over a car with loud exhaust.

Les asked the driver and lone occupant to get out of his car so he could inspect his own defective muffler. Once that was completed, Les informed him that he was going to write him what was commonly known as a fix-it ticket, i.e. fix the exhaust and bring the car into any police station within ten days and the ticket would be dismissed—no points, no fine.

The guy was agreeable to the program and Les invited him into the backseat of the car while we filled out the ticket. Then, as if an after-thought, Les asked him whether he had any guns, weapons, drugs, or any-thing illegal on his person, and the guy replied, "No." Les then told him that policy required us to check any person for weapons prior to getting into a patrol car and directed me to do so.

I frisked him head to toe, including the waistband, and started to open the door for him. Les reminded me to check visually the pelvic area. This is accomplished by pulling the pants away from the stomach at the buckle with one hand while pushing the stomach in with the flashlight while il-luminating the area in question with the other. This is a very effective technique for checking for contraband in a sensitive area without groping a person's privates, but it does not seem to be commonly taught in acad-emies. Yes, you are in a tactically compromised position while doing so, but it beats getting shot by the gun you missed. As if the bell had been rung, as soon as I began to check, the fight was on. I dropped my flash-light and took control of the suspect's right arm. Les took control of the suspect's left arm with his left hand, keeping his flashlight in his right. The suspect was trying to reach into the front of his pants, and we were having a difficult time getting his arms pulled behind his back.

Les then tapped him in the back of the head with his flashlight, which caused the suspect to relax, so we were able to handcuff him behind his back. In his groin area, we found jewels—and not the family ones. We were able to determine the loot was from a jewelry store he had just bur-glarized.

At the end of the month, the training officer has to submit a form called a TD-15; it documents experiences, problems, and progress during that month. On that form, there are specific tasks to be checked off when ex-perienced. For example: Attend Autopsy, Attend Polygraph, Use of Force, Administer First Aid, etc. From this one incident, Les got to check off Use of Force and Administer First Aid since I had to bandage the bleeding head of the burglar.

Being able to patrol alone required a minimum of three months work-ing with a senior officer and the approval of district headquarters. I bet all troopers remember their first day on patrol by themselves, and I'm no exception. While nothing extraordinary happened, it was a milestone to run my own patrol.

During this era, a trooper worked a swing shift: a week of afternoons followed by two days off, a week of days followed by two days off, and then a week of midnights, followed by the coveted long weekend off. A long weekend consisted of getting off at 8:00 a.m. on a Thursday and not having to return to work until the next Tuesday at 4:00 p.m. Otherwise, all days off were during the week. Except for being hard on a trooper's longevity, it wasn't a bad rotation since each shift brought a different flavor of work.

During one of my first stints working days solo, I remember patrolling in rural Lapeer County on a narrow blacktop two-lane road with deep drainage ditches on both sides. I met a car I wanted to stop, so I quickly stopped on the road and tried to back into a driveway, which would enable me to turn around and give chase. The only complication was that I cut the turn a little sharp and dropped my right rear tire off the culvert, setting the patrol car on its frame. How was I going to get out of here without calling a wrecker? An elderly farmer came out of his house and asked whether he could help. He didn't even crack a smile, but I'll bet he was laughing inside. With his help, I was able to get the blue goose back on four tires without calling a wrecker. A benefit to being solo was my colleagues, hopefully, would not learn of my driving skills.

Trooper John Jackson, aka Action Jackson, was my second senior officer. While Les' forte had been patrol, John's was investigations and interviews. Personally, John was suffering through a difficult divorce, which would lead to alcoholism. He taught me to look beyond the obvious in pursuit of what he termed "the big arrest in the sky." Every valid criminal complaint we were assigned became a personal challenge to solve. And while John taught me these skills, I tolerated the burden of his personal problems.

While working midnights, John could suddenly fall asleep. He tried to combat it by driving faster, but it didn't always work. When it was his turn to drive (we usually split the shift), I was on pins and needles watching him, ready to shout him awake or grab the steering wheel. At the end of the shift when I went home, my fear of John falling asleep at the wheel prompted nightmares, disturbing my sleep.

I remember doing my first stakeout with John. Our objective was to arrest a fugitive wanted on a felony assault who was known to be combative. We received information that the fugitive would be at a certain house party and we were provided a description of the car he should be driving. Toward the end of our afternoon shift, we drove by the house, and sure enough, the car was there.

It was a bitterly cold winter night. The house was just off a snow-covered gravel road in the boonies. In the darkness, we sat down the road waiting for the car to leave. When our shift ended, the fugitive's car remained at the party. There was no overtime to be paid and no troopers to relieve us, so we stayed over on what was called V-Time (v=voluntary), which was not uncommon.

About 2:00 a.m., the car in question departed the party. We quickly closed in on it, our headlights revealing only a driver. It is said that waiting is the worst part, and I was shaking in anticipation of a chase and fight.

We positioned ourselves for the stop and turned on the overhead red light. The car pulled over and the guy peacefully gave up, simply replying to our comments with, "Yes, Sir. No, Sir. Handcuff me and take me to jail."

Pumped up on adrenaline, I was shaking and needed a way to burn some off. While John and the cuffed suspect sat in the patrol car waiting for a wrecker, I excused myself and went to the rear of the patrol car where I dropped down and did about thirty push-ups on the snow-covered road. About halfway through, I started getting dizzy from the fumes of the dual exhaust, causing me to stumble back into the patrol car.

Allow me to fast forward in time a moment. When transferring to a new post, the departing trooper gets a roasting party. When I transferred from Romeo to Ypsilanti, my colleagues hosted one for me. I was surprised during the roast when John took the podium and told how I had gotten high doing push-ups behind an idling patrol car since I didn't think he had noticed.

On another note, John eventually had to reckon with his drinking problem. He became a model to overcoming this addiction and was one of the finalists for a position to mentor troopers combating alcoholism. A victim turned victor.

One midnight shift, John and I got dispatched to a trailer park north of Romeo. Apparently, a husband and wife had had a fight and she had fled to a friend's place where she called the post. Among other things, she said her husband was pretty drunk.

Jackson parked the patrol car about four trailers away and we crept up to the couple's trailer in the darkness. We did not go to the front door and knock, but we peeked in the windows and listened. I vividly remember what I saw and heard. A middle-aged bearded man was sitting at the kitchen table, leaning back in a chair. In his left hand, he held a phone to his ear and was talking. In his right hand was a 12-gauge pump shotgun with the butt resting on his front hip. The muzzle was aimed at the front door. I heard him say into the receiver, "I know the cops are coming and when they knock at the door, I'm going to blast them."

We backed off, set up a perimeter, evacuated nearby trailers, and requested the Emergency Service Team, commonly known as SWAT (special weapons and tactics), to assist us. Upon arrival, SWAT relieved us of the inner perimeter. Contact was made with the prosecutor, who would not authorize a felony arrest. So it was a long night, waiting for the estranged husband to sober up. I don't think he knew the police had his home surrounded all night until we talked to him the next day.

This incident reminded me that the grim reaper could lurk anywhere. During my career, I know of three times when, if I had wigged instead of wagged, I likely would have been killed. This was the first.

During this field-training period, probationary troopers were assigned to work with the Detective Sergeant for two weeks. John Flis was the Romeo Post detective, a tobacco chewing grisly thirty-year plus veteran who did fifty push-ups every morning and had a crushing handshake. During my time with him, I heard a lot of war stories, all of which had learning points.

He introduced me to the idea and technique for developing informants, which I would later develop into a huge asset in investigations. It would be under his tutelage that I would develop my first informant and use him to make a controlled buy of marijuana, which was the catalyst to a productive raid. There is nothing like success to motivate, so this episode made me an informant addict, no pun intended.

Over the years I would package these techniques into a class titled "Cultivation & Utilization of Informants," which I would teach to colleagues. On behalf of the officers to whom I taught what I learned from you, thank you, John Flis.

Deb and I had rented a house in the Village of Almont, which was eight miles north of Romeo. One winter night, we were driving to Romeo when I noticed the car in front of us was weaving—the sign of a drunk driver. About that time, the driver went into the ditch and got his car stuck.

Although off-duty, I stopped to check on him, finding him okay but intoxicated. He was a year or two younger than me, taller but with a similar build. I identified myself as a State Trooper and placed him under arrest for drunk driving.

The fight was on, with Deb not wanting to be there. As I gained control of the suspect, I told her to get behind the wheel. I finally got him into the backseat of our car, wishing I had a pair of handcuffs. I had Deb drive us to the Romeo Post while I held the suspect down in the backseat. I turned the arrestee over to the troopers on duty. Deb said she had never seen me act like that and she didn't like it. I supposed it was good that I had never behaved so aggressively in our personal life.

15) Confirmation

After six to nine months of field training, the probationary trooper returns to the academy for three weeks of advanced trooper training. Amongst the myriad of classes was advanced firearms training. There, I was able to improve my score from "Expert" to "Distinguished Expert," which earned me issuance of a stainless steel Smith & Wesson Model 67 revolver with the Michigan State Police logo engraved on the side. Years down the road, it would serve me well in two separate shootings. I would carry that weapon until the department transitioned from revolvers to semi-automatics in 1989, and then I purchased it from the state. After completing one full year as a probationary trooper, I was finally off probation and confirmed as a trooper.

The good citizens of the State of Michigan had now invested much in me, both in training and by granting me the authority of a Michigan State Police Officer. It was now time for me to make good on their investment.

> *"Nearly all men can stand adversity, but if you want to test a man's character, give him power."*
> — Abraham Lincoln

Part D – Romeo Trooper
(June 1977 to November 1978)

16) Father

In early 1977, Deb and I decided to start a family, and not long after, she was pregnant. During her second trimester, she began experiencing episodes of extreme abdominal pain. Diagnosed as an inflamed gall bladder, the doctor said it was too risky for her to have surgery during the pregnancy. Deb would have to "grin and bear" the attacks until after she gave birth. Her due date was mid-October.

As that date approached, I found myself partnered with Action Jackson on the midnight shift. On October 14, 1977, we handled two separate fatal accidents. We normally would have gone off-duty at 8:00 a.m., but the investigation into those crashes found us working over. About 10:00 a.m., Deb called the post to tell me she thought she was in labor. I headed home and we called the doctor. He advised us not to come in until the contractions got much closer.

As I went to bed to grab some sleep, I crossed my fingers that the birth would not occur until the 15th since I felt it would be a bad omen for the birth to occur on the same day I had policed two fatal crashes. About four hours later, Deb awakened me, telling me it was time. We drove to Crittenden Hospital in Rochester. I had already been there twice that day concerning the fatal accidents. We waited for the monumental moment, which I hoped wouldn't occur until after midnight.

Midnight came and went, and while exhausted, Deb remained stalwart in what seemed like the never-ending hours of labor. Finally, Trevor was born at dawn on October 15 to the repeating music of the *William Tell* Overture, more commonly known as the theme song from the television series *The Lone Ranger*. We did not select that song, but we had forgotten to bring our own music, and it was the only tape available in the delivery room. Undoubtedly, that is why Trevor, as an adolescent, would often hum that tune in his sleep.

Deb's episodes of intense abdominal pain continued after the pregnancy so she weaned Trevor in anticipation of hospitalization. Surgery resulted in an inflamed gall bladder being removed. She was hospitalized for about a week, convalescing from her surgery. In Deb's absence, I came to know baby Trevor like a Mr. Mom, which was a precious experience for me. I learned the remedy to most of his needs, and when he continued to cry, I danced before him to Bob Seger tunes, which almost always made him laugh.

Our parents stayed overnight with Trevor when I had to return to work on the midnight shift. One of those rainy nights, my partner and I were dispatched to a pin-in car crash. The car was overturned and partially submerged in a ditch full of water.

While my partner radioed for rescue personnel, I waded to the car and supported the victim's head out of the water, reassuring him that all would be okay. While the rescue workers were the true heroes of this save, I was the only person the trapped man could see during these dire minutes. To that person, I probably appeared as a blue angel.

17) Domestic

It was December 3, 1977, and Trooper Manuel Reyes and I were partnering because his Field Training Officer was on vacation. Manny, as he was known, was an ex-marine and older than me (I was the youngest trooper at the Romeo Post). But, I was senior to him and off probation (he wasn't), so that put me in charge. We were the lone patrol for the Romeo Post that afternoon shift, which evolved into a stormy night.

I was driving when we were dispatched to a farmhouse where a family fight had gone from bad to worse. Sergeant Doug Wilt advised us that he had received information about a drunken husband who had armed himself with a shotgun, fired two rounds in the house, and was threatening to kill his wife. This information originated from the wife's mother, whom the wife had called. As we raced to the scene, we recruited back-up from the Romeo Village Police. Unlike my first barricaded gunman incident with Trooper Jackson when I was on probation, we knew this one was bad from the time of dispatch.

We responded tactically, not pulling too far into the long driveway leading to the dilapidated farmhouse. The Romeo Village Police took a position behind the house, creating a perimeter that would hopefully keep the threat contained.

With our spotlights illuminating the house and us behind the doors of the patrol car, we radioed arrival and requested that the post attempt telephone contact at the house. At that time, the patrol rifle was a 30 caliber M-1 carbine of Korean War vintage. My partner, with the rifle at ready, assumed the cover role while I was to try my hand as a negotiator.

Sergeant Wilt telephoned the house and the wife answered. She whispered the same information her mother had relayed—that her husband was still armed and threatening to kill her. Sergeant Wilt asked whether she could see the patrol car in front of her house and whether she thought she could run to it without being harmed. She said she thought she could. Sergeant Wilt told her to run to the patrol car at her first opportunity; then he radioed us what to expect. Within moments, she burst out the front door of the house, sprinting to the patrol car.

Trooper Rey covered her flight with the rifle, and I called her to me behind the shining spotlights. Out of sight and sound of her husband and behind the protection of the patrol car, she told me the circumstances leading to this situation. While her husband and she had been out drinking, he had become drunk and hostile. As he drove them home, he threatened to commit suicide by driving into a cement abutment. Once home, he loaded a shotgun and threatened to kill her and shoot himself. To emphasize his point, he shot the gun twice in the basement.

I requested that Sergeant Wilt try to get the suspect on the phone; he responded by informing me that no one would answer. We later learned the husband had torn the phone from the wall.

Alone in the Romeo Post, Sergeant Wilt was busy calling the midnight shift in early, briefing the post commander, and requesting the Emergency Services Team be activated. It's during times like these when a citizen will call for directions or road conditions and wonder why the desk officer is so curt.

Members of the Emergency Services Team are troopers with specialized weapons and training for handling barricaded gunman situations. They do normal trooper duties until a call comes in, and then they are summoned to a scene where a team is assembled. Once assembled and briefed, they take over the incident. It usually takes them at least three hours to get a full team on location. Until then, it was our situation to handle.

Through the windows, we got glimpses of the suspect walking through-out the house with a long gun. Although impersonal, I had little choice but to use the public address (P.A.) system on the patrol car to hail him. I verbally identified us, calling him by his first name, and asked whether he could hear me. After a couple of renditions of these lines, a male shouted out the door for us to leave. As I thought, "Good, I have established communication," a shot rang out inside the house. The gunman acted as if he had just shot himself in the stomach, but we held our positions, wary that he was feigning.

Eventually he appeared on the porch, one hand on his abdomen, as if covering a wound, the other steadying the shotgun whose stock rested on the side of his hip, pointing skyward. His body language signaled that he did not intend to remain on the porch.

I dropped the microphone on the seat and shouted, "Can you hear me okay?" I hoped my naked voice would lend itself to more personal communication. He paused a moment, which seemed like an hour. Whether accidental or purposeful, the shotgun suddenly discharged into the sky. The pellets struck branches high in the tree above us, causing leaves and twigs to rain down. I wasn't sure what such an answer meant.

His behaviors were indicative of what is referred to as "suicide by cop," where a deranged person attempts to get the police to kill him. Time is often the cure: allowing a person to fatigue, anger to diminish, and rapport to be built; hopefully, sobriety will return.

It is amazing how time can fly in a crisis situation. I was surprised and relieved when Sergeant Wilt, having been relieved by the midnight shift sergeant, and Troopers Victor Trierweiler and William Gabriel, the midnight patrol, arrived on the scene.

With the suspect's wife and her mother, who had also arrived on the scene, Sergeant Wilt brainstormed on themes that might convince the husband to surrender. A rule of negotiations is not to lie to the suspect.

Using darkness and trees as concealment, Troopers Trierweiler and Gabriel were able to sneak close to the front porch. Trooper Trierweiler called to the suspect and was able to engage him in conversation. In time, Trooper Trierweiler was able to develop rapport with the suspect, who asked to talk with his wife.

Trooper Trierweiler had Sergeant Wilt escort the wife into the light so the suspect could see her. With bait exposed, Trooper Trierweiler then told the suspect that if he would leave his guns inside and come out, he could talk with her. The suspect agreed.

Unable to see the guns pointed at him, the suspect came out unarmed. His wife, escorted by Sergeant Wilt, called to him, and as they talked, the suspect gradually distanced himself from the farmhouse.

From behind trees, Troopers Trierweiler and Gabriel gauged the time it would take them to engage the suspect before he could retreat back to the house and his weapons. As he stepped forward to hear his wife's words, Troopers Trierweiler and Gabriel broke cover in a full sprint and overpowered the suspect before he could take flight. With the suspect in handcuffs, we sighed in relief. In the house, we found a loaded and cocked shotgun and a .22 rifle.

We lodged the suspect at the Macomb County Jail for the night. By the time the first court date came around, the wife no longer wanted to prosecute and the charges were dismissed.

Domestic abuse situations that resulted in dismissed charges were a common frustration during this time period, but action was being taken in the legislature to correct the problem. With time, the law would be changed, empowering the state to pursue domestic violence charges and require the victim to appear and testify with a subpoena. Along with this law change, an officer no longer had the discretion not to arrest in misdemeanor offenses; now a custodial arrest was required in all domestic violence complaints. In other words, no longer would domestic violence be swept under the rug.

18) Kidnapped

During a winter midnight shift, I was partnered with Trooper Bob Ball. He was one of the lead troopers at the Romeo Post with whom I had not yet worked. Bob was driving on a bitterly cold night and chose to patrol a desolate gravel road. I remember thinking, "If I were driving, we would be patrolling where the people are." After a while, we spied a set of taillights in the distance. When Bob caught up to the car, we observed it weaving on the narrow snow-covered road. We activated the overhead red light and the spotlights. Initially, we could only see a silhouette of the driver, but as the spotlights illuminated the interior of the vehicle, we saw a second head rise from the driver's lap. Once the vehicle was stopped,

Bob approached the driver's side while I approached the passenger's.

As soon as Bob initiated contact with the driver, the lone female passenger burst out of the front passenger door screaming, "He kidnapped and raped me, and he has a knife!" Simultaneously, we drew our revolvers.

Concerned it might be a diversion, I took control of the woman, checking her for weapons and handcuffing her. I asked her to be patient with me as I explained that we had to make sure everything was safe. As I had her take a seat in the back of the patrol car, I turned on a tape recorder on the front seat to capture what she might utter in our absence. The recording was legal as she had no "reasonable expectation of privacy" in a police car.

I then assisted Bob, who was holding the driver at gunpoint. Together, we made a felony arrest. Searching the car, we found a knife hidden in the crack of the front seat.

While monitoring the suspect, we conducted an initial interview of the victim in the patrol car. She told us how the suspect had kidnapped her at knifepoint in Mt. Clemens, driven her to the country, and had been forcing her to perform fellatio on him when we pulled them over.

As cynical police officers, we were first skeptical of her story since so often such stories are not true. So many times they are what we label as a "failure to pay," which is an accusation of rape made by a prostitute when a client does not adequately pay her. To see whether she was credible, we asked her further about the weapon. At that time, I was carrying a Gerber double-edged knife as a backup weapon. When I showed it to her, asking whether it was the knife he had, she said, "No," and she described the knife Bob had found in the seat. Then, I grabbed the tape recorder and Bob and I stepped out of the car to see what she might have uttered in our absence, as she had appeared nearly hysterical. The emotions recorded, along with her reaction to the knife, garnered credibility to her accusation.

The prosecutor charged the suspect with this crime and a trial later followed in Oakland County Circuit Court. I was disappointed when the verdict was "Not Guilty."

In our legal system, it is important not to confuse "Not Guilty" with "Innocent." The jury has two verdict options: Guilty or Not Guilty. If they choose neither, the judge will deem them a "Hung Jury" and allow the prosecution to retry the case. A verdict of "Not Guilty" means the government was unable to prove the charges beyond a reasonable doubt. The defendant may or may not be innocent. So having cleared that up, remember this—in the eyes of the law, you are innocent until proven guilty. You've got to love the law!

This case was not the first time, nor would it be the last, when I would have to remind myself of one of the basic concepts of our justice system: we would rather ten guilty go free than one innocent be found guilty.

While I was still at Romeo, Bob Ball was promoted to Detective Sergeant and transferred. He would solve many major cases over the course of his career, retiring out of the Calumet Post. An interesting book written by David Distel, first published as the *The Sweater Letter* and later as *Hunt to Kill*, depicts a murder case Bob solved.

19) Blizzard

History records that the incredible Blizzard of January 26-27th, 1978 evolved out of a winter that was infamous for cold and storms. While there are several contenders for the worst blizzard ever to hit the Great Lakes in relatively modern times (since 1870 when records began in Detroit), the immense and intense Blizzard of January 1978 must rank at or near the top, and its power can be compared to that of the Great Hurricane of 1913.

As troopers, we drove rear-wheel drive Plymouth cars with positive traction and radial snow tires. That automobile, combined with our driving skills, allowed us to do our job throughout this blizzard.

State police posts usually only mounted snow tires on about half of the fleet, but the way this blizzard besieged the area necessitated that more patrol cars be so equipped. I was a young trooper at the Romeo Post and had just had snow tires mounted on another patrol car when Trooper Jackson and I were dispatched to a car-snowmobile accident on Romeo Plank Road.

Much of the ten mile drive found us in a complete whiteout, creeping along with red light, spotlights, and siren on. It was difficult to know where the road was and maintain a sense of direction. How we got to the scene, let alone knew we were there, remains a mystery to me. Probably some awaiting Good Samaritan heard our siren or saw our approach and banged on the hood to get us to stop. We found the young woman lying on the road, clad in a snowmobile suit, and a full-face helmet. Removing my gloves, I checked her for vital signs and found none.

Fatal accidents are to be thoroughly investigated, which includes the recording of detailed measurements. Perilously, we attempted to mark and measure the final resting positions of vehicles and victims, but Mother Nature would not allow it. The bitter cold wind, low visibility, and drifting snow forced us to abandon this part of the investigation. So as quickly as possible, we gathered up the broken pieces, including the lifeless woman, and cleared the scene.

The woman had been the passenger on a snowmobile travelling on the roadway when it struck a car, breaking her neck. It is illegal for snowmobiles to be on the roadway, so this shouldn't have happened; however, I do not remember whether the snowmobile driver was prosecuted.

Regulations prohibited snowmobiles from being operated on the roadways, but the blizzard seemed to have changed that law in the minds of snowmobile operators. Many rode them on the roads as if they were cars, making a bad situation worse.

The next day, I was haunted by the fatal crash when we observed a snowmobile being driven down highway M-53 just like a car, but faster. As we gave pursuit, it fled into a field. As we watched, the snowmobile floundered, and then stopped in the deep snow.

The race was between me traversing the snow to the snowmobile and the rider getting the snowmobile unstuck and underway. When I arrived first, the overweight rider signaled submission by rolling onto his back in the snow as he gasped for breath. As I pulled off his helmet, I was surprised to recognize a local restaurant's manager. We later dropped him off at his place of employment, with citations in hand.

Not long after resuming patrol, we saw another snowmobile travelling the highway. As we went to stop him, he also fled across a field. Luck was with him, and he disappeared from sight. The snow was fresh, the tracks obvious, and my blood hot, so I decided to track him.

Driving the patrol car, my partner kept me in sight, meeting with me when the trail crossed a road. After a couple of miles of tracking, the trail eventually led us to the snowmobile, parked among several others at a farmhouse.

A party seemed to be going on, and our knocks at the door were answered by the resident, a man around thirty years of age. We told him that we needed to talk to the snowmobile's rider, pointing at the machine. He asked us to wait as he closed the door and went back inside the house. A few minutes later, he returned, saying he did not know who had been riding that snowmobile.

We decided to take a hostage—the snowmobile in question. So we summoned a tow truck, a common tactic in such situations. Funny thing, as the wrecker driver began to load the snowmobile, guess who decided to make an appearance? Tickets were exchanged for our hostage once the rider paid the wrecker driver for coming out.

In an odd way, these arrests were helping me cope with the melancholy the fatal snowmobile crash had caused.

20) Ready

It was February 1978, and the Romeo Post was slated to receive one of the recruits graduating from the trooper school. Having only trooped for seventeen months, I was both surprised and honored when the post commander, First Lieutenant Russell Beamish, assigned me as the recruit's field training officer.

I learned that my first cub, Jerry Ellsworth, was twenty-six years old (at that time I was twenty-two), had a bachelor degree in business from Michigan State University (at that time I had no college degree), and had decided to make a career change from business to law enforcement. He was married and his wife had given birth to their first child while he was in recruit school. He had excelled both academically and physically in the academy. I don't remember being intimidated by these credentials, although looking back, I think I would have been.

On his first day at the Romeo Post, we were scheduled to start our shift at 7:00 a.m. There had been no patrol out since 4:00 a.m. It was one of those bitterly cold mornings, where the snow squeaks and nostrils stick together. Wanting to be at the post when Jerry arrived, which I expected to be early, I got there at 5:30 a.m. and busied myself with the never-ending stream of paperwork. It was my practice to be briefed, patrol car loaded, and on a day like this, warmed-up and windows scraped, ten minutes before my shift started. I hoped to imprint Jerry with that habit.

At 6:30 a.m., Jerry had not yet arrived, which surprised me. Not wanting him to compromise my practice, I prepared a patrol vehicle for the shift, staying true to my tenet of being "good to go" ten minutes prior to being on the clock.

At 6:50 a.m., Sergeant Richard Campbell answered a ringing telephone at the Romeo Post. It was the janitor from the Peach Pit, a bowling alley/ bar combination located just south of the Village of Romeo. The janitor excitedly told the sergeant that when he got to work and began cleaning, a white male confronted him with a crowbar and then fled with a bag of money. He described the robber as being in his twenties with long brown hair, a stubble beard, and armed with a crowbar. He said he last saw him running toward the M-53 highway. Sergeant Campbell yelled the information to me in the squad room, and I sprinted to the patrol car, alone.

I raced south in the dim morning light on two-lane M-53 amongst work traffic. I only had the overhead red light activated since I did not want my siren to warn the suspect of my approach. I primarily straddled the center line, prompting oncoming traffic to pull to the shoulder. Often cars overtaken don't see you at first, while those approached head on will immediately yield. The Peach Pit was only about a mile from the post and as my eyes negotiated traffic, they also scanned for the suspect.

Like a dream come true, I saw a person matching the suspect description shuffling through the nearly knee deep snow toward M-53, carrying the proverbial moneybag. He was looking south, as if watching for something, so he didn't see me approaching from the north. Going south, I began to pull to the northbound shoulder. As I did, I saw a newer model white car being driven north by a blonde white female; the car was also pulling to the northbound shoulder. My impression was that she, like the other traffic, was yielding to my flashing red light so I didn't consider her a threat.

I barely had time to radio "226 (my patrol car number) 22 (post number), I'll be out with the suspect on the east side of M-53 just north of the Peach Pit." (Note - since that time radio protocol has changed. In this case, it would now be 22 -226.) Leaping from the patrol car as I drew my service revolver, I did not hear Sergeant Campbell's response, but I knew there was no backup in the area. I shouted, "State police, drop the bag and put your hands on top of your head. (He obeyed.) Turn around and look away from me. (He obeyed.) Interlace your fingers and put them behind your head. (He obeyed.) Kneel down, cross one leg over the other (He obeyed.)." I then moved in and handcuffed him. Checking the bag he had dropped, I found it was full of coins, later determined to have been stolen from the vending machines. The bag also contained a dual-purpose crowbar, which had just served as both a prying instrument and impact weapon.

During this maneuver, which we call a felony arrest, my back and attention were turned away from the blonde in the white car. As I began to escort the handcuffed suspect to my patrol car, she asked me where I was taking him. That was a clue! Keeping her in my peripheral vision, I told her to wait a moment and I would tell her.

After seat belting the handcuffed suspect in the backseat of my patrol car, I contacted the blonde in the white car. She asked where I was taking him and how much the bond would be. When I asked how she knew him, she told me they had come to Romeo together and that she had let him out, but she didn't know he was going to break into the bowling alley. I asked myself, "How did she know he broke into the bowling alley?"

During this period in the evolution of the Miranda Warning, any time the finger of suspicion pointed at a suspect, the police were required to advise the person of those pre-interview rights. Believing I could articulate probable cause, I placed her under arrest, but my handcuffs were on her partner. Grasping her hands behind her, I walked her back to the patrol car where I had other restraints for her wrists. Fortunately, this couple was not Bonnie and Clyde because I undoubtedly would have become a notch in Bonnie's gun while my back was turned to her.

With her seated in the right front seat and her partner in the right rear seat of the patrol car, we waited for the wrecker to tow their car to the post. I did not let them talk and advised them of their Miranda Warning by reading it from my departmental issued card. I did not question them until we arrived at the post and they were separated.

When I later searched their car, I discovered a phonebook, and in the Yellow Pages, I found where the advertisements for various bowling alleys had been circled in red. A telephone call to the bowling alleys revealed that many had been recently burglarized, similar *modus operandi* to the Peach Pit caper. We soon found out that both suspects were from the Detroit area and he had a felony record.

It is not often that you knock off a robbery in progress, and unheard of on the first day on the job, but where was Jerry? It turned out that Jerry had thought his shift began at 8:00 a.m. so he arrived at the post at 7:00 a.m. He was just in time to help process the crime scene, search their car, and be introduced to the best part of the job, paperwork. After he heard about my morning adventure, I didn't have to tell him why I liked to be "good to go" ten minutes before the start of the shift.

21) Prophecy

After a period of time, a cub is cleared to work as a true partner on night shift. Soon after being approved, Jerry and I were working midnights; he was driving the first half, which was considered prime time for drunk drivers. In Police Alcohol Training (PAT), I, and I assumed he too, had been taught that freeways are not typically fertile grounds for drunk drivers. I bit my lip, wondering why Jerry was patrolling M-59, the freeway that runs between Mt. Clemens and Pontiac. I said nothing as it was usually driver discretion on where the patrol hunted, and I did not want to be the training officer who dictated his every move.

As we patrolled, we met a car going the wrong way, westbound in the eastbound lanes of the freeway; radar indicated his speed at 55 mph, the speed limit. I remember my initial confusion: What's going on? Are we going the wrong way? No, he is!

We spun around and gave chase—red lights, siren, and spotlights activated. Jerry got right behind the car, but the driver seemed oblivious to us. We were going up a hill and I could see headlights shining into the sky as approaching vehicles climbed the other side. We were moments from a catastrophe if we didn't stop him and get our vehicles off the roadway.

Jerry floored the accelerator. We roared around and then positioned our patrol car directly in front of the derelict vehicle. Using his rearview mirror, Jerry maintained this blocking position as he braked to a halt. If the vehicle rear-ended us, oh well, we had to stop him. Amazingly, the wrong way vehicle came to a stop behind us without a collision.

I leaped from the patrol car before Jerry had it in park and ran back to the driver's door of the suspect vehicle. I jerked his door open to see a man about my age. He smelled of intoxicants, had bloodshot-watery eyes, and with slurred speech, asked, "What's wrong, officer? Was I speeding?"

I had just pulled him from the car when Jerry got to my side. With no time to spare, I said to Jerry "Take care of him," referring to the drunk, as I slid behind the wheel of the drunk's car and backed it onto the shoulder of the road. I then sprinted to the patrol car, which was sitting on the roadway, facing the wrong direction. I pulled it off the road just before oncoming traffic whizzed past. When traffic cleared, I repositioned the patrol car and Jerry tried to administer field sobriety tests, but the drunk could barely stand. With the drunk arrested and handcuffed, the three of us took refuge in the patrol car.

For liability reasons (the car was on the shoulder of a freeway facing the wrong direction with no reflectors at night), we summoned a wrecker to tow the car. By the time the wrecker arrived, the drunk had lapsed into unconsciousness. Not knowing whether his slumber was only alcohol-related or whether he had some other medical problem, we transported him to the hospital for evaluation, where he was admitted.

When we cleared the hospital, I asked Jerry why he had chosen to patrol the freeway at that time. He said, "Just had a hunch." If you think about it, you can see if we always followed the training we had received in PAT, it could make for a self-fulfilling prophecy, which is the tendency for our expectations to foster the behavior that is consistent with our expectations. As we headed for the restaurant, I thanked my lucky stars that I had allowed Jerry to follow his instincts.

22) Thumb-up

When partners have bonded, they are like left and right hands. I had been Jerry's training officer for his first three months as a trooper and toward the end of that period, we approached this intuitiveness.

The four elements to an arrest are intent, authority, submission, and custody. During my training, troopers were taught when making an arrest that you "ask, tell, and take." This statement means the normal steps for taking a person into custody are to request their submission to custody; if they refuse, you demand their submission to custody; and if necessary, you make them submit to custody. This does not mean fighting fair, but it does require legal use of force. Legal use of force does not exclude the element of surprise, one of the principles Sun Tzu cites in the book, *The Art of War*.

We developed a technique for taking custody of a noncompliant arrestee which we labeled "thumb up." While the contact officer negotiated with the suspect to submit and be handcuffed, the cover officer positioned for a takedown. If the contact officer's verbal judo failed and physical force was imminent, he would simply put a thumb up. This cued the cover officer to take the suspect down to be handcuffed. Some might call it a surprise attack.

One night in the Village of Romeo, we pulled over a BIG drunk driver. He was probably in his twenties, 6' 2", two hundred fifty pounds, and muscled like a bodybuilder. However, as the years pass, I may remember him as bigger than he really was.

Having performed poorly on the sobriety tests, I verbally placed him under arrest and asked him to put his hands behind his back to be handcuffed. Calmly looking down at me, he shook his head, saying "Not going to happen."

While I explained to him that state police policy required me to handcuff all arrested persons, Jerry maneuvered into a takedown position. Jerry stood about 5' 8" and weighed about one hundred fifty pounds. I then told the drunk to put his hands behind his back to be handcuffed. He said nothing as he stared at me with defiant eyes. Having exhausted verbal judo during that "ask" and "tell" phase, I gave Jerry the thumb up signal, which kicked off the "take" phase. Remember, during this era troopers did not carry intermediate weapons, such as tasers or pepper spray.

From behind, Jerry leaped to the suspect's back and set the Carotid Chokehold, which blocks the flow of oxygenized blood to the brain. Like a bull, the suspect began twisting and turning in an attempt to fling Jerry off. And like a rodeo clown, I tried to distract him by restraining his arms from reaching back for Jerry. We knew that if Jerry had the hold set right, it would be a short dance. I positioned to ease their collapse to the ground and then quickly handcuff the suspect. It was over within ten seconds. When the drunk woke, he found himself handcuffed and us brushing off our uniforms.

The Carotid Chokehold was the best hold they ever taught us in the academy, and I have used it successfully several times. However, when cocaine became the drug of choice, a number of combatants and resistors died while receiving it; since most of the deceased had cocaine in their system, it suggested the two don't mix well. Many police departments responded by no longer teaching the Carotid Chokehold and advising those officers previously taught the choke to cease and desist from its use, except when fatal force could be justified.

With the advent of mixed martial arts at the turn of the twenty-first century, the rear naked choke, aka Carotid Chokehold, is taught as a submission hold, making it common knowledge amongst those practitioners. By academies not teaching it, many officers are ignorant to how lethal it might be to them.

With the passing of time, some academies have realized their choice not to teach such a hold has left their officers vulnerable, so now they are teaching the Lateral Vascular Neck Restraint, which is pretty similar to the Carotid Chokehold but more appropriately named. The pendulum swings.

23) Obscene

One day, I was dispatched to a trailer park north of Romeo. A pretty young mother of a one year old had complained about receiving obscene telephone calls from an unknown male that were threatening in nature. Her recital of them was disturbing.

I took her information, installed a tape recorder to record future calls, and arranged for the telephone company to place a trap—a tap in layman terms—on her phone line. Back then there was no caller ID. If she were able to keep the caller on the telephone long enough, followed by a call to the telephone company, it might be able to provide us with the telephone number where the call had originated as well as subscriber information.

A few days later, I stopped by to listen to the taped telephone calls. They were extremely obscene and frightening. As the case developed, I consulted a Macomb County Assistant Prosecutor. After listening to some of the recordings, he was equally obsessed with us catching this pervert. He told me that if we were able to make the trace, I should go to the subscriber's address to see whether I could develop a suspect. If I could develop a solid suspect, who either made an admission, or in my opinion, whose voice matched, he gave verbal authorization to make a warrantless custodial arrest for the misdemeanor offense. Back then, voiceprints were admissible evidence. Since the prosecutor is an attorney and the chief law enforcement officer in the county, I didn't give his instructions a second thought.

Finally one stormy night, the trace was made. Jerry and I headed out to an address off a dirt road in the middle of nowhere. Our knocks at the door were answered by a burly, obstinate man in his mid-thirties. He wouldn't invite us in, and he refused to take a seat in the patrol car, so the interview transpired on his porch, not the preferred stage.

We got as far as him saying that he was the only adult male who had been at the house all day and he was the subscriber to whatever the phone number was. During this conversation, I recognized his voice and accent as being the same one we had tape-recorded making the violent sexual threats.

Jerry went back to the patrol car to radio the post of our status, leaving me alone with an increasingly hostile pervert. Those were pre-handheld radio days so our only means of communication was the mobile radio in the patrol car. While I tried to tread water until Jerry returned, the suspect said he was done talking and ordered me off his property.

I then played the ace of spades, or so I hoped, telling him he was under arrest and asking him to turn around and put his hands behind his back. He wasn't impressed, saying, "I won't go." Taking a defensive posture to prevent a possible sucker punch, I defaulted to verbal judo, an essential skill of a peace officer; "Frank, before this goes from bad to worse, I want to share a couple of thoughts with you." Holding up my index finger for emphasis and distraction, I said, "First, I don't claim to be the toughest guy, but if this gets ugly, you are in for a hell of a battle." Holding up my first two fingers, I continued, "Second, if by some chance you win the battle, I can guarantee you this: you will lose the war as I am absolutely positive that my gang is bigger than yours." And then, opening my hand in a non-threatening manner, I closed with, "Frank, consider this: the penalty for resisting arrest is more serious than obscene telephone calls. I will ask (tell) you again to turn around and put your hands behind your back."

As I paused to catch my breath, our eyes met for the moment of truth as Jerry returned. I am not sure whether it was the speech or Jerry's return or some combination of both, but the suspect submitted to arrest. With him handcuffed in the backseat of the patrol car, I breathed a sigh of relief. We lodged him in the Macomb County jail.

A couple of weeks later, I got a call from the assistant prosecutor I had consulted on this case. He explained that he had just had a telephone conversation with the pervert's attorney and we had a problem—I had made a false arrest. The heat of the chase had apparently blinded us both from following basic criminal procedure, meaning he couldn't authorize me to make a warrantless misdemeanor arrest for an offense that hadn't occurred in my presence. What had we been thinking? As prosecutor, he was immune from any legal action, but I was not. The remedy: drop charges and they would not pursue any legal action against me for false arrest.

And so it was. As often said, "Lessons learned hard are lessons learned well." Did you know you could legally resist an illegal arrest? If he had, well who knows what it might have escalated into? In a sense, I won the battle and he won the war.

What I should have done was what the pervert had told me—left his property. Then I could have submitted a warrant request to the prosecutor's office, and signed the complaint before the judge, who then would have issued a misdemeanor warrant. I then would have been empowered to go back and arrest him. It probably would have taken a week, but we would have had our day in court, and having followed proper procedure, I wouldn't be the defendant.

But at least, our complainant did not receive any more phone calls from him.

24) Speeder?

During this time, a spike in violent crimes committed on Detroit freeways occurred. Until now, such crimes had always been the responsibility of the Detroit Police Department. In response to a hue and cry of citizens, however, the Governor of Michigan assigned the state police to make the Detroit freeways safe again.

While initially a temporary detail, it was so successful and well-received by the public that it was decided to make the Detroit Freeway Post permanent. It would be the largest post in the state with over one hundred troopers assigned. The department first looked for volunteers, but when the total fell short, they readied for mandatory transfers. At the Detroit Post, troopers provided only Highway Patrol services. While I liked patrol, I equally liked investigations, so I looked to dodge a mandatory transfer there.

The Ypsilanti, Flint, and Benton Harbor posts were considered the highest crime posts in the state. Ypsilanti was close to my and Deb's families in the Irish Hills, and within the same district as Romeo, which made me eligible for an intra-district transfer. If I got transferred to Ypsilanti, I wouldn't get transferred to Detroit. I requested an audience with the District Commander, Captain Walter Anderson, whose office was at district headquarters in Northville, to try to persuade him why it would be best for the state police to transfer me to Ypsilanti.

The appointment was scheduled at Northville District Headquarters, a place I, surprisingly, had not yet visited. I was given directions there and told the drive would take about an hour and a half.

It was a beautiful summer morning when I set out in full uniform driving a sleek blue goose. It was the kind of day when almost everybody speeds and I soon saw a car speeding in the far distance. Michigan law permits a police officer to exceed the speed limit, without emergency equipment activated when necessary, to enforce the law. I exceeded the speed limit to get close enough to the suspected violator to do a pace speed check. That day, everyone seemed to be watching his or her rearview mirror and would slow down before I got a solid pace in excess of the speed limit.

And so it went, all the way to Telegraph Road where I came across a disabled car in the right lane blocking traffic. I stopped to render assistance, learning that a wrecker was already en route.

As I walked back to my patrol car, I noticed a new Cadillac parked behind it and a well-dressed, middle-aged man standing behind my patrol car. When I asked whether I could help him, he said he wanted my name and badge number because he had been following me since Utica and I had been speeding. Suddenly, the tables were turned and I was at a loss for words, but I did provide him with my name and badge number as required by policy.

I made it to the meeting with Captain Walter Anderson and things seemed to go well. I kept my fingers crossed that I would get transferred to the Ypsilanti Post.

A couple of weeks later, I was called into the Post Commander's office. Lieutenant Beamish told me a complaint had been filed at the governor's office that accused me of speeding. He showed me the letter from the governor's office and the citizen's complaint. It was written by the man in the Cadillac, and it concerned the day I drove to Northville. And so, I would author another "special" to the Colonel.

Things are not always as they appear, and this citizen's perception was that I was violating the very laws I enforced. I regretted that. It was a reminder to me that police officers live and work in a glass house and should be aware of how their actions appear to the unknowing public. And since most police officers are "risk takers," they must resist the temptation to abuse their authority.

25) Garbage

It was August 11, 1978 and I was working the 2:00 p.m. to 10:00 p.m. shift alone. During this era in the MSP, daylight patrols were solo and during the hours of darkness we were paired. I had picked up some health food at McDonald's—a Quarter Pounder with cheese and fries—and was eating it while standing in front of the window air conditioner at the Romeo Post. It was hotter than blazes and the wool uniform pants and body armor made it punishing.

Since the desk sergeant was busy, I answered the telephone when it rang at 5:05 p.m. "State Police, Trooper Edwards." The caller said a young woman had walked to their farm and told them a man had tried to kill her. As I told the caller I would be en route from the post, I thought it smelled like a domestic dispute.

This conjecture was probably a symptom of my flirting with what the departmental psychologist labeled "the John Wayne Syndrome." During advanced trooper school, we were warned about it in hopes that knowledge equated to prevention. It happens when all of an officer's training and experiences come together in a bad way that makes the officer become a cocky know-it-all. It's not a good place to be, and every once in awhile, you'll meet an officer who didn't evolve past it.

I gulped down my food and headed north, not realizing I had just begun what I would later consider my premier case while serving at the Romeo Post. I would handle it alone since there were no other patrols available to assist me.

Following a twenty minute response time, I arrived at the farm. First, I observed an eighteen-year-old white female standing to the side whom I thought to be the victim. On the ground was a middle-aged white male, whom I surmised was the suspect; he was being restrained by what appeared to be the farmer and a young man, whom I would later learn was the farmer's son.

I relieved them from holding the suspect down, ordering the suspect, a forty-eight year old white male, to put his hands behind his head and interlace his fingers, which he did. With one of my hands, I grasped both of his, holding them behind his head, and with my other hand, I frisked him for weapons, finding none. He said his name was Cheyenne Brody and the driver's license in his wallet supported that claim. I then had him stand up and walked him to my patrol car where I told him to keep his hands on the hood while I interviewed the victim and witnesses. Apparently, he didn't realize, or maybe hoped, I wasn't keeping an eye on him since he tried to sneak away. He hadn't gotten far when I grabbed him. I then handcuffed him and secured him in the backseat of the patrol car.

The farmer told me that the victim had run to his farm looking for help, with the suspect trailing her. When she had told him what had happened, the farmer had his wife call the police, and he stood by the suspect, keeping him away from the victim while they awaited the police.

The farmer's eighteen-year-old son, seeing his father standing with a stranger, joined them. Suddenly, the suspect grabbed a nearby rake and struck the son in the stomach, knocking him back. The father retaliated by striking the suspect in the head with his fist, knocking him down. They held the suspect until I arrived.

The victim told me that she knew the suspect as John; he was the uncle of a good friend who had recently shown up in their Detroit neighborhood. John had helped her move into her new apartment, and she had agreed to return the favor by accompanying him to meet a friend about some business. When she got off work that day, he was waiting for her, wanting to take her up on the offer. Looking back, this was my first clue that his real name was not Cheyenne Brody, but at the time, I thought, "If my name were Cheyenne, I too might prefer to be called John."

They departed Detroit and ended up in this farmer's field, where he said they were to meet someone in a blue car. As the trip unfolded, she became increasingly worried. She did not know where she was, but she felt dependent on him to get home. This tactic of control, and I make analogy to a spiderweb, is often practiced by many predators, and it certainly was part of his *modus operandi*.

Once in the farmer's field, they got out of the car. He produced a set of homemade brass knuckles and struck her in the chin, knocking her to the ground. He then tied her hands behind her back with yellow telephone cord and forced her into the backseat of the car, convincing her he was going to kill her. During this struggle, she was able to get her hands loose and escaped out the other door. She ran toward the farmhouse with "John" in pursuit, but he couldn't catch her.

With the suspect detained for officer safety reasons in the backseat of my patrol car and my initial witness interviews complete, I waited for Trooper Thomas Garvale to arrive to assist me. While Tom had hazed me as a cub, now that I had completed probation, he treated me as a colleague. The victim got into Tom's patrol car, keeping the victim and suspect separate, and we drove back to where he had left his car in the field to pursue the victim on foot.

I advised "John" of his pre-interview rights known as the Miranda warning and then requested and received written permission to search his car. It is surprising what people will tell you and give you permission to search if you ask them nicely.

As I searched the area around the suspect's car, I found the brass knuckles wrapped in gray duct tape the victim said he had hit her with and the yellow telephone cord he had tried to bind her with. In the glove box, I found a female billfold. In the billfold was an attorney's business card and a birth certificate for an eighteen year old female I will call Jane Doe II; the victim I was currently dealing with had another name and it was not Jane.

When I searched the trunk of Cheyenne Brody's car, I found it full of personal belongings, including old letters to a John Weeks with the envelopes bearing the address of San Quentin Penitentiary in California. I was becoming suspicious that John was Cheyenne's real name, but he refuted it, saying he was simply keeping the stuff for a friend. I now felt I had probable cause to make a warrantless felony arrest for assault and did, transporting him back to the post for processing.

That evening, I interviewed Cheyenne Brody at the Romeo Post for nearly an hour. He was twice my age, and unknown to me at the time, he had been in prison as long as I was old. Fortunately, he was not as smart as he thought, and I fed his ego using a tactic I would later call the "double con" by appearing to believe his statements—statements I hoped I could later prove were lies to a jury, destroying any credibility he might have.

After discussing the incident at hand, I explored his true identity and then did a blind interview on the mysterious female wallet in his glove box. He described Jane as an attractive teenage blond with whom he sometimes socialized. Having no information to dispute what he might tell me, I encouraged him to talk by listening intently. As I tape recorded this interview, my objective was to lock him into a story that could later be investigated for its veracity. As I wrapped up the interview, "Cheyenne" wanted to press charges against the farmer for assault, kidnapping, and robbery. He was proving to be a real piece of work.

The man known as Cheyenne Brody was fingerprinted and then lodged at the Lapeer County Jail by Troopers James Tyler and Dennis Woizeschke. The next day he was arraigned before a judge, to whom I provided information that supported my concerns about his true identity. At arraignment, the judge asked him his name and he said, "Cheyenne Brody." The judge asked him whether he might be "John Weeks," which he denied. The seriousness of the charges and the questionable identity prompted the judge to set a high bond, insuring the suspect remain in jail while we sorted out his true identity.

John Weeks Jr is demanding changes at jail.

Compliments of the *Saginaw News*

I took another set of fingerprints from him and had them sent to Lansing headquarters to be classified and checked against others on file. Back then fax and scanning did not exist so they had to be driven there. The fingerprint unit matched the fingerprints to a set on file under the name of John Matthew Weeks, taken by the Pontiac Police Department back in 1948 on an auto theft charge. The match proved that Cheyenne Brody was really John Matthew Weeks Jr. with an extensive criminal history, including over twenty years of prison time. His criminal history included rape and robbery. Faced with this proof, "Cheyenne Brody" now admitted to being John Weeks Jr. Having lied to the judge would be the least of his troubles.

Curious, I looked further into his background. Information surfaced that suggested he was the product of incest, his mother also being his sister.

An area teletype was broadcast via LEIN (Law Enforcement Information Network) concerning the arrest of John Weeks and his *modus operandi*. It prompted many inquiries from various police departments investigating similar incidents in which the suspect's identity was unknown. Trooper Craig Nyeholt was assigned as the liaison to these investigators, allowing me to remain focused on our primary case. Through this departmental cooperation, John Weeks was found to be responsible for several cases of a similar nature.

On March 1, 1979, the first capital felony (penalty could be life sentence) jury trial of my career would begin in the Lapeer County courthouse, where legend has it Abraham Lincoln once tried a case. The trial would take two days. I would testify for about ninety-five minutes, during which time I played the taped interviews of Weeks from the day at the farm. The recordings proved to be damning to his defense.

It took the jury only two hours to find John Weeks "Guilty of Assault with Intent to Commit Murder." He was subsequently sentenced to life in prison. The evidence supported this conviction, but I believe his true intent was to rape her. Either way, the penalty would have been the same.

Other than the courage of the victim, farmer, and his son, nothing was really spectacular about the case in Lapeer County. Finding the female named on the birth certificate in the billfold found in the glove box of Week's car would be a more challenging path.

All my queries in the state police computers concerning the name on the birth certificate came back with no records. I ended up calling the attorney whose card I had also found in the same billfold. This attorney was hesitant to share any information because he didn't want to violate any attorney-client privileges. I finally convinced him that I had good reason to be concerned about his client's welfare, and he provided me with the address and telephone number of the young woman's grandmother. He also described his client as thin and blonde, which matched the description of an unidentified murder victim found at a gravel pit swimming hole near where I had arrested John Weeks. When found, that murder victim was wearing a two-piece yellow bathing suit.

When I telephoned the grandmother, she told me Jane was a troubled wayward girl who had disappeared a couple of weeks ago. I asked whether Jane had a yellow bathing suit. She said, "No," but Jane's sister did, and Jane sometimes borrowed it. She checked the sister's dresser for the yellow bathing suit, only to find it missing. The grandmother asked why I was interested in the bathing suit. I dodged the question by telling her I needed to speak to her granddaughter concerning a case I was investigating and to contact me immediately if she heard from her.

Detective Sergeant John Flis was investigating the murder of the yet unidentified female. As I prepared to brief him with my concern, I heard, "Clif, phone call on line one." When I picked the phone up, it was Jane's sister. She had just talked to her grandmother and wanted to let me know she had seen Jane a couple of days ago and could probably locate her.

The unidentified murder victim had been discovered over two weeks ago so she was clearly not Jane then, but she was still somebody's daughter. Detective Sergeant John Flis investigated Weeks as a possible suspect in his investigation but cleared him of it. When I was transferred to the Ypsilanti Post some four months later, the murder investigation was ongoing and I never learned its outcome. Many major investigations include wild goose chases and this one serves as an example.

Meanwhile, I requested that the sister contact Jane and ask that she meet with me. A few days later, I received a call from the sister who then put Jane on the phone. I told Jane I needed to talk to her about her wallet being found in a car owned by John Weeks, also known as Cheyenne Brody. I could sense the fear in her response. I assured her that he was in jail on serious charges with a high bond. After some convincing, she agreed to meet me at the Romeo Post.

On August 14, 1978, Jane was brought to the Romeo Post by her sister, who sat by her side during the interview. Jane was a pretty thin blonde with a seemingly quiet, reserved nature. She was hesitant to talk with me. After being assured that John was in jail and it was unlikely that he would get out, and with the encouragement of her sister, Jane shared her sad story of how she knew John.

A couple of weeks earlier (we later determined it to be July 23, 1978), Jane and her boyfriend were at a residence in Detroit when one of her girlfriends showed up with John. The girlfriend had been hitchhiking and John had picked her up. The four of them decided to go ride around in John's car. After awhile, Jane's boyfriend was dropped off because he had other business to attend to. The remaining three rode a while longer, and then Jane's girlfriend took off, leaving only Jane and John in the car. John told her that he knew a place where they could score some dope and she agreed to go with him. He asked her to drive, which she did, with him giving directions.

He directed her north, out of the city, and then had her turn right on what she remembers was signed as 26 Mile Road. After a while, he pointed out an abandoned two-story farmhouse and told her that was where the meeting was to take place. A party store was nearby so they stopped to purchase a bottle of Boone's Farm Strawberry Hill wine and a pack of cigarettes.

They then went to the abandoned farmhouse, which was unlocked. He led her upstairs to a bedroom and began looking out the window as if watching for someone. During this time, she sat down on the bare mattress. As they waited, he said, "See the red stain on the mattress; that's where I killed a girl last week." Startled, she became scared. He then pulled something out of his pocket and tapped on the window as if signaling someone to come in. When she asked him what the object was, he briefly showed her duct tape covered brass knuckles. Suddenly, he drew back his right arm and punched her in the mouth, knocking her back onto the bed.

As she struggled to maintain consciousness, he tied her hands behind her back and convinced her he was going to kill her. She pleaded for her life. He then gave her a choice: have sex with him, or with the fifteen guys downstairs. At the time, she feared there really might be fifteen guys downstairs so she submitted to having sex with him. He then untied her, made her undress, and then retied her. Next, he took off his clothes and sexually assaulted her.

After the act was completed, she pleaded with him not to kill her. As if pondering her plea, he proposed not to kill her if she would live with him. When she agreed, they left in his car. Once in the car, he showed her a jar filled with brown liquid, telling her it was acid, and if she tried anything, he would throw it in her face.

They drove back to Detroit where Jane's girlfriend was staying in a runaway shelter. John told her to go in and get her. Jane, leaving her billfold in his glove box by accident, went in and found her friend. She told her girlfriend what had happened. They took refuge in the shelter; however, the counselors did not believe Jane's story and ordered her to leave.

Fortunately, John had become wary and left the area prior to her exit.

Jane told me she had never reported the incident to the police because she feared John would then find and kill her. Since then, she had lived in a constant state of terror, fearing that John would find her and fulfill his threat of throwing acid in her face.

Quite a story! But I would need a lot more pieces of the puzzle to make it a prosecutable case. I had Jane describe the person who had assaulted her and the car he was driving. Both descriptions matched John Weeks and his car. She identified the billfold I had found in his glove box as hers. Further, her sister also identified it, saying she had gifted it to Jane. When I showed Jane the duct taped brass knuckles that I had found near his car, she also identified them. Now we needed to find the abandoned house she had described to see whether anything there was of evidentiary value.

We had started our interview at 8:45 p.m., and when we finished, it was after 11:00 p.m. While it was late, I was anxious to locate this abandoned farmhouse she had described. When I asked Jane and her sister whether they were up to searching for it tonight, they said they were. By now my shift was over, but the sergeant authorized me to work over.

Following Jane's direction, she, her sister, and I drove south in a patrol car on Van Dyke Rd. to 26 Mile Road and then headed east. We watched for the party store she had described to be on the south side of the road. It was not long before we departed the Romeo Post area, putting me in unfamiliar territory. Where was the store? Was she confused or worse yet, lying to me?

Suddenly, like a big buck magically appearing when you are hunting, she said without question, "That's the party store." As I turned on the spotlight and began illuminating the south side of the road, I thought to myself, "Okay, now we will see if there is an abandoned two-story farmhouse as she described." And there it was!

The next question to answer was mine: "Where were we?" I radioed the New Baltimore Post of the Michigan State Police and learned we were in Ira Township in St. Clair County. While the initial case would go to trial in Lapeer County, if there were any prosecution on this developing case, it would be in St. Clair County. When I requested assistance in checking the abandoned farmhouse, an Ira Township Police Officer responded since no other troopers were available.

The ramshackle house was definitely uninhabited—no cars, no lights, no electricity. The door was open and a real estate "For Sale" sign was in the overgrown yard. I was anxious to look inside, but what were the legal ramifications? Did I need a search warrant? Would one of the ten exceptions to the search warrant rule apply? I decided not to wait under the legal premise that John Weeks, aka Cheyenne Brody, would have no legal standing to object to a search in a house where he had trespassed.

Everything was just as Jane had described, right down to the red stain and Boone's Farm wine bottle. I photographed the scene and collected many items as evidence for the crime laboratory to process. It was eerie.

It had been a long and productive day, which had corroborated information and produced evidence. The garbage (John Weeks) was in the can (jail). Now we had to try to get it to the dump (prison), but that would have to wait for future days.

Unlike many cases where it is a race against time, in this instance, time was somewhat on our side since the suspect was in jail on the other charges with a very high bond.

Trooper Nyeholt and I returned to the ramshackle farmhouse a few days later with crime lab personnel; they processed the crime scene thoroughly, finding and collecting more potential evidence. All the evidence collected was sent to the crime lab for analysis.

A likely defense was that the suspect would claim consensual sex between adults. Because of the manner in which the incident was reported—delayed and solicited—future jurors might find the victim's story incredible. The victim agreed to take a polygraph test, which she passed, strengthening our position.

Next, I would engage the suspect in another interrogation, which would focus on the incident involving Jane. This time, it would not be a blind interview. While I would hope for a grand slam confession, just his denial of ever being in the abandoned farmhouse with the victim could be very damning because I could now put both the victim and suspect in the farmhouse's upstairs bedroom with physical evidence.

In previous interviews, my tactic of the "double con" had served me well, but now I was concerned that Weeks was on to it and that approach might not be effective in the upcoming interview. I solicited the assistance of Trooper Jerry Ellsworth for the upcoming interview. To have the right partner in an interrogation can be a huge asset, particularly when they are lengthy ones. Jerry and I had learned how to team interview effectively while I was his field training officer. In team interviews, it is imperative that you agree on who is the lead.

We did our homework, developing themes and picking the time and place. In learning Weeks' personality, I knew he fancied himself as a jail house lawyer. We decided to patronize his apparent ego and hope to revive the "double con" by asking him whether he was the Weeks responsible for the landmark Supreme Court case "U.S. v. Weeks" which had produced the "exclusionary rule," making evidence seized illegally inadmissible in court. While I knew he wasn't because that case came down in the early 1900s, I would hope he didn't and would buy into my pretense of being impressed if it were him. I would take my police procedure manual to the interview in case I needed a visual aid, to be used only for flash and not review. Remember, the courts have never said that the police could not use trickery in pursuit of the truth.

Trooper Jerry Ellsworth and I spent the morning of August 28, 1978 interviewing John Weeks at the Lapeer County Jail. He was a bit surly in the beginning. I decided to cast what I thought was my best lure, the police procedure manual that summarized the court case "U.S. v John Weeks." He sniffed it a few moments and then bit. Why he now claimed to be the infamous John Weeks in the Supreme Court case I am not really sure. What did matter was that he thought we were in awe of him, so my "double con" was back up and running. Acting is a good skill in an investigator.

The suspect told us that not long ago, he had spent time with a Jane Doe. They had driven around in his car and spent the night in his car in a parking lot near the Detroit Zoo where they had sex. He was proud to tell us that he'd had sex with this young attractive woman. We continued to feed his ego. The next day, he and Jane had driven to Marine City where he had introduced her to his sister.

John Weeks denied any and all knowledge of the abandoned farmhouse and taking the victim there. In his denial, he strengthened our case since the crime lab had physical evidence that put both of them in that farmhouse and crippled him from later saying they had consensual sex there. I thought to myself, *Thank you very much!*

I now believed I had collected all the pieces available for this puzzle.

I began assembling it in the way of a report and warrant request to be presented to the St. Clair County Prosecutor's Office. Because the Romeo Post's primary area of responsibility was the townships of Macomb, Oakland, and Lapeer Counties, I was a total stranger to the St. Clair County Prosecutor's Office. But I was a Michigan State Trooper and St. Clair County was in Michigan.

On September 18, 1978, at age twenty-three, but looking twenty, and with two years and one day experience as a Michigan State Trooper, I arrived at the St. Clair County Prosecutor's Office in Port Huron. I asked to meet with a prosecutor concerning a felony warrant request. After a short wait, I was taken to the office of an older assistant prosecutor.

He listened patiently through the overview, but as I transitioned to the warrant request presentation, he interrupted me. He told me this case was way too big for someone of my age, rank, and experience. He wanted me to return to the Romeo Post and to turn the case over to a detective sergeant.

For a moment, I felt devastated! I had invested my heart and soul into this case over the past month. I had sought the direction and approval of my superiors. I believed the case was good, and I knew I could handle it. Calmly, I apologized to him for apparently not making a quality presentation and asked to meet with the prosecutor. Fortunately, he was available, so after a few minutes, I was escorted to his office. Again, I gave my overview as he perused the report. As I began the warrant request presentation, I was once again interrupted. He told me he was comfortable with my handling of the case and would assign it to another assistant prosecutor, who authorized felony warrants. I was back on track!

From there, the case went forward, with the suspect being charged with two counts of Criminal Sexual Conduct-First Degree in St. Clair County, in addition to the charges filed in Lapeer County. I kept my fingers crossed that John Weeks' days of preying on young women were over.

On October 16, 1978, I served a writ of *habeas corpus* (Latin for "bring me the body"), issued by Judge Hamm in Port Huron on John Matthew Weeks at the Lapeer County Jail. I then transported him to Port Huron where he was arraigned. We now had the wheels of justice turning in two counties, Lapeer and St. Clair.

My request for transfer to the Ypsilanti Post came through in November 1978, but court appearances on these cases, one in Lapeer County and the other in St. Clair County, would have me returning to Romeo many times.

One of those court dates was scheduled for 9:30 a.m. on January 8, 1979 in Port Huron. That day, I started a week of midnight shifts. Those who have worked the graveyard shift know that it is always hard to get any sleep before that first night, and this time was no different. I started that first shift at midnight, and at 6:00 a.m., I broke off from patrol.

In uniform and a marked patrol vehicle, I headed for Warren to pick up my victim, Jane, and her grandmother and drive them to Port Huron for court. Providing transportation to victims is not a service police usually provide, but I would be traveling near their home, and they did not have a car available to make the long drive into unfamiliar territory.

This route had me traversing morning work traffic in metropolitan Detroit. After waiting in court all day, the case was adjourned to allow the defendant another psychiatric evaluation. I was now traversing afternoon work traffic in metropolitan Detroit with the victim and her grandmother, intending to take them home before driving on to Ypsilanti.

Having not slept for thirty-two hours, I began nodding at the wheel. Jane's grandmother noticed and said, "Trooper Edwards, if you would like me to drive, I do have my driver's license." That was a wake-up call in the truest sense; I initially declined her offer, but it soon became apparent we would not make it if I kept driving.

In busy work traffic on westbound I-94 near Mt. Clemens, I pulled the patrol car to the shoulder of the freeway. Grandma climbed behind the wheel of the blue goose and I, in full uniform, laid down in the backseat to rest. As Jane's grandmother accelerated out into traffic, I wondered what people were thinking. Good thing there weren't cell phones then or I am sure someone would have called a post to report a trooper kidnapped by a grandmother! Once lying down in the backseat, I was wide-awake with worry.

Once we made it to the grandmother's house, without a crash, she fixed me some coffee. Getting my second wind, I made it home okay to grab a couple of hours of sleep before going back in to work at midnight.

ALMONT-IMLAY EDITION ONLY The Adviser Newspaper August 16-22, 1978

Attempted murder, assault, rape warrants sought
Detroit man faces felony charges

By MARYANN KRYZANOWICZ
Advisor Staff Writer

A 48-year-old Detroit man has been arraigned in Lapeer County District Court on charges of attempted murder and felonious assault, following an incident in Almont Township Friday evening.

State Police at the Romeo post said three additional warrants are being sought in St. Clair County to charge John M. Weeks, 48, Detroit, with three rapes. He currently is lodged in the Lapeer County jail in lieu of $80,000 bond.

Weeks was arrested under the name Cheyanne J. Brody after he allegedly attempted to kill 18-year-old Lori Decker, Detroit, in a field on Kidder near Hough Rd. and later attacked Donald Malburg, 18, 7705 Hough Rd. The incident was reported at 6:50 p.m. Friday.

POLICE SAID Decker and Weeks were acquaintances, and were supposedly enroute to Imlay City on business when Weeks drove into the field and instructed Decker to go to the road to watch for a car. She told police she became uneasy and returned to the car, and Weeks then went to the road. When he returned, he struck her face with an instrument similar to oversized brass knuckles.

The impact knocked Decker to the ground, and Weeks then bound her hands with a telephone cord.

Decker told police that during the struggle, Weeks said, "I'm going to kill you. They're going to find you here because you're not going home again. Go ahead and yell all you want. No one will hear you."

Decker said she was then forced into the vehicle, but while Weeks walked around the car, she managed to free her hands and escape. She then ran north on Kidder Road to the home of an unidentified woman, who sent her children to get their neighbor, Henry Malburg, 7705 Hough Rd., Almont.

MEANWHILE, WEEKS arrived at the woman's home, where Decker was being sheltered. Malburg and his son Donald arrived shortly afterward and took Weeks to a barn to await the arrival of police.

While waiting, Weeks struck the younger Malburg in the abdomen with a rake. To protect his son, Henry Malburg struck Weeks, knocked him to the ground and pinned him down until police arrived. Police later confiscated several knives and a gun from Weeks' vehicle.

State Police Trooper Clifford Edwards said Weeks confessed his intention to kill Decker, and said he was acting at the request of her boyfriend.

Edwards said Henry Malburg recognized Weeks as the man he had towed from a ditch at the same field in Almont Township where the crime against Decker occurred.

ACCORDING TO EDWARDS, Weeks has served at least 20 years in prisons in California and Florida on charges ranging from writing checks against accounts with nonsufficient funds to rape.

Because of his extensive criminal record, police are continuing their investigation into other unsolved crimes in the area in which Weeks could have been involved. The Federal Bureau of Investigation also has been consulted regarding Weeks' record.

Police have investigated the possibility that Weeks could have been involved in the drowning death of a still unidentified woman found floating in a grave pit in Armada Township August 25.

Edwards said a search of Weeks' vehicle turned up a ladies' wallet, which belonged to a young woman in Detroit.

"WE HAD TO CONSIDER him in the drowning case because he was seen in the area prior to his arrest, and he has an extensive record of crimes against women," Edwards said.

Weeks will appear in court for preliminary examination on August 24.

Conviction of attempted murder carries a maximum penalty of life imprisonment. Felonious assault is punishable by up to five years in prison.

Compliments of the *Advisor* Newspaper

The trial in St. Clair County was scheduled, but with the conviction and life sentence in Lapeer County, a plea-bargaining deal was made with the defendant being allowed to plead guilty to a reduced charge. He received a similar sentence to the Lapeer County prison term. The garbage was now in the dump!

Trooper Craig Nyeholt and I received a Professional Excellence Award for this investigation.

A few years after retiring in 2001, I was visiting my son Trevor. We found ourselves on the Internet at the State of Michigan's website where we queried the name John Matthew Weeks in the Offender Tracking Incident System (OTIS). I was initially concerned to see that it listed him as released in 1992 until I read further and learned that he had died in prison. I guess that garbage won't be recycled.

26) Onward

In October 1978, my request for transfer to the Ypsilanti Post was granted, to be effective in November. Deb and I borrowed five thousand dollars from her Uncle Cliff and Aunt Jesse for a down payment on the purchase of our first house. It was a small three-bedroom home with a full, finished basement and unattached garage. We would have to get used to hearing sirens several times an hour since it was in Ypsilanti Township. We felt like we were going to be on top of the world.

One night, during my final month at Romeo, I was able to monitor the Ypsilanti Post radio frequency. A man named Billy Hardesty was on a killing spree and Ypsilanti troopers were hunting him. Two troopers out of my recruit school, Dave Koetsier and Gary Cuperus, were the first to locate him and gunfire was exchanged. Later, a reporter asked Trooper David Koetsier what he was thinking when he was pinned down behind a small tree by hostile gunfire; he replied, "I was thinking, skinny," meaning he was afraid the tree was not big enough to provide him adequate protection from the shots fired at him. In the end, Billy Hardesty was captured and no police officers were hurt.

However, the incident made me realize that Deb and I were moving to a more dangerous place, and one where, when I was eighteen years old, I had vowed never to live. But with our first home awaiting us, we could not wait to get there.

Part E - Ypsilanti Trooper
(November 1978 to February 1983)

27) Melons

My first day of duty at Ypsilanti found me scheduled to start at 10:00 a.m. When I walked into the squad room, there sat Trooper Joe Payne doing paperwork. He was a cub, more commonly known as a rookie, working midnights. Joe had been off the clock for two hours, but like all good cubs, he was still working.

An ex-marine and previous Port Huron Police Officer, standing 6'3", weighing about 220 pounds, and full of enthusiasm, Joe appeared to have all the qualities sought in a Michigan State Trooper. As we went through our introductions, we seemed to hit it off immediately.

Good thing...because we had been visiting about five minutes when I was dispatched to a semi-truck/tanker rollover on east bound I-94 west of the State Road overpass. I welcomed Joe's offer to help and we jumped into my patrol car, racing to the scene with red lights and siren activated.

As we slipped onto westbound I-94, traffic quickly became congested. In this area, eastbound and westbound I-94 is divided by a cement median wall with a narrow paved shoulder on each side that joins the roadway. As I pulled onto that median shoulder and raced west, with only a couple of inches to spare between the wall and traffic, I remember asking Joe whether we (Ypsi troopers) do this (drive the narrow shoulder), to which he answered, "Hell, yes!"

As we neared the scene, we could see the rig lying on its side, smoke rising. We planned our arrival. I would bring the blue goose to a momentary stop adjacent to the wreck and open the trunk, via a remote button on the dashboard, where the first aid kit was kept. Joe would hop out, grab the first aid kit, and slam the trunk, which would be my signal to take off. He would then jump the wall and render assistance. Meanwhile, I would race to the next interchange, flip around onto eastbound I-94, and detour traffic away from the accident. Hearing the trunk slam, I accelerated away. Glancing into my rearview mirror, I got a glimpse of Joe leaping the median wall in a single bound.

I don't remember the outcome of this crash; it has melted into the memories of many. I do remember, however, that during this period we had a rash of tanker accidents. The State responded with new safety regulations for tankers and mandated the state police to conduct inspections to insure compliance. This action greatly reduced tanker-involved accidents. Police officers also received training on how to respond properly to tanker crashes because they often released hazardous materials. In future crashes of this nature, we would respond much more cautiously and intelligently.

For just having met, Joe and I seemed to click. When we cleared the scene, we critiqued our actions so we might learn from our mistakes. This incident was the first of hundreds we handled as partners during the next five years.

In time, Joe and I liked to think of our partnership as E (Edwards) & P (Payne) Wrecking since we prided ourselves in wrecking crime. Joe liked to quote his father saying, "Two heads are always better than one, even if one is a melon." We often argued who was the melon head.

28) Instincts

In high schools, I believe the two primal warrior sports are cross-country running and wrestling. They are individual sports with no implements where pain must be embraced for success. They directly correlate with the survival instincts of flight and fight which are valuable skills whether we are prey or predator.

One day toward the end of my shift, I was patrolling the northern part of Ypsilanti Township. It was nearing dusk when I stopped a car for a minor traffic violation. The driver and sole occupant was a man named Ira Bryant, a forty year old from Kentucky. Guys like him prompted the area's nickname of "Ypsitucky."

His blurry eyes, slurred speech, and the odor of alcohol about him were clues he might be drunk. His performance on sobriety tests supported that suspicion, so I arrested him for drunk driving—not his first offense, I later learned. When I told him to turn around and put his hands behind his back to be handcuffed, he turned around but made a run for it.

The chase was on as I pursued him behind a closed business and into a stubble field. Within fifty yards, I had closed within leaping distance, placing my hands on his shoulders and pulling my full bodyweight onto him. Unable now to support his forward momentum, we toppled to the ground.

My running skills had served me well; I quickly transitioned to grappling. My 170 pounds spread over a 5'11" frame prevailed over his 190 pounds spread over a 5'10" frame, and I was quickly able to handcuff him. The next time would not be so easy.

Ira Bryant pled not guilty to the charges of drunk driving and attempted fleeing and eluding. The trial was scheduled for March 20, 1979. When Bryant failed to appear, Judge Robert Fink issued a bench warrant and directed me to find and arrest Ira as soon as possible. It was the only case he had scheduled that day and he hoped to dispose of it.

Court records indicated that the current address for Ira Bryant was 220 S. Washington St. near downtown Ypsilanti. When I arrived, alone, I found the address to be a large old dilapidated house that had been converted to three apartments. Not knowing which one Ira stayed in, I knocked at the first apartment I came to—number two. The resident told me Ira resided in apartment three with a man named Homer.

As I paused outside the door of apartment three, I could hear a television inside. I began a crescendo knocking on the door until eventually a man opened it...Homer, as it turned out. When I asked him if Ira was home, he said he didn't know.

In search of Ira, I entered the apartment, lit by a flickering television and dim daylight coming through thinly draped windows. Generally speaking, search warrants are for things and arrest warrants for persons. Since I was searching for a person in his residence of record, I was authorized to do so with an arrest warrant. What I lacked was a flashlight, a tool an officer should carry day and night. In the bedroom, I spied what appeared to be a person sleeping beneath blankets. When I pulled down the covers, *bingo*, I recognized Ira Bryant.

When my verbal commands did not arouse him, I shook his shoulder. Eventually, he opened his eyes, once again to see that he would have to deal with Trooper Edwards. I told him he was under arrest for a bench warrant issued for his failure to appear in court. He responded by saying he was not Ira Bryant but rather George. I told him I knew he was Ira Bryant and to get up and put on his clothes; I was taking him directly to court.

It seemed like a few minutes passed before Ira slowly sat up in bed, and in a matter-of-fact tone, stated he would not be going with me today. I told him he had no choice, to which he said he would not go without first calling his attorney; then he admitted he had no attorney. Seeing that Ira had pants on, I told him to put on a shirt and shoes because it was time to go. Ira grabbed a sweater from the floor and I walked him from the bedroom, passing by a pair of shoes that looked like they would fit him.

As Ira walked to the kitchen table, I again told him he was under arrest and to grab a pair of shoes and put them on his feet. He sat down at the kitchen table and began to light a cigarette while he calmly told me he would not be going with me today. Again, I told him he had no choice but to go with me because he was under arrest, and I presented him with the actual warrant.

Ira glanced at the warrant and then tossed it aside as his roommate, Homer, entered the drama and told me to leave. I told Homer I would not be leaving without Ira. It was now two against one. I ordered Ira to stand-up, turn around, and put his hands behind his back. When he refused, I pulled him from the chair. As if the bell had been rung, the fight was on.

I tried to put Ira's hands behind his back for handcuffing, but he pulled free. I then did a leg sweep, causing him to cut his lip when his face struck the floor. Ira scrambled to his feet while I attempted to place a wrist-lock on him, but he wiggled free. The brawl attracted the attention of other tenants whom I noticed were peeking in the apartment door.

In situations like this, a police officer must also combat what is known as tunnel vision—being so focused on the immediate threat that he is oblivious to potential peripheral threats. We carried no handheld radios at this time, so I couldn't radio for back-up. Nor did we carry any type of intermediate weapon such as pepper spray, baton, or a taser. Not knowing whether these gawkers were friend or foe, I yelled to them to telephone the police and report, "Officer needs assistance." I could only hope!

Once on his feet, Ira grabbed a kitchen chair and began to swing it at me. I countered by quickly kicking him in the chest, followed by repeatedly kicking him in the legs until he dropped the chair. As he fell to the sofa, he grabbed the torso of Homer, who was positioned like a referee.

Like maggots, the three of us squirmed on the smelly sofa as I tried to separate Ira from Homer so I could handcuff him. Eventually, I realized that as long as Ira was conscious, I would not be able to handcuff him, so I applied a Carotid Chokehold, rendering him unconscious.

When Ira awakened, he was handcuffed but still full of fight. I gave up on the shoes and tried to walk him from the apartment. He resisted one more time, with us going to the floor, but handcuffed, he was more manageable. Finally, I got him on his bare feet and down the stairs, just as several police cars, emergency lights on and sirens wailing, arrived.

Trooper Gary McGough and his cub, Garry Gray, came to the scene to transport the prisoner to jail. Trooper McGough, a more seasoned trooper than I, took me aside and asked me what the hell I was thinking to go make a warrant arrest by myself? Lesson learned!

29) Trimester

I was assigned as Joe Payne's Field Training Officer (FTO) for the second trimester of his probation period. Typically, the trooper's field training with his first FTO lasts for three months, his second FTO for three months, mostly solo for his final trimester, and then back to Advanced Trooper School for confirmation.

Joe had worked with Trooper Al Jones for his first three months, during which time more than one internal investigation had been initiated against Al surrounding allegations of excessive use of force. On Al Jones' locker door was the name "C. Eastwood." While some would call Al unconventional and heavy-handed, he solved major cases where others had failed. Many of these cases are worthy of a book in and of itself. But Al was going through a difficult time in his life—his first divorce—and it was affecting his work.

Joe Payne had five years experience as a Port Huron City Police Officer and three months as a state trooper. This would be my first experience as a field-training officer for the second trimester. While Joe may have had a few rough edges, he certainly had a lot of polish that only needed a little buffing. Joe would teach me much.

Most city police officers conduct an initial investigation and turn the case over to the detective division for follow-up investigation. State troopers investigate all crimes they are assigned, except for the most serious, from beginning to end. In my assessment of Joe, the only thing I saw pending in his transition from city officer to state trooper was accepting this responsibility and challenging himself to try sincerely to solve every legitimate case he was assigned, whether big or small.

One evening, as we headed to a restaurant to meet some other officers for dinner, we were dispatched to a burglary. We were starving, so after acknowledging the radio traffic, Joe said to me we would only be fifteen minutes late, insinuating we should take a quick report and continue to dinner.

I took pause to collect my thoughts. Joe was a couple of years older in age and in experience as an officer, but I was his FTO. My responsibility was to teach him the state police way. I told him that if it were a legitimate complaint, we might have to forego dinner to investigate.

This call did turn out to be a valid complaint. We ended up skipping dinner that night, but by the end of the shift, we had a suspect in custody for breaking and entering. There is nothing like success to motivate, and that lesson would not have to be repeated for Joe.

--

One precision-driving maneuver not taught in recruit school is the "J-turn." To teach it in the academy is to condone it and to condone it is to pay for it. The maneuver is advanced and very hard on cars, particularly emergency brakes and transmissions. If the department started teaching it in the academy, I would consider purchasing stock in the company that manufactured those replacement parts.

I had learned the J-turn from Trooper Dave Smith, who was probably the best driver at the Romeo Post. It enabled a driver to make a 180-degree turn on a narrow paved road with no shoulders and was much quicker than the Y-turn taught in the academy for this maneuver. An officer might use it when meeting a wanted car on such a road when he needed to spin around quickly to stop it.

One early morning, around 4:00 a.m., Joe and I were patrolling east on the M-14 expressway when I asked him whether he knew the J-turn maneuver? He responded by saying "Negative," but in true Payne fashion, he was eager to learn.

There was a lull in traffic and we were on a flat section where we could see for miles, so I decided it was a good time to teach him. First, I would demonstrate while giving the following instructions: Make sure there is no traffic in front or behind you. Come to a complete stop. Put the car in reverse and accelerate to about 35 miles per hour (speedometers don't work in reverse so you have to estimate). Do a jig-jag with the steering wheel to cause momentum to pull the front end of the car around. Slam on the emergency brake, which locks up only the rear brakes. This action, combined with the jig-jag, causes the front end to pivot around the rear end (pinwheel). Shift from reverse to forward gear while spinning around. When the 180-degree pivot is complete, release the emergency brake and stomp on the accelerator. Done right, a driver can spin around on a twelve-foot wide paved road very quickly. Impressive when it works... embarrassing and worse when done incorrectly.

After one demonstration, Joe said he was ready and took the wheel. Just as I began to tell him he was going too fast in reverse, he jig-jagged the steering wheel and set the emergency brake simultaneously. We did a couple of complete pinwheels down the expressway, sliding off the pavement, down the grassy embankment, and coming to rest against the fence. When Joe tried to pull out, our tires spun.

"Joe," I yelled, "since your dumb ass got us into this mess, you can take *your* big ass and try to push *my* sparrow ass back onto the freeway." So he waded into the mud with his size 13 spit-shined Oxfords and pushed while I steered. I was afraid we were going to have to radio for a wrecker, and then the sergeant would know, which could mean another letter to the director.

As Joe pushed, I accelerated, spraying him with mud. I would have bet against him, but he did it, pushing us onto the paved shoulder. We checked the patrol car for damage and were relieved to find nothing but mud. About that time, the sergeant radioed us and we answered, neglecting to tell him our location. He dispatched us to check on a report of a car in the ditch at our location. We told him we were close and would check on it.

Enough of that. If Joe wanted to learn J-turns, he would have to do it on his own! We radioed the post and told the sergeant we were UTL (police talk for "Unable to Locate") a car in the ditch at that location as we headed for the carwash.

--

That Christmas, Joe and I worked the midnight shift. We were both married and couldn't wait to get home to wake our families for the unwrapping of gifts. It was policy to end your shift by refueling the patrol car. The gas pump at the post was broken, so we were refueling at Eastern Michigan University Police Department's gas pumps. EMU PD was on the north side of Ypsilanti while the post was on the south side, meaning we had to traverse the city to go off duty.

As we did, we saw a brown, older model Lincoln Mark 7 with Alabama registration plates driving slowly with no lights on; even though it was approaching dawn, lights were still needed. We decided to make one last patrol stop. A male was driving the vehicle, with a female in the right front passenger seat.

As we activated the red light and spotlights, the Lincoln pulled to a side street and stopped. Joe approached the driver's side while I approached the passenger side. As I did, the female suddenly stepped out and began walking back toward me, demanding to know why we had stopped them. She was carrying a purse; I recognized her behavior to be a possible diversion. Concerned for our safety, I quickly checked her purse for weapons. I found it contained a large quantity of suspected powder cocaine. I shouted "3500" to Joe, code for a narcotic violation, and we simultaneously took both persons into custody.

Beneath the driver's seat, Joe discovered $10,000 in cash in a brown paper bag. Keeping the two suspects separated, I attempted to interview the female. I remember her telling me I was no mental match for her. She was probably right.

Call us Scrooges, for we had undoubtedly ruined someone's *white* Christmas that morning. In fact, by the time we had counted the money and jailed the suspects, we had missed Christmas morning with our families.

30) Suspicious

I think this incident represents what my second training officer, Trooper John Jackson, meant when he encouraged me always to look beyond the obvious in pursuit of the "big arrest in the sky."

Original to Director
1st Copy to District
2nd Copy to Post

Michigan Department of State Police
REQUEST FOR CITATION

5 Jun 79   0   21

Complaint No. __26-4697-79__ 2300
File Class. No. __26-4704-79__ 1200

Date ____June 27, 1979____

Date of Complaint __6/19/79__

1. In accordance with Official Order No. 19 it is requested that an appropriate departmental citation be awarded to each of the following individuals for extraordinary acts of duty performed as described in the official departmental complaint report bearing the above number:

    1. Trooper CLIFTON EDWARDS   3. _____

    2. _____   4. _____

2. Following is a brief description of the extraordinary service:

    Trooper EDWARDS was sent to the Lake-in-the-Woods Apartments to investigate a suspicious vehicle possibly involved in a larceny investigated by the Monroe Police Department. The investigating officer located the owner of the vehicle, RONALD REDDING, who after questioning admitted a limited involvement in the incident. However, REDDING did also implicate a second suspect who was reportedly responsible for the actual theft.

    The second suspect, THOMAS HEDGER, was also identified as an escapee from Jackson Prison and was possibly living in an apartment in the city of Ypsilanti. Based on that information and in spite of the fact that the landlady initially offered resistance to the investigation Trooper EDWARDS was finally able to get consent to search the house. At that time HEDGER was found hiding in the bedroom.

    Upon questioning HEDGER a full confession to the larceny was obtained and all of the stolen property was recovered from two seperate locations.

    The assistance complaint was carried on 26-4697-79 2300 with all property/evidence being released to Monroe PD for prosecution.

    At this point Trooper EDWARDS continued to question both suspects regarding their involvement in any additional criminal activities. As a result of that questioing and by using one suspect against the other, Trooper EDWARDS was also successful in getting full confessions from both suspects regarding their involvement in a prior robbery armed reported to the Washtenaw County Sheriff.

    The weapon used in that robbery (knife) and the stolen property were also recovered by Trooper EDWARDS and released to the Washtenaw County Sheriff's Department for prosecution.

    The assistance complaint was carried on 26-4704-79 1200.

    As a result of Trooper EDWARDS' initiative and timely interrogation he was able to clear two seperate complaints and make prosecution possible for the originating jurisdictions.

Signature of person preparing the request ____ D/Sgt. _James P. Tuttle_

MSP request for citation

31) Home

Shortly after transferring to Ypsilanti, Deb and I decided to try for our second child. It would not be long before she was pregnant. Again, it would be a long difficult labor for her. Finally, the doctor said she would give Deb another hour for a natural delivery to occur, and if not, she would perform a caesarean. And when that hour ended, guess what? No anesthesiologist was available! So after hours of being told to push, Deb was told to resist the urge when it came. I was livid!

After what seemed like a period of cruel and unusual punishment, Deb finally got called into surgery with me in tow. How do you spell relief? S-P-I-N-A-L. Finally, Eric's blonde head popped out of the incision in Deb's abdomen and we were relieved to welcome him to planet earth. Eric's debut later reminded me of a scene in the movie *Alien*.

--

Life rushed on during this period of time with home ownership, trooping, parenting, and completion of college. When Trevor, our first son, started kindergarten, the school was located adjacent to the housing projects on the south side of Ypsilanti. One night, Trooper Joe Payne and I made a miscellaneous patrol arrest within a block of that school. Just as we had placed the handcuffs on the suspect and were escorting him to the patrol car, shots rang out from the darkness.

It's odd how you can tell from the muzzle blast that a gun is pointed in your direction. We instantly pulled the suspect to the pavement and made sure none of us were hit. We then crawled back to the cover of the patrol car and radioed for assistance. Within a minute, Ypsilanti City Police cars flooded the area, but nothing else happened; the shooter had vanished. We transported our prisoner to jail and went off-duty. Within eight hours, I was back to nearly the same spot, dropping Trevor off at kindergarten.

--

On another night, Joe and I were part of a team of officers who had surrounded a house in response to a domestic dispute where a man armed with a rifle and standing on his porch was telling police to go away. While we were busy on this call, Deb telephoned the post, afraid. She had been awakened by the sound of breaking glass and checked our sleeping boys, finding them to be okay. She then looked out the window and saw two men throwing rocks at our house. When the desk sergeant radioed this information to Joe and me, we cleared the gunman call as quickly as possible and responded to my home, but the culprits were GOA (police talk for "gone on arrival").

It seemed that somewhere in the course of my duties, I had made an enemy. An enemy who had figured out where I lived and probably knew I was at work. Frightening! You would think we could have solved this case, but we never did.

Somewhere along the line, I adopted the adage that a cop or a family member should be a victim of a crime every couple of years. Not that I wish anything bad on my brothers and sisters, but such events can be a benefit because they tend to prevent a cop from becoming hardened to crime. Vandalism of a mailbox is not a big deal, unless it's your mailbox. Call it sensitivity training reality style.

--

We lived about three miles from the post. Deb was not working outside the home since she was busy tending to the boys. To make ends meet, we decided to have only one car. On days when Deb needed the car, I would run to work. The most direct route took me through the projects on the south side of Ypsilanti, often after dark.

Regulations require that a state police officer be armed at all times. When I ran to and from work, I would carry my snubnosed revolver concealed in a leather mitten in my hand. Upon meeting a youth gang on the sidewalk, I was the one who had to run onto the lawn to get by. One time as I passed a group, I heard, "What's you got in the mitten?" I answered, "Life insurance."

32) Belligerent

My mother always told me that if the police stopped her, she would jump out of her car and quickly walk back to the officer. She felt this behavior would increase the chances of getting a break rather than a ticket. Try as I might, I could not convince her that her best action was to wait in her car, with her hands in plain view, since you never know what else might be going on in that officer's day.

By October 1979, Joe Payne and I had worked together enough to become like left and right hands. We continued to refer to our partnership as E&P Wrecking, wrecking criminal lives.

We had modified the method of making a two-officer patrol stop. Once the violator's car and patrol vehicle had come to a stop, the passenger officer, acting in a cover role, would exit quickly and approach the passenger side of the violator's car. He would peek into the passenger side windows, first checking hands and the area near them. Meanwhile, the officer who had been driving, acting in a contact role, would exit the patrol car cautiously, as he had traffic beside him. He would position himself between both vehicles and wait for his partner to signal that it was okay to initiate contact with the violator. Usually, the attention of the violating vehicle's occupants was focused on the contact officer, oblivious to the cover officer who was peering in their passenger windows. If the cover officer saw something suspicious, he would signal to the contact officer by pointing from above the roof to the area of concern and whispering a code for the nature of the suspicion. If a weapon were observed, the officer called it clearly and firearms were drawn. This type of approach was not anticipated by the vehicle's occupants, making it more difficult for the evildoer to spring an effective ambush.

We did not often patrol in the city of Ann Arbor, but one night, Joe decided to pass through it. As we crossed into the city on Washtenaw Avenue, we met an older Volvo, weaving with two persons aboard. Joe spun around and we activated the red light and spotlights.

Curiously enough, the vehicle made a left turn into a nearly vacant shopping center parking lot and came to a stop. When the violator chooses a place to stop rather than just pulling over, it can be an indicator of trouble.

As cover officer, my door was open as the patrol car came to a stop and I began my approach. I was adjacent to the passenger side of the violator's vehicle and beginning my sneak-and-peek when the college-age female driver jumped out of the Volvo, oblivious to me. Her hands were empty and she appeared agitated. She stomped toward Joe, demanding to know why she had been stopped!

While Joe dealt with her, I continued my plain-view check of the vehicle's interior with the aid of my flashlight, confirming no one was in the backseat. As I moved forward, I noticed the right front passenger to be a college-age male, who was glancing back over his left toward Joe and the driver. He was unaware of my presence. His empty hands rested on his lap and stuck in his belt was a snubnosed revolver. I shouted, "Gun!" as I drew my pocket gun and took control of the suspect.

Meanwhile, Joe was dealing with a belligerent intoxicated University of Michigan coed who apparently wondered who the hell he was to order her to halt and put her hands on the trunk. While one shouldn't generalize, this type often seemed to think they didn't have time to be bothered by law enforcement.

Having heard my alarm, as she entered Joe's "reactionary gap" (the six foot safety zone officers try to maintain between a suspect), Joe drew his pocket gun with his right hand and with his left hand, he picked her up off the ground and placed her on the trunk of the Volvo. Can you imagine her shock?

When I took custody of the revolver, I realized it was a replica toy gun. When I looked in the owner's face, I saw he was wearing masquerading make-up. He explained that they were coming from a Halloween costume party where they had posed as Bonnie & Clyde.

Okay, time for the storm troopers to stand down, but we still had to deal with a suspected drunk driver. With all that had transpired, there was no turning back now. In this situation, Joe would have normally administered the FSTs (police talk for "Field Sobriety Tests"), but the woman hadn't forgiven Joe's actions and felt as if she had been assaulted.

Consequently, I administered the FSTs and arrested her for what was then labeled "Driving Under the Influence of Liquor." Prior to driving her to jail, Joe looked into the backseat to make sure she had on her seatbelt. When he did, she looked him square in the eye and said with venom in her voice, "You are the product of ill breeding!" What a hoot.

We had a delay in getting her a breathalyzer test, and its results indicated a blood alcohol content of .07 percent—at that time the legal presumptive level was .10 percent. Nevertheless, we went forward with the case and subsequently had a jury trial in the Ann Arbor City Court, a place where neither of us had testified before. The jury found her guilty as charged, and surprisingly, one of the jurors wrote a complimentary letter to the Post Commander about our demeanor.

Lieutenant Pifer
Michigan State Police
1501 Wittaker Road
Ypsilanti, Michigan 48197

Dear Lieutenant Pifer;

    I was a member of the jury on January 24th at which officers Edwards and Payne were witnesses for the prosecution. The incident occurred November 1, 1979 when the officers stopped the defendant who had been speeding, was un-cooperative, had been consuming alcohol, and was accompanied by a passenger who had a very realistic toy pistol.

    Officers Edwards and Payne were very professional in their conduct and testimony. However, a few of us agreed that these men showed more than good judgement. It was a situation where someone could have been hurt and questions asked later. The driver was upset with Officer Payne and a discussion led to officer Edwards conducting the sobriety test after allowing the "lady" to calm down. Officer Edwards was patient in this manner.

    That is briefly what transpired, it is somewhat lacking from the actual event or being in court. Again, good judgement, conduct, and courtesy was shown on the part of both men. I'm sure you hear more than enough negative things about the police. If this one situation is an indication of the way Officers Edwards and Payne handle most of their calls - they are doing a fine job. Thank you.

            Sincerely,

33) Cadillac

Unlike most state police/patrol agencies, Michigan troopers were not issued their own take home patrol cars. Patrol cars were pool cars, so theoretically, a patrol car could find itself on the road 24/7 until it broke down. A fact of life is that pool cars are not treated like issued cars. In an effort to increase care of the patrol cars, one vehicle would be primarily assigned to three troopers, each from a different shift. However, if your patrol car (goose) were in the shop, you drove whatever "goose" was available.

I was assigned patrol car 261 and my partner, Trooper Joe Payne, was assigned patrol car 262. When on patrol, the car number was your radio number. The first two digits, 26, made up the number assigned to the Ypsilanti Post, and the next number indicated the car number. Joe and I took pride in having our assigned cars looking good and running well.

Patrol car 261 was a semi-marked 1978 Plymouth Fury with a 440 cubic inch engine. A semi-mark was a patrol car that was a color other than the patented state police blue, did not have the red bubble light on top, and displayed a door shield only on the right side. 261 was a sweet light green color. Semi-marked patrol cars allowed you to blend with traffic, often seeing things you wouldn't otherwise. For some reason, 261 had a high speed rear-end that increased top speed, but made it a bit slower out of the hole.

Trooper Joe Payne's 262 was a traditionally marked patrol car. It was the same make and model, but had a standard rear-end, making it faster out of the hole, but about five to ten miles per hour slower on the top end.

At that time, patrols during dark always consisted of two troopers. That policy would change with time, although Lieutenant Colonel William Hassinger would resist it. In his efforts to keep that policy in place, I recall him declaring, "I never knew two troopers who would not stop the devil himself, and I never want that to change."

In April 1980, with spring well on its way, Joe and I were working a week of midnight shifts, which would be followed by our one weekend off per month. It was Joe's night to drive so we were in his assigned patrol car 262.

We had received a BOL ("Be On Lookout") for a new model black two-door Cadillac that had twice outrun troopers from the Northville Post. On the initial contact, Troopers Ted Monfette and Kelly Hillary had seen it idling alongside the road; when they had stopped to investigate, it had taken off. In that chase, the speeds had been up to 120 miles per hour, but the reason for its flight was a mystery. Later, another Northville Post patrol had spotted it and futilely given chase. The Cadillac was fast!

Author and Tpr. Payne

Joe and I patrolled toward the north side of our patrol area to position closer to where the Cadillac had last been seen. Dawn was approaching when we saw a Washtenaw County Sheriff car sitting on a side road, monitoring southbound Prospect Road. The deputies were in one of the newer model Chevrolet patrol cars, powered by a 350 cubic inch engine. The Chevy lacked the top end of the Plymouth. Just as we pulled alongside them to talk, the Cadillac in question crossed their bow, southbound toward Ypsilanti. The deputies jumped right on its tail while we had to spin around. The chase was on!

As we caught up to the deputies, the Cadillac was pulling away, so we passed, taking primary in the pursuit. While Joe drove with red lights and siren activated, I radioed the post. Prospect Road was a blacktop two lane road with no paved shoulder, and our speeds were approaching three digits, when the Cadillac's brake lights flashed as the driver braked to negotiate a right turn on Clark Road, a hilly narrow two lane. When you brake from high speeds, your ability to brake again is compromised until the pads, rotors, and shoes cool. High speeds with little or no brakes are especially scary. As soon as we had made the turn, it was again "pedal to the metal" with the speedometer soon nearing 120 miles per hour.

I knew we were on a dead-end road that ended at a two-track dirt lane leading into a gravel pit. The last time I had been there, the two-track had been blocked by a large pile of dirt and rocks, keeping people out of the gravel pit. I needed to communicate that to Joe, right now!

When I looked over at him, he was in what we called a white knuckle trance. Like a lion in pursuit of a gazelle, he was totally focused on the task at hand. Over the roar of the four barrel carburetor and the siren's wail, I yelled, "Joe, this is a dead-end road blocked by a mountain of dirt! Slow down!" He didn't seem to hear me.

As we crested the final hill before the dead end, I again yelled my warning, shouting at the top of my lungs. And there it was—the dead-end, with no dirt/rock pile blocking the two-track as the Cadillac entered the gravel pit. Did I feel relief? No, something less.

Our speeds diminished immensely as we entered the gravel pit, but we were still on the edge of control. I did not want this chase to spill back onto the road and continue since kids would be waiting for school buses.

Joe must have been thinking the same thing as he said, "Shoot off some warning shots; maybe he'll stop." It seemed like a good idea, so I rolled down my window and drew my .38 revolver from my cross draw holster. When I fired a couple of rounds, the Cadillac's brake lights came on. Two more rounds and the vehicle stopped, as did we.

With only two rounds left in my six-shooter, I left it in the car. I told Joe to stay in the patrol car since earlier the suspect had pulled the old trick of taking off when both officers exited the patrol car. As I jumped out, I had my steel Streamlight flashlight in my left hand as I drew my snubnosed revolver from my right pocket. I ran up to the right front passenger door and peeked in. The driver and sole occupant was hunkered down behind the steering wheel and the door was locked.

With all my might, I struck the right front door window with my flashlight, hoping to break it. Wrong! The flashlight ricocheted back, causing my left ring finger to be sandwiched between the end of the flashlight and the door jam. Luckily, I had my wedding ring on, which the impact collapsed, pinching my finger, but undoubtedly, saving it from being broken, or worse yet, severed.

In response to my hitting the passenger window, the suspect jumped out of the driver's door and ran around to the back of the car with me scrambling to intercept him. Like charging bulls, we collided by its trunk and the fight was on. He seemed to be grabbing at my flap holster as if trying to get my service revolver. Unknown to him, I had left the near empty gun in the patrol car.

When the suspect came out of his car, so did Trooper Joe Payne with the .30 caliber M-1 carbine patrol rifle. When the opportunity presented itself, Joe (probably having a flashback to pugil-stick training in the Marines) struck him with the rifle's butt, breaking the wooden stock. The impact stunned the suspect, cutting a portion of his ear, during which time I was able to get him handcuffed. The cut was minor and did not require any immediate medical attention.

When we got him secured in the patrol car, we were still overdosing on adrenaline, screaming, and jumping around like we had just scored the winning touchdown for the Super Bowl. No contraband was found in the car, although it could have been discarded during any of the three chases that night. We would never really know why he fled.

When we got to the Ypsilanti Post, we were still high, although my left ring finger was now beginning to hurt. We got a pair of pliers and squeezed open my wedding ring to get it off. Ruined, I never wore that ring again.

Sergeant Leonard Rukkila sent us to the basement to calm down so we could get our facts straight before we wrote our report. Years later, research determined that recall immediately following a crisis type incident is often not as accurate as the day after. Sergeant Rukkila was a wise man. At an arraignment that morning, with a bandaged ear, the suspect pled guilty to the charges stemming from his attempt to flee and elude the police. After taking care of his sentence, he moved to Texas. To my knowledge, he was never seen in these parts again.

Months later, I filed a grievance against the Ypsilanti Post Commander concerning his denial of two hours of overtime incurred during the Republican National Convention in Detroit. Sometime after that, I received a reprimand for shooting the warning shots. Coincidence?

At the time, I thought this incident should be an exception to the rule. In retrospect, I agree with the policy of "No Warning Shots." Often when one cop shoots, it's the green light for all cops to shoot. For example, in this case another officer in the chase might have assumed the shots he heard had been shot by the suspect so the criteria for justification for the use of lethal force had been met, and then he might shoot the suspect. This phenomenon, where if one cop shoots, they all shoot, is often labeled "sympathetic gunfire."

Michigan Department of State Police
WRITTEN WARNING NOTICE/COUNSELING MEMO

☒ WRITTEN WARNING NOTICE   ☐ COUNSELING MEMO

Employee EDWARDS, TPR, CLIFTON L.	Social Security Number	Date Sept 4, 1980
Job Title Trooper	Work Station Ypsilanti Post #26	Date of Employment 9-17-76

If Written Warning Notice, state:		If Counseling Memo, state:
Date of Violation 4-2-80	Time 6:50AM	Location Ypsilanti	Date of counseling

Description:

On APRIL 2, 1980, Troopers C. Edwards and D. Payne were involved in a High Speed chase involving a black 1978 Cadillac that had eluded other officers twice earlier that morning. Upon entering a gravel pit in the area of Clark & LeForge Rds in Washtenaw County, Ypsilanti/Superior Township Trooper Edwards fired 4 rounds from his service revolver into the sky in an attempt to get the violater to stop. This action was not in keeping with departmental policy as outlined in Official Order No. 71.

Trooper Clifton L. Edwards is given written warning notice that he is not to use a firearm in any manner to help effect a traffic arrest.

A repetition of the above violation or occurrence of any other may result in disciplinary action.

Signature and Title of Supervisor *Robert L. Pifer*	Date Given to Employee 9-4-80

2-B—THE DETROIT NEWS—Thursday, April 3, 1980

Wild chase ends in a gravel pit

By MARTHA HINDES
News Staff Writer

A 27-year-old Ypsilanti man driving at speeds of up to nearly 130 m.p.h. eluded state police and sheriff's deputies for nearly two hours yesterday in a wild chase that ended at a gravel pit in Ypsilanti Township.

Pursuing officers lost him twice before he was spotted a third time, when he drove off a dead-end road into the gravel pit and was arrested by state troopers.

Troopers Kelly Hillary and Ted Monfette of the Northville post first spotted the man about 5:10 a.m. rummaging in the trunk of his black 1978 Cadillac on the shoulder of Ann Arbor Road (M-14) at Sheldon in Plymouth Township. When they stopped to investigate, the man drove off at a high speed, Hillary said.

"WE STOPPED to see if he needed any help and he said no," he reported. "Then my partner wanted his name to check if it was a stolen car. I walked back and he had gotten in and started to drive away.

"We put on our red flasher. He drove about 100 yards and slowed down, then he just took off."

Hillary said the officers chased the suspect along M-14 to southbound Ford Road then onto eastbound Ann Arbor Road, where he was driving

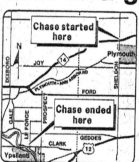

Chase started here

Chase ended here

"about 115 to 120 miles an hour."

"We lost him because that's a very hilly, curving two-lane road with traffic on it and we didn't want to hit someone head on," Hillary said.

Two state troopers in a second Northville Post car spotted the suspect again about an hour later on Geddes Road near Prospect in Superior Town-

ship and took up the chase. They lost him after about five miles when he turned just before reaching a Washtenaw County Sheriff's Department roadblock at Dixboro Road.

The man was spotted again a third time about 6:30 a.m. by two Ypsilanti Post State Police troopers as he drove west on Clark just west of LaForge, in Ypsilanti Township. He drove about a mile at speeds of nearly 130 m.p.h. before reaching the gravel pit, Hillary said.

AFTER DRIVING a half-mile into the gravel pit, the suspect stopped, got out of his car and was arrested after putting up a fight, Hillary said.

He said a check of the man's identity showed the car probably belonged to the suspect.

"We talked to the wife of the owner who said he was at work in Ypsilanti," Hillary said. "The suspect matched the description she gave, so we figured the car wasn't stolen. When troopers asked why he fled, he said it was because he had no insurance on his car."

The suspect was released from the Ypsilanti State Police Post on $100 personal bond pending arraignment April 17 in 14th District Court.

State police say he will be charged with two counts of reckless driving, two counts of fleeing and eluding police and one count of resisting arrest.

Compliments of *Detroit News*

34) Time

It was a Sunday night and Trooper Joe Payne and I were again working midnights. Prior to our shift starting, the Payne and Edwards families had enjoyed an evening meal together. We had watched a rodeo on television, and Joe and I had commented on how the calf ropers would quickly lasso and tie the calf and then raise their arms yelling, "Time!"

It had been a quiet night, so Joe and I were at the post, plugging away on typewriters at reports, carbon charged forms, and using white-out (a trooper's best friend) to correct mistakes. Suddenly, three telephone lines lighted-up with incoming calls. All three callers had the same complaint: two teenagers on an un-muffled motorcycle were tearing up and down the sidewalks, throwing eggs at houses. We responded from the post with me at the wheel of my beloved 261.

As we neared the subdivision, we rolled down our windows, hearing the rat-tat-tat of an un-muffled two-stroke engine going through the gears. It made it easy for us to find the obnoxious motorcycle, and we were soon paralleling it as it rode on the sidewalk and we on the street.

When we activated our emergency lights to signal it to stop, the chase was on. At the end of the block, the motorcycle transitioned from side-walk to street. The residents had thought the motorcycle was loud until we added a siren and roaring-screeching patrol car.

As we chased them, I didn't realize the street dead-ended into a town-ship park until the barricades came into view. There was certainly enough gap for the motorcycle to pass between the poles, so I could only hope the patrol car could squeeze through since there was no way to stop in time. And it did, but just as I sighed with relief, the patrol car went sidewise, sliding on the dewy grass that was as slippery as ice. While the dirt bike was in its environment and the patrol car was not, on the slick grass, nei-ther of us could abruptly change direction. While I maneuvered around a swing set, the Viking saying, "Don't praise the ice until it's crossed," flashed through my mind.

Again, it is amazing what the mind can process while under the influ-ence of adrenaline. As I steered through the obstacle course, known as a playground, I had flashbacks to precision driving training on the skid pad and visualized tomorrow's front pages of the Ypsilanti and Ann Arbor newspapers featuring a color picture of a State Police patrol car entangled in a playground slide. In a few moments, which seemed like an hour, we came to the end of the park.

I now prayed I could get the angle right to fit through the barriers at what would be my exit from the playground. Was I good! When we left the slippery grass and entered the blacktop, the tires screeched as they regained traction.

The chase continued south on the subdivision street until it ended at Grove Street, a four lane highway. The motorcycle turned right and decided to try to outrun us on a straight road. No way! I quickly positioned the patrol car in front of them, and using my rearview mirror, kept them dead center behind me as I quickly braked down, matching the stopping capabilities of the motorcycle to the patrol car so they would not hit me yet deny them the opportunity to turn out from behind me.

Nearly stopped, I shifted the patrol car to park, hearing the clicking of the transmission, reminding me not to do that. In a flash, Joe and I sprung out of the patrol car and sprinted back to the motorcycle where the two riders were trying to pull the bike around in hopes of getting away. Using our extended arms like a clothesline, we knocked them to the ground and raced to get them handcuffed. And then, nearly simultaneously, we both jumped to our feet, and with our arms outreached, yelled, "TIME!"

On this night, Joe learned what I had learned the night we chased the black Cadillac with him at the wheel—assuming you don't crash, the worst chase to be in is the one in which you are not driving.

35) WAIT

> *"All men who feel any power of joy in battle know*
> *what it is like when the wolf rises in the heart."*
> *— Theodore Roosevelt*

In early 1981, I was assigned to the Washtenaw Area Intelligence Team, known as WAIT. It was an informal multi-jurisdictional team that consisted of eight officers from four different police agencies: Washtenaw County Sheriff Department, Eastern Michigan Police Department, Ypsilanti Police Department, and Michigan State Police. It was an excellent example of police agencies pooling resources to investigate non-drug targets of mutual concern in an unconventional way.

The reason WAIT didn't target drug dealers was that another similar team was dedicated to those crimes. The trooper, who was drawn from the Ypsilanti Post, was rotated in and out every three months. WAIT would be my first exposure in surveillance and undercover work.

I grew my hair and beard long so I could blend with the population we were most often investigating. Don't misunderstand me; criminals have a variety of appearances. However, a person can transition from an unkempt appearance to a high and tight appearance in about an hour. It takes weeks to grow hair.

Picture taken day of "Flintstone" incident when I stopped home for lunch.

Toward the end of my tour with WAIT, the Jackson Post sent over a subpoena to be served on a person I will call Fred Flintstone. Flintstone was viewed as a hostile witness in an upcoming court hearing in Jackson County. Hostile witnesses are often one of the defendant's friends or family who are likely to try to avoid a subpoena so they don't have to testify against them.

Flintstone had been the passenger in a vehicle that had been stopped by troopers from the Jackson Post. The driver, an associate of Flintstone, was arrested for "Carrying a Concealed Weapon—Pistol," and a large amount of cash was seized from him. Jackson troopers suspected Flintstone would try to avoid conventional subpoena service, so it was decided to task WAIT with serving the subpoena.

I was tasked with coming up with the operational plan, which would be reviewed for approval by Lyle Schroeder, the Michigan State Police Detective Sergeant assigned to WAIT. First we did our background checks on Flintstone, discovering that he was a wanted felon on charges out of Wayne County that originated from organized dog fighting. We learned that he lived on a farm in rural Sumpter Township where it was suspected that he raised, trained, and fought pit bull dogs.

Because Flintstone was a black man, we decided to utilize our one and only black officer on the team, Michael Wells, who was assigned from the Eastern Michigan University Police Department. First, we needed to determine whether Flintstone was home. The plan was for Officer Mike Wells, clad in plain clothes, to knock at Flintstone's door and ask about buying a dog.

I would be Mike's closest backup, and we would have a marked patrol car with two uniformed troopers briefed and in the area. Mike studied booking photographs of Flintstone before going to the house so he hopefully would be able to identify him if he saw him. If Officer Wells determined that Flintstone was there, he would leave, report his findings, and we would immediately return with the uniformed troopers to arrest him on the felony warrant and serve him the subpoena.

I followed Mike to the long driveway that led to the house and parked on the dirt road, just out of sight. Mike first met a teenage boy in the yard; he asked whether Fred was home and explained that he wanted to talk to him about buying a dog. The boy indicated that he would get Flintstone and walked away. A few minutes later, a man matching Flintstone's description appeared, so Mike asked whether he was Fred. This person denied being Flintstone and ordered Mike to leave his property, which he did. As Mike drove east on the dirt road, he updated me via radio, saying that he thought the man was Flintstone, but he couldn't be positive.

I held my position while Mike drove east. As I did, a pickup truck left the same driveway and sped east as if in pursuit of Mike. I radioed Mike my concern and took off after them. In maybe a minute, Mike radioed me that he could see the pickup truck gaining on him in his mirror, and it was driven by the man he suspected to be Flintstone along with the same teenage boy as a passenger.

The pickup truck followed Mike as I raced to catch up from behind. I radioed our direction of travel to the uniformed troopers, Eric Humphrey and Tadarial Sturdivant, and I told them we would surveil the pickup truck until they caught up, at which time we would break-off so they could perform a patrol stop on it.

The plan was holding until Mike approached a red traffic light at Sumpter Road. As Mike stopped in traffic, the pickup truck swerved to the left, against traffic, and began to pull alongside Mike. Watching his rear-view mirror, Mike saw that he was going to be blocked in, so he pulled into the left lane ahead of the pickup, but he had to stop at the intersection because of cross traffic. As this transpired, I observed the pickup's occupants bending down as if to get something. I radioed this concern to Mike.

Like a chain reaction, Mike stopped, the pickup stopped, and then I stopped; three vehicles in a neat little row, all in the wrong lane. The uniformed troopers hadn't caught up to us yet.

Mike stepped from his car and faced the pickup, displaying his credentials. As he did, he saw that the man was aiming a shotgun at him through the pickup windshield. In just the nick of time, Mike dove into his front seat as the man shot through his windshield, shattering the driver's door window right behind where Mike had just been standing.

While I couldn't see Mike draw his 357 magnum revolver with six-inch barrel from his shoulder holster, I heard him return fire toward the pickup. We would later see that the rounds had skipped off the sloped windshield, not penetrating it.

As I leaped from my car, I yelled, "State Police!" over and over and drew my issued .38 caliber Smith & Wesson revolver from my shoulder holster, the one I had been awarded for qualifying as a "Distinguished Expert."

I remember wanting my shotgun so badly, but it was cased in the trunk of my undercover car, and I realized this battle would be settled long before I would have time to retrieve it. As I yelled, "State Police, drop the gun!" I observed the man aiming the shotgun toward where Mike hid. Fortunately, it was awkward for him to maneuver the shotgun in the cramped space of the pickup cab. But as he raised the shotgun toward Mike's car, I felt no hesitation in firing all six rounds at him.

I was trying to shoot the suspect through the back window of the pickup and a two-inch space of the cab not protected by the pickup truck's bed. All of my rounds hit in the target area, but apparently, they were not penetrating the glass, sheet metal, and seat cushion to strike the suspect. As the suspect dropped down out of sight, I began reloading my revolver, crouched behind the open driver's door of my car.

And then it happened—the police officer's nightmare. When I had ejected my six spent cartridges, one had dropped behind the ratchet and become jammed, preventing me from reloading. I thought to myself, *All right, calm down! Look at the jam and finger the cartridge clear just like they taught you.* Fine motor skills and functions are always challenging under an adrenaline dump, but it worked, and I used my Bianchi speed strip quickly to reload six rounds.

During the reloading process, I retreated behind my car for better cover. As I came up to reengage, I realized I might have a better angle from the passenger side. As I repositioned, the marked patrol car with Troopers Humphrey and Sturdivant slid in behind me. They were unaware that shots had been fired, but they observed my revolver in my hand as I maneuvered to aim at the pickup.

At that moment, Flintstone apparently decided it was too crowded in the cab for a firefight so he jumped out the driver's door, armed with the shotgun. Trooper Humphrey and the suspect's eyes momentarily met. Although Trooper Humphrey was in full uniform and armed with a shotgun, Flintstone continued to ignore orders of "State Police, drop the gun!" He apparently decided the inside of the pickup's cab wasn't so bad after all and jumped back in. You would have thought with the arrival of uniformed reinforcements, Flintstone might have waved the white flag, but he was apparently determined.

Unknown to Trooper Humphrey, Officer Michael Wells was lying down in his car's front seat just ahead of the pickup with a now empty revolver, and his driver's door was still open with the shot out window. While Mike was a slim guy, I'm sure he was thinking "real skinny" when Trooper Humphrey shot at Flintstone with the 12 gauge slug, which missed him but put a big hole in Mike's car door.

Flintstone was back in his pickup and positioning his shotgun to shoot again when I shot three more rounds into the back of the cab from my new vantage point on the passenger side of my car. The third bullet succeeded in penetrating through the glass and seat cushion to drill Flintstone in the shoulder. Who says a .38 Special lacks knockdown power? The Speer 125 Grain Jacketed Soft Point round dropped Flintstone like a rock, even after penetrating the back window. He rolled out the driver's door into the road, leaving behind his shotgun and the teenager.

We pleaded with the teenager to throw the shotgun out, but to no avail. As the youth maneuvered the shotgun around, we held our fire. Finally, he responded to our repeated commands and threw the gun out the door. We then ordered him to get out of the pickup and to lie face down on the ground. He did as ordered, lying down on the shotgun he had thrown out. Again, we held our fire. We ordered him to roll away from the shotgun, which he did. We went forward and handcuffed the two suspects whom we later learned were father and son.

By now, backup was arriving and the scene was being secured. I was worried that an innocent bystander might have been hit, but thankfully, our scan of the scene revealed no collateral injuries. As I realized the battle was over, lower back spasms bent me over. I was puzzled since I had never experienced this pain before. Like a muscle cramp, they passed within a few minutes. I suppose it was just the tension of the battle since I was not injured. In my career, little did I know I would experience it only one more time, at my next shooting.

Because of my role in the shooting, my responsibilities at the scene were minimal. I was relieved of my revolver and returned to the post to write my report. I called Deb to tell her I had been in a shooting, but that I was okay and would tell her about it when I got home. The guys took me out for a couple of beers at the Roundtree Bar, but I didn't stay long.

When I got home around 11:00 p.m., with our sons asleep, I told Deb what had happened. She seemed indifferent to what I told her and said she was tired, so she went to bed. I did not consider what she was feeling, but looking back I can imagine many scenarios. At the time, I felt somewhat abandoned by her as I sat alone in the dark living room until the wee hours of the morning. The mental tape of the shooting continued to rerun in my head. Like a song that keeps singing in your brain, it was driving me crazy. It took a lot of effort to think of something else, but it was worth it. Finally, sleep came.

The next day, Deb was gone to work and I was on administrative leave while the shooting was investigated and then ruled on. I canceled the boy's daycare for the rest of the week because I would be home and available to take care of them, or more accurately, they would take care of me by keeping me busy.

On the second day after the shooting, I received a call from the Assistant Post Commander, Lieutenant Doug Swix. He advised me that the shooting has been ruled justifiable and for me to report for duty. After I explained that I had cancelled my boys' daycare, I requested one more day off, which would get me to my weekend, and then I would return to work on Monday. Lieutenant Swix agreed to this.

When I returned to duty, my service revolver was returned to me. When I inspected it before returning it to service, I discovered that it had been discreetly marked as evidence in the event that the shooting had been ruled unjustifiable and I had to be prosecuted.

Back then, contact with a mental health professional following an officer-involved shooting was not required. At the time, I didn't feel like I needed any. Little did I know the ghosts would come later. I was scheduled to return to uniform in a week, but I was asked to extend my tour with WAIT. I declined.

Fred Flintstone was charged with felony level crimes in Wayne County and the preliminary examination was held before Judge James Stone in the 34th District Court in Romulus. At a preliminary examination, the prosecution has to establish that a felony crime had been committed and there was reason to believe the defendant had committed the crime; then it could be sent to Circuit Court for trial.

The prosecutor viewed the case as very solid, and as I recall, only one witness testified. I was sequestered, meaning I was not allowed in the courtroom to see the proceedings because I was a potential witness. We were shocked when Judge Stone dismissed the charges! The prosecutor stated he would appeal the ruling to Circuit Court, having six months to do so.

Somehow, the case fell through the cracks at the Wayne County Prosecutor's Office in Detroit, and the six months expired without the appeal being filed. Fred Flintstone would not be legally punished for trying to shoot Officer Michael Wells.

Officer Wells and I did not know each other very well. At the time, he was new to the team and I was in my last couple of weeks. It was not long after the shooting that he left law enforcement, choosing another profession. Looking back, I wonder why we didn't get together and talk about it.

The trauma of the shooting did not haunt me until about six months later. I was not troubled in the least iota about what I had done or my performance. But I was stressed by how fast it had happened; that it had felt "done, said, and over with" before I realized it had even happened. I suppose many significant events in a person's life are like that. And while

I drew comfort from how my training had kicked in, and that I had gone on "automatic pilot," I began to doubt myself. What if it happened again? Could I do it again? Being too macho to seek professional help, I quietly dealt with it in silent turmoil.

Eventually, Fred Flintstone filed a civil lawsuit against me for shooting him. Since the Department and Prosecutor's Office had ruled the shooting justifiable, the State of Michigan offered me legal counsel through the Attorney General's Office.

The wheels of justice turn slowly, and the ordeal of depositions would not transpire until after I had become a dog handler for the police. I remember being deposed in an air conditioned office at the Ypsilanti State Police Post, and because of the heat outside, having my police dog "Cisco" lying beside me. As Flintstone's attorney attempted to illicit statements from me that would support his lawsuit, he visibly suffered because he was allergic to dogs. That didn't bother me.

Two weeks before the civil trial was scheduled to begin in Wayne County, Fred Flintstone said he would settle out of court for the sum of $10,000. The Assistant Attorney General telephoned me and made me aware of the offer, asking what I thought, and explaining that if accepted, the State would pay it. I told him that while I did not look forward to the stress of trial, I did not want Flintstone to be rewarded in any way for trying to shoot my partner.

A few days later, the Assistant Attorney General contacted me again and told me that it would cost the State more to take the case to trial than settle, and the possibility existed that the jury would rule in Flintstone's favor. The long and short of it was that the State had decided to settle; if I wished to contest the matter, it would be at my expense and risk. Talk about forced choice and justice.

36) Character

The Special Operations Division of the Michigan State Police consisted of three units; Underwater Recovery (scuba divers), Canine (dog handlers), and Emergency Services (special weapons and tactics). When the department announced that it would be selecting twenty troopers for six weeks of Emergency Services Team (E.S.T.) training, Joe and I were all about it. EST troopers provide traditional trooper duties, but they are on continual call for emergency situations such as barricaded gunmen and high risk raids. Their selection, training, and equipment made them among the best for emergencies of this nature. No doubt they were an elite cadre, and Joe and I aspired to be among them.

The prospective candidate had to have a minimal of two years of trooper experience and submit a letter of interest endorsed by the post commander. Seventy-five candidates from around the state competed for the twenty positions.

The selection process would consist of a fitness test: a 40 yard dash, 1½ mile run for time, the number of continual 150 pound bench press repetitions that could be completed before failure, and the number of push-ups, pull-ups, and sit-ups that could be completed within a minute. That fitness test score would accompany the candidate to the afternoon interview. The interview would be before a board of three persons, the EST Commander, departmental psychologist, and the Special Operations Division Commander. The first step was to submit a letter of interest.

In our own minds, Joe and I had become the dynamic duo. We were spit and shine troopers in the prime of our lives, which was accented by our fitness program. We regularly ran to and from work, and at the end of our shift, we lifted weights in the basement of the Ypsilanti Post. We felt tried and tested in both performance and experiences. In addition to our various Ypsi trooper escapades, we had been on mobilizations to the Kalamazoo tornado disaster and two prison riots.

PERIMETER PATROL — Trooper Clifton L. Edwards of the state police post at Ypsilanti was one of scores of county and state police officers from around the state called into Kalamazoo Tuesday night to establish a cordon around heavily damaged downtown and westside areas. This scene is from N. Westnedge and Water streets, looking east.   — Gazette photo by Robert Maxwell

Compliments of the *Kalamazoo Gazette*.

MICHIGAN STATE POLICE
Interoffice Correspondence

Date : March 8, 1981

Subject: Request for assignment to the Emergency Services Team

To : Colonel Gerald L. Hough, Director

From : Trooper Clifton L. Edwards #854, Ypsilanti Post

Please be advised of my continued desire to become a member of the Emergency Services Team.

Since my enlistment in the department, I have always had a keen interest in the E. S. Team. Upon graduation from recruit school, I was assigned to the Romeo Post. I was a member of the Service Trooper Recruit School (89.5) and was sworn as a trooper on September 17, 1976. My initial training officer was Trooper Leslie G. Hasler, an original member of the E. S. Team. Through him, I became acquainted with the extensive training, specialized equipment, and maintenance program of the team. This served to increase my respect and interest in the team.

While assigned at the Romeo Post I became directly involved in three incidents in which the services of the E. S. Team were requested. In one of these cases the scene was secured prior to the arrival of the team and I later received an award for professional excellance for my role in it.

On October 30, 1978, I was transferred to the Ypsilanti Post. The diverse situations encountered here have continued to broaden my police experiences.

Since graduation from recruit school I have constantly strifed to increase my competency as a state trooper. I have achieved marksmanship rating of distinguished expert, gold physical fitness badge, Oscar G. Olander award, and three citations for professional excellance. I received my associate degree in criminal justice from Washtenaw Community College in December of 1980, graduating with a grade point average of 3.31. On two seperate occassions I was selected as a training officer for probationary troopers.

If selected, I pledge my total commitment to this important function of the M.S.P.

Respectfully submitted,

Clifton L. Edwards

Trooper Clifton L. Edwards

Recommend Approval at this Level. Tpr. Edwards is a dedicated, excellent young officer who certainly has the desire and makeup to become an excellent EST Officer.

Respectfully submitted,

Robert L. Pifer

Robert L. Pifer, Lieutenant
Post Commander, Ypsilanti

APPROVED
ASSISTANT DISTRICT COMMANDER
OA (REV. 1-75)

When test day arrived, five Ypsi troopers met at the post to travel together to the academy in Lansing to compete. Of those five, one would be late, something we could not fathom. This delayed departure made our arrival just in the nick of time—not the way Joe and I operated.

When the day of testing was done, Joe and I came home feeling we had performed well, both physically and mentally. The days of waiting passed slowly. Finally the long-awaited letter arrived. Neither Joe nor I had made the cut. Of the five Ypsi troops who had tried out, only the trooper who had nearly made us late had been selected. We couldn't believe it! You would have thought we had just learned of our mothers' deaths.

Later that day, Joe and I met at the Roundtree Bar to cry in our beer. After a couple of rounds of whimpering, whining, and beer, Joe said to me, "You know, Clif, I've never—I repeat never—not gotten what I've gone after. This builds character."

Neither of our careers would ever include being members of the Emergency Services Team.

MICHIGAN STATE POLICE
Interoffice Correspondence

Date   :   June 1, 1981

Subject: Selection of Emergency Support Team Personnel

To   :   Trooper Clifton Edwards, Ypsilanti Post #26

From   :   Major Michael J. Anderson, Commanding Officer, Uniform Division

This is to notify you that you were not selected for Emergency Support Team training. There were a total of 75 men who appeared for the testing and interview process, excluding those who either rescinded their applications or failed to appear. During the interviews we found, with few exceptions, that the applicants were well qualified and would be an asset to the team. Unfortunately, we were authorized to fill only 20 positions. This leaves us with the task of advising many good men that we are unable to accept them at this time. We sincerely hope that you will not be discouraged and that you will consider applying again when conditions permit another school.

All applications will remain on file for further consideration if alternates are needed. You are to be commended for your efforts and dedication to the department.

MJA/od

37) Gangster

Gangster Goodloe

It was the summer of 1981 and my stint in WAIT was over. I was now back in uniform and trooping with my good hunting partner, Joe Payne. It was late into an afternoon shift when we observed a black 1976 Cadillac stopped at the red light for westbound Michigan Avenue in downtown Ypsilanti. The driver, a middle-aged black male wearing a floppy gangster hat, appeared to be the lone occupant. As we passed by, we noticed that the Cadillac had a broken tail lens, causing it to emit white light to the rear; a violation of the Michigan vehicle code. As I turned the patrol car around to stop the Cadillac, it bolted through the red light.

The Cadillac traveled only a block before turning right on Washington Street, without signaling, and raced north with its lights now extinguished—it looked like the driver was trying to elude us. Patrol Car 261 was closing in like a heat-seeking missile when the Cadillac attempted to turn right on Washtenaw Avenue, lost control, jumped the curb, and crashed into the glass garage door of a closed service station, causing shattered glass to rain down on its hood.

I positioned the patrol car tight, my front bumper to the Cadillac's rear bumper, to prevent it from driving away. Joe and I were exiting the patrol car when the Cadillac's backup lights came on and it crashed into 261. The impact caused our open car doors to spring shut, nearly hitting me with a velocity that would have likely knocked me to the ground. With revolvers drawn, we approached the Cadillac, whose driver's door was already open. I ordered the driver to put his hands on the car's ceiling. He ignored my commands and continued to shift the car and adjust its steering wheel in an effort to wiggle his car free of the vise in which it was pinned.

To end the volatile situation, I struck the suspect in the upper body with my flashlight, which persuaded him to comply with my orders. We arrested him for "Attempting to Flee and Elude a Police Officer," handcuffed and searched him, and then placed him in the patrol car's backseat.

We determined that the driver was Robert Lee Goodloe and that the license plates on the Cadillac were expired. While we probably could have justified a warrantless search of the car for "search incident to arrest," we bolstered that exception to the search warrant rule with requesting "consent," which Goodloe granted us. In the car, Joe found a lone marijuana cigarette and a used syringe. Then we summoned a wrecker to tow the car, and the Ypsilanti City Police to deal with securing the gas station. We transported Goodloe to the Ypsilanti Post for an interview and processing.

Once we had placed Goodloe in lock-up, prior to the interview, we checked his criminal history. It was extensive, and the FBI listed his occupation as "Hit Man." Interesting!

About that time, Ypsilanti City Police Dispatcher Cindi Agge called and told us that while the wrecker driver had been sweeping up the broken glass from the glass garage door, he had come across a Luger Pistol. Were we interested? Affirmative—we said we'd be right over to collect it. The scene was only about three miles away, so we were there in a matter of minutes. Undoubtedly, Robert Lee Goodloe had thrown the pistol from his window about the time he crashed into the door, but could we prove it?

We protected the pistol for latent fingerprints while making it safe. It was loaded to capacity with 9mm rounds with one round in the chamber. We packaged it as evidence and later sent it to the crime lab along with a set of Goodloe's fingerprints. We crossed our fingers that the lab would develop a latent lift from the Luger that would match one of Goodloe's. We returned to the post to conduct our interview.

To say the least, the interview with Goodloe was interesting. He was both personable and charismatic. While he was willing to discuss issues generally and hypothetically, when our questions became more specific, he crafted his answers so they were not incriminating.

He told us things he knew about the police that we hoped he and his colleagues never learned. In his street slang, he said, "I know about you troopers cross draw flap holsters. While a brother be looking at it and thinks I can beat him to the draw, and makes his play, you give him a third eye with that snubnosed revolver you got your hand on in your pocket."

His statement reminded me of the teachings of Miyamoto Musashi in *The Book of Five Rings*, written in 1643: "It is the duty of all warriors to wear two swords." For modern day warriors, that means carrying a backup gun.

When we asked Goodloe about his criminal history listing his occupation as a hit man, he did not deny or admit to it, but suggested (not to be confused with admitting) that he had killed seventeen people. He denied any knowledge of the Luger, and at the end of the day, we could only charge him with misdemeanors, for which he was able to post bond. We asked him what the tattoo "GG" on his arm stood for. "Gangster Goodloe," he told us, and he went on to say that when asked by kids, he would say it stands for "Good Guy." Who's to say he didn't aspire to being a good role model?

Ten days later, we got the news that a Goodloe fingerprint had been found on a 9mm round loaded in the Luger. With near Godspeed, we obtained a felony warrant for carrying a concealed weapon (pistol), entered it into NCIC (National Crime Information Center), and began our hunt. Street sources directed us to Ann Arbor, a sister city to Ypsilanti, and indicated Goodloe was now carrying a sawed off shotgun. During the hours of darkness, Joe and I parked the patrol car and crept through lawns, peeking in houses where the informant said he might be staying.

One of those nights, we overheard Ann Arbor Police being dispatched to a motel about a person who had checked into a second floor room and appeared armed with a sawed off shotgun. The person's description matched that of Goodloe. Joe and I headed for the motel.

We arrived after the Ann Arbor Police, who had initiated a knock and talk at the room in question. Fortunately, they had stationed an officer on the ground beneath this room. Their knocks on his motel room door prompted a sawed off shotgun to be thrown out the back window, followed by the landing of Robert Lee Goodloe. Bingo!

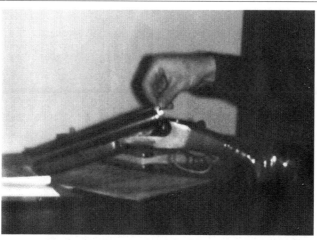

Sawed-off shotgun Goodloe tossed out motel window.

The next day Goodloe was arraigned on our felony charges of "Carrying a Concealed Weapon," in reference to the Luger and the additional charge of "Possession of a Short-Barreled Shotgun." Because he was charged with "victimless crimes" and the jails were full, Goodloe's bond was not very high. Within a few days, he posted bond and was released. When his court date came around, he did not appear, so bond was forfeited and felony bench warrants were issued for his arrest. Hunt as we did, we never found him. Eventually, the Ypsilanti City Police did find him, murdered. "Live by the sword; die by the sword."

Tennessee man sought in killings

By STEPHEN CAIN
and SUSAN OPPAT
NEWS STAFF REPORTERS

YPSILANTI — Drugs and a possible "contract hit" are being mentioned in the double murder of two men in a southside Ypsilanti apartment building Wednesday night.

Ypsilanti police say they have a suspect in the killings, but after two days of searching it now appears likely that he has fled the area.

Detective Michael Duncan said the officers and detectives were out all night again last night searching for a 30-year-old man wanted in Tennessee on drug charges and in Ypsilanti on weapons charges. Police refused to release the suspect's name.

Duncan confirmed that the motive for the shootings at 209 S. Grove Street just before 7 p.m. Wednesday was probably drugs, since both victims were believed to be drug users. Neither was armed or robbed.

The two men were shot in the hallway of a Four Hills apartment building. Most of the Four Hills complex is condemned for housing code violations.

A handgun is believed to have been used to kill Thomas Bigham, 33, who lived at Four Hills, and Robert "Gangster" Goodloe, 53, of Maybee. Goodloe died at Beyer Memorial Hospital minutes after the shootings, and Bigham died at St. Joseph Mercy Hospital at about 9:15 p.m. the same night.

Police would not say whether there were any witnesses to the shootings.

One federal law enforcement official familiar with Goodloe said there were street rumors that the ex-convict, whose nickname was "Gangster," had been "running protection" for drug deals in the Ypsilanti area.

A second federal official, who had had contact with Goodloe off and on for nearly a decade, said he had been told that a major Ecorse drug dealer "has had a contract out for Robert for some time."

Although Goodloe had continued to list his parents home in Maybee as his home address, he operated out of Detroit in the 1950s and 1960s and had been a fixture of the Ypsilanti area underworld from the 1970s until his death.

His trademark was a sawed-off shotgun, and he had a fearsome reputation in the Ypsilanti area, according to interviews The Ann Arbor News had conducted with small-time drug dealers for a different story.

"I'm surprised he wasn't killed a long time ago," said the second federal official, who added that he could not be quoted by name because his department's rules forbid talking to the press.

Goodloe's record of felony convictions began in June of 1950 with a guilty plea in Detroit Recorder's Court to an unarmed robbery charge — plea bargained down from armed robbery.

His last two convictions stemmed from a July, 1981, carrying concealed weapon (a 9-mm German Luger) incident, and a November, 1981, arrest for possession of a shotgun.

38) Knight

On September 16, 1981, I had just ended a long weekend off and started a week of afternoon shifts. I had not yet completed my self-briefing of police activity when the desk sergeant walked back to the squad room and assigned me a burglary case. The same house had been broken into a few days earlier, and the woman who lived there had been sexually assaulted and stabbed. No arrests had been made at the time. That case had been assigned to Trooper Henry Tyler, but he was now on vacation.

At this point, you might be asking, "Where is Trooper Joe Payne?" Back then troopers worked alone during daylight hours, Joe was handling his own caseload, so I went to the site of the burglary alone.

I responded to the home, which was in the area of Ypsilanti Township known as West Willow. It was a deteriorating, racially mixed neighborhood, begun during World War II when the nearby airport of West Willow manufactured bomber aircraft. It was a small single story Cracker Jack box shaped house on a postage stamp size lot, pretty similar to the one I lived in on the other side of town.

When I arrived at the scene, I contacted the homeowner and previous victim of the assault. Jane Doe was a divorced middle-aged blonde who lived alone. She was visibly shaken and in the company of her adult daughter. She told me that a few days earlier she had been home sick, sleeping on the sofa, when she was awakened by the odor of cat urine. She opened her eyes just in time to see a teenage black male covering her face with a rug from her basement. A struggle ensued and she pleaded with him not to rape her, using her period as a reason why he would not want her. During her resistance, the suspect cut her with a knife. When the suspect discovered that she was in fact menstruating, he abandoned his attempt to rape her and fled with a few valuables.

I contacted Trooper Tyler at home and was updated on the status of his investigation. He was now on vacation, and since both crimes had undoubtedly been committed by the same perpetrator, the investigative responsibility was passed to me. Trooper Tyler had worked hard to solve the case. He had processed the crime scene and summoned a police dog in hopes of tracking the suspect, which proved fruitless. He had developed a possible suspect upon whom he conducted a background investigation, interviewed, and then presented in a photographic line-up to the victim. While initially this person appeared a likely suspect, he would be cleared.

Jane explained that since that incident, she had been staying with her adult daughter; they had just stopped by to check on the house, discovering that it had again been broken into the same way. As she told me all this, Jane's composure melted and she began to sob uncontrollably. Her daughter wrapped her arm around her to console her and I floundered. I then did something I had never done before; I grasped her hands and asked her to look in my eyes. As our eyes met, I said, "I promise you I will catch the person who did this." Her daughter then drove her to the hospital emergency room where she was sedated. I began my investigation, determined to leave no stone unturned.

Statistics indicate that if a crime is not solved within the first twenty-four hours of occurrence, the chances of it being solved are greatly reduced. To me, that statistic is a cop-out and reflects one of two things—either lack of initiative or time to conduct a skilled follow-up investigation. This case was not going to be easy. Understandably, my victim was an emotional mess, unable to live at home since she felt as if she were prey. I hoped my promise would provide Jane some peace of mind and that I could make good on it.

As I wrapped up my on-scene preliminary investigation, I turned to my neighborhood canvass. There is an art to a proper neighborhood canvass, and it involves earnest communication. Too often, this probe (which I define as an action taken to produce a lead, suspect, or evidence) is neglected. Obviously, the objective of a neighborhood canvass is to learn of any suspicious persons the neighbors may have seen. The less obvious is to learn the background of the victim and evaluate the potential of neighbors or other persons who frequent the neighbor's house as possibly being involved.

More often than not, the culprit in crimes of this nature resides within a mile radius. In other cases, during such probes, I have spied shoes placed by the door that matched the suspect's shoeprints along with other evidence, such as the stolen property. Unfortunately, that would not be the case in this investigation.

Trooper Tyler had previously completed a neighborhood canvass, so mine was the second in a week. The neighborhood had never experienced so much state police attention, which was cultivating positive police-citizen relations. This blossoming relationship produced more tips from the neighbors, each requiring investigative hours to resolve. An elderly black woman, who lived across the street, told me of a teenage black male who had been hanging around and seemed to be watching Jane's house. She did not know his name, but the description she provided matched the glimpse the victim got of the suspect before being covered with the urine-soaked rug. After considerable leg work, I was able to identify him, and he looked promising as the suspect. In fact, the victim also made a tentative identification of him in a photographic line-up. However, he too was eventually cleared.

With the description provided by the victim, I polled various officers of the many police agencies that served this geographic area. Detective Kennon of the Washtenaw County Sheriff's Department told me that the description and *modus operandi* were very similar to a past case of his that had resulted in the conviction of a Paul Byars. Paul Byars had lived in the same neighborhood, but Detective Kennon was pretty sure he was still in prison.

Initial inquiries indicated that Byars was currently in prison, but experience had taught me that things were not always as they appear. Just perhaps Byars had been furloughed for a short period of time for some reason. I dug deeper, only to confirm that Byars had been in custody when these two crimes were perpetrated.

Why do I share these dead end leads? Real police work involves a lot of wild goose chases, often not shared in action-packed police shows. Sadly, my investigation into Paul Byars was not in vain. He would later cross my path twice; I'll share those stories later. Meanwhile, other criminal activity continued and calls had to be answered. An officer must be mindful of persistence and careful not to get distracted or he will give credence to the "cop-out" cliché.

During the evening of September 30, 1981, the victim, in the company of her sixteen-year old nephew, decided to spend the evening at her house in an effort to get comfortable with home again. They had been watching television for a couple of hours when they heard someone breaking into the home through the basement window, the same entry point as the previous two burglaries.

They telephoned the State Police Post, but all troopers were on calls, so the desk sergeant requested the assistance of the Washtenaw County Sheriff's Department, with Deputies Curby and Smith being dispatched. As the deputies neared the area, they observed two black males walking away and carrying a brown paper bag of pop bottles. Ask yourself, should they take the time to stop and identify them or go straight to the scene? They decided to stop briefly to identify the persons, who turned out to be brothers, one named Joseph Poole, and they lived in the vicinity.

When the deputies arrived at the scene, they learned the perpetrator had already fled. As is the practice, they held the scene down until troopers could respond since the original call had been to the state police, and it appeared related to the two previous incidents currently under state police investigation.

Troopers Johnson and Breedveld relieved the deputies at the scene. The deputies told the troopers of the two brothers they had identified and their descriptions. This information would later be relayed to me. Of the two brothers, Joseph Poole's description most matched the description provided by the victim from the first incident.

State Police Detective Sergeant Roy Turbett processed the crime scene, lifting a shoeprint from the lid of a washing machine, where the suspect had crawled into the basement. That print would later prove valuable.

Within nineteen days, the residence had either been burglarized or attempted three times with the same method of operation. An MSP profiler confirmed what we already suspected—this predator would continue to hunt this prey until successful. We scheduled a night for the victim to return home with Trooper Joe Payne and I secretly inside the house. If this plan worked, it would be just like television police dramas and a dream come true.

But that night, we got tied up on another serious call which we could not clear so we postponed the plan until the next night. The next day, the victim again had an emotional breakdown and had to be readmitted to the hospital. Waiting for the victim to become available, I began investigating Joseph Poole. Would it be just another wild goose chase?

I learned that during the evening hours of October 1st, Sergeant Kirby of the Ypsilanti City Police responded to a prostitute's complaint that a "John" had threatened her with a knife. When Sergeant Kirby arrived, he interviewed the prostitute and the client, Joseph Poole. Poole did have a knife, which Sergeant Kirby examined, but it was legal and had not even been opened in the alleged assault. Sergeant Kirby felt the complaint lacked merit, so both persons were sent on their way.

Nearby, and less than two hours later, a citizen saw a black male crouched down by a basement window of a home. He then heard glass break. As the brave citizen approached, the suspicious person fled into the dark. The citizen, whom I will call Captain Courageous, gave pursuit and caught him, at which time a struggle ensued. Finally, the suspect was able to break away, making good his escape. Captain Courageous summoned the police, and Officers Chan and Savage of the Ypsilanti City Police responded.

Captain Courageous supplied a detailed description to the police officers and showed them where he had heard the glass break. There, officers found a cut screen, broken window, and knife. They collected the knife as evidence.

The description provided by Captain Courageous and the knife seized by Officers Chan and Savage matched that observed by Sergeant Kirby on the earlier prostitute complaint involving Joseph Poole. As previously mentioned, Joseph Poole matched the glimpse the victim had of the man who had assaulted her. This information now sat in a large stack of pending cases on the desk of Ypsilanti City Police Detective Mutchler.

Years later, I would be a task force commander. I would review all "leads" (also known as "tips") received and give them a priority of either "probable, possible, or doubtful" before assigning them to an investigator. The mission of the investigator was to return that lead either cleared or solved. The investigator's opinion of "cleared" would then have to be seconded by me, the task force commander, before being closed. I prayed I would never clear a lead that would later prove to be the perpetrator, like what had happened in the Yosemite Murders of 1999. In that case, a person named in a lead was initially cleared but later proved to be the murderer. While the previous leads in this case would have been rated as "possible," the Joseph Poole lead was knocking at the door of "probable."

The next morning, I caught Detective Mutchler in his office just before he left for court. I shared with him my suspicions of Joseph Poole. I requested he seek a warrant for Poole, charging him with attempted breaking and entering, and then allow me to serve it, making for an opportune time to interview him on my case. While Mutchler was willing, he was currently in a trial so it might be days before he could get to it. Time was of the essence, so I asked Mutchler for permission to take over this city case. Mutchler gladly gave me the green light, reducing his waiting in-basket by one.

I put the paperwork together and presented the package to Jack Sims, Washtenaw County Assistant Prosecutor. He authorized a felony warrant for Joseph Poole, charging him with attempted breaking and entering. I signed the complaint and the warrant was issued by Judge Thomas Shea. I now had the authority to arrest Joseph Poole, at which time I hoped to interview him on my case.

A skilled interviewer can conduct a competent cold interrogation. But a skilled interviewer, given the opportunity, will always choose to prepare for an interrogation. This situation provided me that luxury.

Other than what I've previously shared, I discovered no indicators in Poole's background of sexual assault. Had he just become deviant, or had been getting away with such crimes for some time? A confession was imperative to making this case as our victim had tentatively identified two other persons in previous photographic line-ups that had been cleared. I needed to manipulate every possible condition in the interview to promote exposure of the truth.

By now, Trooper Joe Payne and I had become quite skilled as a tag team in conducting interviews and interrogations. Two persons conducting an interrogation can be disastrous or powerful, depending on their style and practice together. I would choose to do an interview solo if I did not have the opportunity to rehearse it with my prospective partner. Joe being black while I was white was another reason to have him assist.

So, partners first prepared for a most important interview, and then, with felony warrant in hand, hunted Joseph Poole. The predator had now become the prey.

It was October 6, 1981, some twenty-five days since Jane had initially been assaulted, undoubtedly long days for her. Trooper Payne and I first went to the address of Joseph Poole, but he wasn't there. His brother directed us to his girlfriend's place, where we found him and made a low key arrest. We told him we had a felony warrant for him, but we were vague about the specifics. We treated him with respect and transported him to the Ypsilanti Post to be fingerprinted and photographed, but more importantly, interviewed. We read him his Miranda warning, and he agreed to talk with us.

At the onset of most interviews, the majority of the talking is done by the investigators as they carefully study their subject. A mental stage is elaborately set in preparation for the first BIG question—a question that is often anti-climatic and more general than specific. A tenet of an interrogator is "The more you know, the less you tell, and the less you know, the more you tell." This strategy should be carefully considered.

In this case, like most, Poole was told we were investigating a crime of a felony nature, in which he was involved, and we wanted to give him an opportunity to tell his side of the story. Often, as the suspect tries to figure out which felony we know about, he will ask for specifics, to which we will simply respond, "Surely, you have not been involved in so many crimes that you don't know what we are talking about?" Now, if the suspect is involved, he must guess which one we are onto. On many occasions by using this technique, I have obtained confessions to crimes I knew nothing about.

Poole gambled that it was the September 30th burglary of Jane's home we were interested in, first confessing to it. When we were not satisfied with that, he then chose to tell us of the attempted burglary in the City of Ypsilanti when Captain Courageous had chased him. When that did not quench our thirst, he finally confessed to the burglary, attempted rape, assault, and robbery of Jane. Bingo!

Our immediate challenge was to sit there calmly while inside we were jumping up and down. Poole shared that he had become attracted to this victim one day when he witnessed her arguing with a man in her front yard.

This entire interview only took an hour, and a tape-recorded confession was obtained. The Converse tennis shoes Poole wore to the interview matched the shoeprint lifted from the washing machine by Detective Sergeant Turbett so they were seized as evidence. While they would not have the weight of a positive identification, it was a class identification which would have circumstantial evidence value in a court trial.

Bond was set at $100,000, and Poole would await court proceedings in jail. At age twenty, Poole had lost his freedom, but in a sense, Jane had lost hers on the day they first met. While the situation was far from over, Jane could now begin her transition from victim to victor.

A defendant, in this case Joseph Poole, is entitled to a Preliminary Examination within twelve days. At a Preliminary Examination, the prosecution must accomplish two things for the case to be sent to trial. First, that there was a crime committed absent any confession, and second, that there is "reason to believe," also termed "probable cause," that the defendant committed the crime. The confession can be used to connect the defendant to the crime. This is a lesser test than "beyond a reasonable doubt" required for conviction. The preliminary examination was held on October 14, 1981, and the case was sent to the Washtenaw County Circuit Court for trial. Poole remained in jail.

Eventually, after a series of plea bargaining sessions spanning seven months, Poole pled guilty to "Armed Robbery and Breaking and Entering with the intent to commit Criminal Sexual Conduct." On May 3, 1982, Judge Henry Conlin sentenced Poole to serve two concurrent (meaning served simultaneously) sentences of ten to fifteen years in prison. So in this case, Poole's total prison time would be ten to fifteen years, which meant he could be paroled in about eight years. If he had been sentenced with two consecutive sentences, the time would be added together, making it twenty to thirty years.

As I drove the victim home in a patrol car from the final court proceeding, she said to me, "Thank you. You are my knight in shining armor." I had kept my promise.

October 16, 1981

```
Colonel Gerald Hough
Michigan State Police
East Lansing, Mich. 48823

Dear Colonel Hough:

I would like to formally thank Trooper Clifton Edwards of the
Michigan State Police, Ypsilanti Post for his outstanding per
formance as an Ypsilanti police officer. His concern and per
serverance in dealing with my case aided in the arrest of my
assailant. He is a fine officer and a credit to the police
force. I am greatly relieved that the ordeal is finally over
and I wish to thank him for making that possible.
```

Thank-you letter from victim

39) Hogs

By now, Joe and I had been in enough tough spots that I was sure he was fearless. We were working the midnight shift one bone-chilling night with about four to six inches of snow on the ground when his Achilles heel of fear was exposed. When you work midnights, there is normally a lull in the action during the period between party-time and work traffic, when most citizens sleep. It was then that we tried to eat.

Our usual spot was a 24-hour restaurant just off the I-94 freeway named the Big Apple. By 4:00 a.m., the drunks were usually gone and the restaurant was quiet, except it always seemed they vacuumed the floors then. Each booth had its own personal jukebox, so we tried to listen to Neil Diamond's hit song "Forever in Blue Jeans" over the irritating hum of a vacuum sweeper. The lyrics seemed to speak to us, both being married, both having young families, and both having a career in which financial wealth was not a goal.

We talked about what we would do when we retired as I would likely be eligible at age forty-five. Passionate about being a police officer, I dreamed of just starting over at another police department, maybe somewhere far away like Alaska or New Mexico.

Cops develop a bad habit of eating fast out of necessity, never knowing when they might get called away from chow to answer an urgent call. When the waitress came to our table and said we had a telephone call, we knew it would be the shift commander, Sergeant Larry Copley.

Sergeant Copley told me that a semi-tractor pulling a livestock trailer full of hogs going to slaughter had overturned on eastbound I-94 near Ann Arbor. Further, the truck driver was injured and there were hundreds of hogs, weighing over two hundred pounds apiece, running wild on the freeway, posing a significant traffic hazard. We had about an hour before work traffic would start.

I envisioned what it would be like: the hogs as bowling balls; the cars as bowling pins. Fortunately, the median wall would confine the threat to only eastbound traffic. Unfortunately, morning work traffic was heaviest on eastbound as workers headed to the Detroit metropolitan area.

Take a cold night, light traffic, and an emergency. Add a pair of troopers in a Plymouth Fury with dual exhaust, four-barrel carburetor over a 440 cubic inch V-8 engine with a flashing red light, and things go so fast it is surreal. That Plymouth Fury could really roar. Thinking now about the hundreds of such runs during my eleven years of trooping, I find it amazing more of us didn't crash and burn.

Prioritize! First things first! Upon our arrival, we saw an ambulance on scene with the injured driver being tended to by the paramedics. We had another patrol car divert traffic off the freeway while we confronted our conundrum—how to conduct a "hog roundup."

In the darkness, with the help of our lights, we saw chaos, smelled manure, and had to yell above the squealing hogs. Hogs being scheduled for slaughter in a couple of hours had made a break for it. Many already lay dead from the crash, one had already been hit by a passing motorist, and the surviving hogs, too many to count, were scurrying about in a frenzy.

A colleague of the injured truck driver had been summoned to the scene with a livestock trailer and portable corrals. We had him back one of the trailers off the shoulder into the grass where we staged the portable fencing to make a chute. Our plan was to herd the hogs into the chute and onto the trailer for transport. The only problem was that the jump up into the trailer was too high for the hogs, unless they were assisted.

The elderly hog farmer who had brought the trailer told us what we needed to do. It was a briefing like I had never had before and would never have again. He said we needed someone to get into the trailer. The others would herd the hogs to the tailgate. The person in the trailer would then reach down and grab a hog by the ears and pull. He told us that hogs have really sensitive ears and would likely jump into the trailer to alleviate the pain. In defensive tactics training, we call that pain compliance. The farmer told us that when he was young, he had done it many times, but he was too old now. Oh yeah, he told us one other thing. Hogs can bite, and when you grab their ears, their jaws will likely start snapping. So don't get your wrist in there because a bite would likely snap your wrist like a toothpick. As he explained this, I found myself peering at the hog farmer's wrists and hands. They didn't appear crippled.

In the dim light, Joe and I looked into each other's eyes. That was the one and only time I ever saw fear on the face of Joseph Payne. Joe, never at a loss for words, said, "Since you spent your childhood in Missouri, and I know there are a lot of pig farms in Missouri, you should be the person to be in that trailer." While I had grown up in Missouri, what made him think there were a lot of pig farms in Missouri, or that I had ever been on one?

And so the roundup began. It wasn't long before we were covered in pig blood and manure. It was just like the old hog farmer said. Just when you didn't think a hog could squeal any louder…I would grab one by the ears and pull back with all my might; then the squeal volume would go full blast, with the snapping jaws keeping a beat to the moment. Before long, the trailer floor was slick with a concoction of excrement, blood, and snow, in which I hoped I would not slip.

Dawn found us trying to do a head count to see whether all the pigs were accounted for, dead or alive. The snow, now stained with defecation, blood, and the tracks of both man and beast, appeared as a place where a battle had been waged. Of the 211 hogs headed to slaughter, about 31 were killed in the crash and we rounded up about 150. So just where did the remaining 30 hogs disappear? I like to think they made good their escape, living out their lives as free pigs in Ann Arbor under the ruse of a U of M Wolverine.

Did we stink! When we got back to the post, we stripped out of our parkas, pants, and boots in the garage and placed them in plastic garbage bags. We then got into a hot shower; however, no amount of soap could remove the stench.

When our shift ended, we went straight to the dry cleaners to leave them a surprise and then to the Roundtree Bar to debrief. In the books written by Joseph Wambaugh about police, he describes this activity as "Choir Practice." You just don't go home from something like that and go to sleep.

By noon, with dark blinds pulled and the white sound machine humming, I was slipping into the cool sheets of bed. Deb would try to keep things quiet, including our infant son, in the small house so I could get some sleep. As sleep approached, I'm sure I smelled pig manure!

100 hogs break out on way to death row

By CAREY ENGLISH
Free Press Staff Writer

About 100 hogs with less than two hours to live got a brief reprieve Friday morning when they broke free from an overturned truck taking them to a Detroit slaughterhouse.

"It was a big 'ol roundup," said 36-year-old Norm Briggs, one of the volunteers who joined police at the accident scene along I-94 near Ann Arbor to help coax the hogs into makeshift corrals.

The hogs, worth about $90 each, skittered off the highway to the side of the road and startled early morning motorists. The truck overturned shortly before 5 a.m. just two hours before the hogs were scheduled to be butchered at Frederick and Herrud — a Detroit slaughter and packing house.

Truck driver William Roland Jr., 32, of Monticello, Ind. was taken to the University of Michigan hospital with abdominal injuries. He was reported to be in good condition.

ABOUT 30 OF THE 211 hogs on the truck were crushed to death when the truck overturned. One hog was struck and killed in highway traffic. Eighty-nine remained in the truck while their colleagues romped about.

"There was just pigs running all over the place," said 24-year-old Jim Dawson, who was called out of bed early Friday morning by his employer, Sakstrup's Towing of Ann Arbor.

The hogs, weighing about 230 pounds each, were being shipped from the Heinold Hog Market in Hamilton, Mich., to Frederick and Herrud.

Gary Nelson, the hog procurer-manager for Frederick and Herrud, said the hogs, worth a total of $18,830 were scheduled to arrive at the slaughterhouse and be butchered at 7 a.m. Friday.

Instead, only 150 of the hogs reached the slaughterhouse and were being kept alive into Friday afternoon, Nelson said. He said the firm hoped to have the hogs slaughtered sometime Friday, however.

DAWSON SAID POLICE and volunteers cut through a nearby fence and herded the hogs into fields where they were kept until trucks could haul them away.

Authorities said the truck overturned in a roadside ditch. The hogs on the upper level of the truck got out through the roof, which had been peeled back in the accident. The truck blocked one lane of eastbound traffic at the Ann Arbor-Saline exit.

"It was a unique experience," said Trooper Clifton Edwards, who was investigating the accident with his partner, Daniel Payne.

DAWSON SAID MOST of the hogs "were pretty scared. The policemen were running around beating on 'em with flashlights and cussing.

"It was really sort of funny," Dawson said. "They didn't want to do what you wanted them to. They're ornery."

Traffic had to be stopped occasionally on access roads to get the stray hogs on trucks. Authorities said traffic on I-94 slowed until the truck could be towed away.

A State Police spokesman said a citation was issued to Roland for careless driving.

The metal roof of the truck appeared bent in the shape of a pig after the rig was righted.

Free Press Photos by CRAIG PORTER

Compliments of ***Detroit Free Press***

40) Battle

In the academy, we had a class on cultural diversity, but at the time it did not seem very important. In my youth and naivety, I thought all you needed to know was to treat all people the same: firm, fair, and friendly. In a country enriched by cultural and ethnic diversity, human relations are not always that simple. Effective communication skills are essential for a police officer to be successful, and understanding cultural and ethnic diversity is a required ingredient toward that goal. To learn something in full, you usually must experience it. While doing so, hopefully you don't spark a riot.

One afternoon shift during my first summer in Ypsilanti, I was working the same shift as Trooper Tom Jones—no relation to Trooper Al Jones whom I previously introduced. Tom was a hardworking trooper, who had some rough edges when it came to communication skills. I smile when I remember some of Tom's legendary court testimonies. One time when Tom was called to the witness stand, the judge routinely instructed him to state his full name for the record and then spell it for the court stenographer. After walking to the witness chair and taking a seat, he responded, "Tom Jones," and then turning to the stenographer, and in all apparent seriousness, asked, "Which one are you having a problem spelling?" Another time while Tom was testifying, the prosecutor asked him to tell the court, "Why did you stop the defendant?" Tom testified, "The car was clean and he was dirty!" In both instances, I would have burst out laughing in a solemn courtroom had it not been for the self-control I learned to practice during recruit school inspections.

The Ypsilanti City Police were investigating another violent incident in which an arrest warrant for attempted murder had been issued for a person I will call Barney Rubble, a young black male. He was on the run and the Ypsilanti Police had put out a BOL (police talk for "Be On Lookout") broadcast to area agencies, warning them to consider him armed and dangerous.

Trooper Tom Jones had just arrested a person known to be an associate of Barney Rubble and who likely knew where Rubble could be found. Having struggled with getting people to share this type of information, I was flattered when Tom asked that I try to "flip" this person—police slang for persuading a person to be an informant. Tom told me I could use the charges he had on the person as leverage to win his cooperation.

While developing trust and rapport with this person, I explained his other option to resolve the charges Trooper Tom Jones had on him, that option being what I labeled as "unconventional community service." Unconventional community service is where a person's charges are reduced or not prosecuted in exchange for information that leads to an arrest or recovery of stolen property. This discussion persuaded him to be an informant.

The now informant told us that Rubble would be attending a party that evening at a townhouse on Grove Street in the city projects of Ypsilanti—a party to which the informant had also been invited. Realizing that the chances of uniformed officers approaching the party and arresting Rubble were next to none, I knew any hope of success would require an unorthodox approach.

After some brainstorming and convincing of the informant, we came up with a plan. Trooper Mel Owens, a black trooper clad in plain clothes, would drive an undercover panel van to the projects with the informant in the right front passenger seat. Hidden in the back of the van would be several uniformed state troopers and Ypsilanti City Officers. Once the van was parked at the townhouses, the informant and Mel Owens would saunter up to the party for the purpose of determining whether Rubble was in attendance. Mel would wear a brightly colored Hawaiian shirt that would hopefully aid us in finding him in a crowd. Mel and the informant would then return to the van and Mel would advise us "Yea" or "Nay." If it were "Yea," they would then exit the van and re-approach the party.

In the van, we would count to ten by thousands, giving Mel time hopefully to reacquire a visual on Rubble. On "one thousand and ten," the informant would fade away and we uniformed officers in the van would burst out and run to Mel, who would point out Rubble for arrest. Ah yes, the best laid plans of mice and men!

On that steamy summer night, eight of us were squeezed tight in the back of that van. Soon, it began to smell like a locker room. As we quietly smoldered in our wool uniforms, which covered our ballistic vests, we heard something. A couple of guys were trying to break into our van! Can you imagine what their surprise would have been? But before they completed the evil deed, Mel and the informant returned, frightening the would-be vehicle burglars away.

Having retaken the driver's seat of the van, Mel said, "Yea." He continued his briefing, saying there were about thirty to forty people in attendance, both inside the townhouse and outside where they had a barbecue going. Further, the informant had pointed out the wanted fugitive whom Mel believed to be Barney Rubble based upon a mug shot he had previously studied. All of this information was said toward the windshield so anyone walking by wouldn't realize he was talking to people in the back of the van. With the briefing complete, Mel and the informant exited the van and headed back to the party. Countdown time!

"One thousand and one...One thousand and ten!" We burst from our self-imposed confinement into the darkness, shadowed by the hazy streetlights, where the humid night air was welcomed. As we charged toward the front of the town house, we scanned for Mel in his Hawaiian shirt, hoping he was pointing out the fugitive.

In retrospect, the partiers' response was very predictable. They would default to one of the three basic survival instincts: fight, flight, or freeze. Since they had home court advantage, numerical superiority and little respect for the police, their reaction would not be to freeze. It is so very clear now. No wonder they say hindsight is 20/20.

With remarkable swiftness, the partiers herded into the house with us in hot pursuit, believing Barney Rubble was among them. Just as Trooper Tom Jones and I stepped onto the porch, the partiers slammed the front door shut and locked it. With repetitive kicks, we broke the flimsy door open and six of us forced ourselves into the living room while Troopers Darrell Dixon and Dan Thomas went to the back door in a futile attempt to keep the occupants contained.

In an instant, time went from fast forward to slow motion as we shoved our way into the living room, shouting that we were there to arrest Barney Rubble. While doing so, I became engaged in what would be the brawl of my career, standing toe-to-toe with the enemy we had created. While they swung chairs and lamps as weapons, we countered with flashlights and batons.

It is amazing the amount of information your brain can process while under the influence of adrenaline. While engaged in close quarter combat, I envisioned myself escaping out the front door and running down the adjacent railroad tracks to safety.

I vividly remember one person picking up a chair and beginning an overhead swing aimed to crash upon my head and shoulders. I remember thinking there was no way I could beat his swing. But, with a preemptory strike of my flashlight to his face, I did. And down he went, with the chair toppling onto him. The battle continued.

To my left, I saw Officer Jim Daugherty, nickname Toad, being taken to the floor by three combatants. I thought, "How can this be? Toad is tough as a bull!" as I pulled assailants off him.

As I struggled to stay on my feet, I saw two persons pin Officer Larry Savage against the refrigerator while a third tried to take his holstered revolver. Savage was able to break their hold with a head butt.

Immersed in chaos, my brain continued processing multiple thoughts at once. Having just witnessed a head butt thwart disaster, I remembered a story M.S.P. Detective Sergeant Mike Knuth had told me about attending a Ypsilanti Police social event where they chartered a bus to a Tiger baseball game. On the way home, apparently too much beer had been consumed by some as they started head butting each other. When Mike came to work the next day, he had a huge goose egg on his forehead. Evidently, police had good reason to practice head-butting.

Gradually, we gained control of the ground floor of the townhouse, but no Barney Rubble was to be found. I decided to check the upper floor and recruited Trooper Mel Owens to back me up. I crept up the narrow dark stairs with my revolver at the ready. Until now, I had been using my flashlight as an impact weapon, and when it wouldn't light, I deduced the bulb had broken in the melee. I hoped there would be a light switch at the top of the stairs.

About halfway up the stairs, I heard officers from the ground floor call to me that they had found Barney Rubble. Objective met, I immediately returned to the main floor. Believing we had Barney Rubble in custody, we took pause to make a coordinated withdrawal to prevent leaving an officer behind. Once back at the post, we learned that our success had really been a failure. The person arrested was Barney's look-a-like brother.

The next morning, Detective Lieutenant John Shewell of the Michigan State Police called me into his office and expressed his concern that we had bled more than our assailants. I assured him that was not the case. Later that afternoon, Barney Rubble surrendered himself to authorities, apparently fearing more police raids. Perhaps our failure had been a success.

In Rubble's debriefing, he confirmed that he had been at the party when the police raided. He had retreated to the second floor of the townhouse where he waited with a sawed-off shotgun, planning to shoot the first officer who came up the stairs. He said he was on the verge of pulling the trigger when the officer suddenly turned around and left.

This was the second time I learned that had I wigged instead of wagged, it likely would have been the end of the game for me. Little did I know a similar incident yet awaited me.

Looking back, I am surprised the shift supervisors at the state police post and city police station authorized this raid. Today, I think the risk of injury, poor public perception, and the possibility of sparking civil unrest would outweigh an operation of this nature. Perhaps I am getting soft in my old age. On the other hand, we had prevailed, at least in that incident.

Eddie Rickenbacker, famous World War I Ace Fighter Pilot and Medal of Honor recipient, said, "Courage is doing what you are afraid to do; there is no courage if there is no fear." When I envisioned myself running away from this battle, I came to understand what he meant.

41) Soaked

Informant generated intelligence was the catalyst to many of the cases E & P Wrecking solved. These arrests often closed cases that, more often than not, would have gone unsolved. We had molded the informant lessons that Detective Sergeant John Flis had taught me long ago into an effective crime fighting tool that many officers fail to develop.

One night when Joe and I reported for our early midnight shift, 10:00 p.m. to 6:00 a.m., we learned that the Washtenaw County Sheriff's Department had received reports of the coin operated laundry machines at the Russell Street apartment complex being burglarized. These apartments provided a place for low income citizens to live, but as their police, we struggled to keep it safe and secure.

Joe and I had recently cultivated an informant in that apartment complex so we called him in hopes of some leads. Bingo, we learned the first names and descriptions, and further, that the suspects planned to hit it again that night. We shared this information with the sheriff's department, but it had no deputies available for a stake-out.

It was a night of pouring rain when we reluctantly approached our sergeant about allowing us to conduct the stake-out. He agreed, as long as we stayed available in the event that the other patrol got overloaded or needed back-up.

So we donned our rain gear, parked away from the complex, and sneaked in on foot. There was more than one laundry room, so we split up to monitor the entrance doors, secluded in the shadows of the mercury lights. Before long, the cold rain had shrunk our wool pants short and made our leather Oxfords squish with each step. The night passed slowly as damp chills crept up our spines.

Patience was a virtue that paid off when Joe whispered over the radio that two males, matching our suspects' descriptions, had entered the laundry room that he was monitoring. I crept to his location, where our ears strained to hear the banging and bending of metal over the pitter-patter of rain. When the rain paused, we heard it.

The laundry room only had one door. When Joe and I filled the doorway, clad in glistening long black slickers and wearing black berets, the sick feeling of being trapped was apparent on the thieves' faces.

A big deal? No, but most of police work isn't. But, I do believe we were doing what the good citizens were paying us to do.

Police surprise thieves

YPSILANTI – A night spent on foot patrol in a drenching rain paid off early today with two state troopers surprising a pair of suspected coinbox burglars in the laundry room of an Ypsilanti Township apartment building. "I think we were the last people they expected to see at that hour of the day," Trooper Daniel Payne said of the early-morning arrests at 137 Russell St. "They had pried open a couple of coinboxes, but we showed up before they had a chance to take any of the money." Payne and his partner, Trooper Clifton Edwards, patrolled the complex on foot after receiving a tip that two men were planning to burglarize coin-operated laundry machines at the complex. About 1:35 a.m., the two rain-soaked troopers heard noises in one of the apartment buildings. According to reports, they found two teen-agers at work on the coinbox of a washing machine. "They were, to say the least, quite surprised to see us there," Payne said. A 19-year-old suspect was taken to the Washtenaw County jail to await arraignment later today on burglary charges. A 15-year-old suspect was taken to the county's juvenile detention center pending further investigation.

Compliments of the *Ypsilanti Press*

42) Molester

At 6:10 p.m. on February 16, 1983, Joe and I were busy combating the endless war of paperwork a state trooper waged with a typewriter and carbon charged forms. In the background, we heard the ringing of incoming telephone calls being answered by two officers at the front desk. Remember, this time period was pre-911 dispatch centers. When too many calls came in at once, which is the way it seemed to go, one of us would break from our typing and answer the phone. It was my turn. "State Police, Trooper Edwards."

A distraught woman told me her six-year old daughter had just told her she was raped. I determined that her daughter was in a condition to be transported to the hospital by the mother. I advised her not to bathe her daughter or remove her clothing and that we would meet them at the emergency room. Before Joe and I departed the post, I called the hospital and arranged for a social worker to meet them.

Medical personnel treated the six-year old girl, using a sex motivated crime kit to collect evidence during the examination, along with bagging her clothes. She was then allowed to bathe and change into fresh clothing.

The victim, who was undoubtedly traumatized, met with Joe and me in the company of her mother and the female social worker. The mother was near full-term with her third pregnancy. The victim reminded us of Joe's daughter, who was about the same age and also of mixed race. With time devoted to rapport building, and with the support of her mother and the social worker, this courageous little girl, whom I will call Melissa, was able to tell us what had happened.

Melissa told us that after leaving her school, where she was a first grader, she went to a neighbor's home. After dinner, she was picked up by Chuck, a family friend, and taken to his house. Earlier, I had learned that Chuck was twenty-six years old, just a year younger than me. The two of them went to his bedroom in the basement where he told her to lie on his bed.

Melissa obeyed partially by sitting on the bed's edge. Chuck pushed her onto her back and clawed down her pants and panties. She tried to hold them up, but he was too strong for her. Holding her down with one hand, Chuck used his other to unzip his pants and pull out his penis. He then lay on her and forced his penis into her "private part." Melissa screamed in pain, but no one came to save her. When done, Chuck removed his penis from Melissa, and relieved her of his 295-pound bodyweight. Melissa noticed that his penis was bloody. Crying, she quickly put on her pants and panties.

Chuck dropped Melissa off at home, where her mother had returned from the hospital, where she had been treated for pregnancy complications. Because Chuck was her mother's friend, Melissa was afraid to tell her what had happened. Eventually, she couldn't conceal her emotional and physical pain and shared her ordeal, yearning for the comfort of her mother's love.

While Melissa's mother was shocked by what her daughter said, she unequivocally believed her. So did we! And the doctor confirmed that there had been a sexual assault on the girl's vagina.

Based on our interview with Melissa and the doctor's finding, we had probable cause to make a warrantless felony arrest. We immediately went hunting for Chuck and found him at home. We placed him under arrest, handcuffed him, and searched him. We did not tell him the specific charges, which is not required of the arresting officers but is required of the arraigning magistrate or judge. Undoubtedly, he knew why he was being arrested.

We took him to the post and placed him in the interview room. Monitoring him via a two-way mirror and trying to calm our rage, Joe and I discussed themes for the interview. We knew by then that Chuck had no criminal history of sexual deviance.

Game plan in place, we abruptly entered the interview room, changing the atmosphere of solitude to the bustle of our presence. The nearly barren room seemed to echo every movement. I removed Chuck's handcuffs and we sat without desks between us. Joe read Chuck his Miranda Warning. Chuck freely explained his knowledge of his rights and willingly spoke to us without an attorney. The crime was so fresh and despicable that we anticipated a quick confession in which he would blame Melissa for his seduction. Since Chuck and I were of the same race, I took the lead in the interview, laying the groundwork and then passing the ball to Chuck by asking him to tell us, in detail, about what he had done from the time he picked up Melissa that day until we arrested him.

He convincingly told us about babysitting his friend's daughter, Melissa, absent any indiscretions. We asked whether he might have had to bathe the girl or whether she had made any sexual advances toward him. He calmly replied, "No."

We then played our first card, asking him whether he had an injury to his penis, to which he replied that he did, having injured it masturbating. We upped the ante by asking him how Melissa might know that he had a bleeding penis, to which he responded that she must have seen it as he left the bathroom after peeing.

Confronted with these bald faced lies, our patience began to wane. We tried to calm ourselves, knowing our best chance for a confession lay in us convincing him to tell the truth.

We suspected that some of the blood found on Melissa's panties was Chuck's, so we speculated on what the crime lab would determine and played our bluff trump card—we asked him how it is that his blood was on Melissa's panties. Maintaining his poker face, Chuck told us that when she used the bathroom after him, she must have dragged her panties through his blood that had dripped on the toilet.

The innocence of this six-year-old girl, her resemblance to Joe's daughter, the heinous crime, and Chuck's calm cold lies tripped us. We could no longer play the role of the understanding counselor placing blame on the victim. We vented our rage by telling Chuck what we thought of him and where he would be spending the foreseeable future.

On television, this moment is usually when the perpetrator confesses. In real life, it is when the interviewer has failed to obtain a confession, as was the case now. Unable to subdue our rage, our emotions had spoiled our best chance for success.

Placing Chuck in the lock-up, we obtained search warrants. With them, we collected evidence from Chuck, and in doing so, witnessed his bleeding penis, which we photographed as evidence. Requesting medical attention, we transported him to the hospital where a doctor closed the tear-type laceration to the underside of his penis with six sutures.

We sought the assistance of Detective Sergeant Lyle Schroeder and Troopers Dean Sanderson and Tom Jones to investigate the crime scene. They served the search warrant on Chuck's house, seizing clothes and bedding. None of the other persons in the house at the time of the crime reported hearing or seeing anything relevant.

The next day, Chuck was arraigned on the felony charges of "Criminal Sexual Conduct in the First Degree." The wheels of justice had begun to turn.

That same day, Melissa's mother gave birth to her third child. By March 3, 1983, the crime lab had confirmed that the bloodstain on Melissa's panties was the same type as Chuck's. Remember, DNA evidence was still a dream at this time.

With the legalese, days turned to months. On October 24, 1983, Chuck pled "No Contest" to the charges. On December 9, 1983, he was sentenced to eight to thirty years in prison with credit for the 297 days he awaited trial in the county jail.

While horrific, this crime was not spectacular. It may even lack on the interest scale, but it does illustrate the sexual deviance an officer is exposed to in the course of a career, the frequency of which most good citizens are unaware. But this reality can shade the prism in which the police officer views society.

43) Cold-blooded

Joe Payne and I had just reported for duty when Trooper Mel Owens briefed us on a heinous crime he was investigating in which he had no suspects. We learned that when a fifty-year old emergency room nurse had arrived home from work late the night before, she had seen a car pulling from her driveway. As she pulled in, her house appeared secure and empty, as it should have been since her husband worked nights.

As she entered her bedroom, she was confronted by a stranger who grabbed her and muttered, "I think I'll kill you and just get it over with." He then repeatedly stabbed her and fled the scene. Incapacitated by multiple wounds, the woman feared she would die. Abandoned, she struggled to her phone, finding it had been torn from the wall. She debated whether to attempt to crawl across a field to her neighbors for help or to hope to hang on until her husband returned home in the morning. Fearing she would pass out in the field and not be found for days, she decided to try waiting it out.

When her husband arrived home that morning, he found his wife barely alive. She was rushed to the hospital in a delirious state where Trooper Owens was only able to interview her minimally, obtaining a description of the vehicle and the man who had stabbed her. The description of the car included what appeared to be a Confederate flag in the back window. Hearing that, Joe and I looked at each other because it matched the description of a car we had stopped a few nights earlier that was being driven by a sixteen-year old male.

We dug out our dailies from that day to retrieve the license plate number of the car and the driver's name. Then we departed in hunt mode. Within the hour, we found the car being driven by the same young man. We stopped it and made some low key inquiries, leading us to believe we were on the right trail. We took custody of both car and person and transported them to the Ypsilanti Post.

We placed the juvenile in the interview room and paused to assemble a strategy. Based upon our information, we believed this juvenile had provided transportation for the burglar turned stabber. Based on the victim's descriptions, we believed the stabber to be older than the juvenile we had in custody. We felt certain this juvenile was not the stabber, but we believed he knew who was. He, however, claimed no knowledge or involvement of the incident.

We enlisted the assistance of Troopers Arnie Phillips and Al Jones in interviewing the youth. As one pair of troopers interviewed, the other observed from behind the two-way mirror. As one pair exhausted themes, the other pair took over with different approaches. In effect, we were tag teaming the juvenile, and we knew we were pushing the envelope for legal procedure, but we were willing to sacrifice prosecution of this juvenile to get the stabber.

As our marathon continued, Sergeant Ray Beamish telephoned Detective Lieutenant John Shewell and updated him on the investigation. Shewell contacted Detective Sergeant Jack Beeson at home and assigned him to assist us.

It has been my experience that young criminals are often infatuated with the macho loyalty that is echoed in the lyrics, "Don't do the crime if you can't do the time." As first-timers, they will often take a fall while their partner goes unscathed. It has also been my experience that this youthful loyalty evaporates once they become repeat offenders and realize there is no loyalty among thieves.

As one pair of troopers watched through the two-way mirror, eventually the juvenile told the other pair who and where the stabber was. The stabber, Robert Rose, was holed up at the Harmony House motel in Ypsilanti with his young girlfriend.

Detective Sergeant Beeson arranged a ruse to lure the girlfriend out of the motel room while we carried out the arrest of Rose. Later, Detective Sergeant Beeson interrogated Robert J. Rose while we watched through the two-way mirror. He was as stone cold in custody as he had been in telling the nurse he was going to kill her.

From the juvenile we learned in what area the stabber had thrown the knife out the window of the car, so the next day, troopers combed the shoulder of the road. Trooper Al Jones found the bloody stabbing instrument in the grass.

In my career in the Michigan State Police, Robert Rose was among the most cold-blooded criminals with whom I ever crossed paths. He was sentenced to thirty to seventy-five years in prison for assault with the intent to commit murder. Twelve years later, he would be shot, but not killed, while attempting escape from prison.

On March 8, 2011, Robert Rose was paroled.

Go to www.michigan.gov/otis and enter offender number 172110 to view Robert Rose's photograph.

THE JACKSON Citizen Pa

1/20/95

35 cents   **FRIDAY**

Ingenuity of escape attempt worrie

Articles by Sara Coppernoll
Staff Writer

Robert J. Rose had been crafting his plot to escape from Southern Michigan Prison for some time.

He wove a 129-foot rope from mop-head strands, created a hooking device out of fingernail clippers, and made a knife using a razor blade and a toothbrush.

Thursday, his tools were ready and fog hung over Central Complex.

So Rose padded his body with towels to protect himself from the razor-edged wires that top the perimeter security fences, grabbed his handmade escape tools, and planned to take off for freedom while the rest of his cellblock headed for breakfast.

Although his plan didn't work, officials say his creative tools are prompting a closer look at the property in-

mates are allowed.

"His ingenuity in creating these devices brings about reactions that range from amazement to disconcertment," said Department of Corrections Spokesman Warren Williams.

Investigators today were piecing together the details of Rose's failed attempt to break out of the Central Complex Thursday morning.

The 29-year-old Ypsilanti native veered off the chow line in the yard, and ran toward two electronic fences. He was shot in the back as he was trying to clear the second of two 8-foot fences on the east side of the facility.

He underwent surgery Thursday in Foote Hospital and remains in critical but stable condition.

If Rose had made it over the second

Please see WORRY, A-2

Robert J. Rose

A former Ypsilanti resident, Rose was convicted of stabbing a 50-year-old emergency room nurse in 1983. He is serving a 30-75 year sentence for assault with the intent to commit murder. The Ypsilanti Township woman returned from work about 11:30 p.m. to find Rose and four other teens burglarizing her home. When she tried to flee, Rose stopped her and said: "I think I'll kill you and just get it over with." He stabbed her numerous times in the back, neck and chest. Now following his attempted escape, the 29-year-old Rose could face another five years in prison.

172110
ROSE
MDOC   07 24 93

Compliments of the *Jackson Citizen Patriot*

Part F – Dog Handler
(February 1983 to November 1986)

Fatigue uniform insignia for MSP Dog Handler

44) Seed

Looking back, my first interest in being a dog handler was probably sparked by the newspaper article about Trooper Harms and K9 Thor tracking down the killer of Howard Stoker that I recounted at the beginning of this book. As you may recall, that tragedy caused me to recognize the fragility of life and redirected my career choice from business to law enforcement. And beneath that calling and quest to be a state trooper lay a seed someday to be a dog handler. This seed would lay dormant for some ten years, awaiting the right time to sprout.

Jackson did not boast of having the world's largest walled prison, one reason being frequent escapes. These occurrences created many tracking calls for the canine team serving the Jackson Post of the Michigan State Police.

During my tour as a service officer at the Jackson Post, my dog handler seed was nourished through my association with Trooper Pat Darrow and his tracking dog Zeke. Like the Trooper Harms and K9 Thor team that had preceded them, they too would become a legend in their own time, at least in my mind.

I would often lay training tracks for Zeke, and I cared for him when

Trooper Darrow went away on vacation. One night while riding patrol, Trooper Darrow and Zeke were sent on a dog call. Arriving at the scene, Trooper Darrow harnessed Zeke and then tethered Zeke and himself together by a lead. They then disappeared into the darkness, tracking the escaped convict. Within the hour, they emerged from the shadows with the convict in handcuffs. How could any hunting be more rewarding than that?

My first tryout for the canine team occurred in 1978 when I was a rookie trooper at the Romeo Post. I knew the odds of my being selected were miniscule since I didn't quite have the required two years of trooping experience, unless they counted my service officer time. Further, I was competing against seasoned Romeo Troopers Vic Trieweiler and Warren Miller. While disappointed, I was not surprised when I was not selected. However, having participated in one interview would give me insight for the next one, whenever that might be.

45) Selection

It was late 1982 when the department announced plans to conduct a twelve person canine school to begin in March 1983. I was now a twenty-seven-year old seasoned trooper, serving at Ypsilanti, and one of the vacancies was at that post. In addition to a favorable service record, being married with two young sons was advantageous for me since the department preferred handlers to have a family so the dog would be friendly with children. These attributes placed me in an ideal position to compete for the K926 spot, the radio name of the Ypsilanti Post canine team. In the past, selection was based only upon service record, post commander recommendation, and an interview. This time, a two-mile cross country run was added to the screening process. I liked that.

And while I was married, unknown to the department, my marriage was in trouble. Deb and I had realized our different interests, and that, combined with the stressors of police work, were taking their toll. Statistically, law enforcement is plagued with a very high divorce rate, and we were about to contribute to it.

Laymen often blame the high police divorce rate on stressors surrounding the danger of the profession. If I fast-forward ahead thirty years and then look back, I would say that has not been my experience or observation. While the job description does include intentionally walking in harm's way, the workman's compensation insurance rates for many other occupations is higher, meaning they are more dangerous.

A trooper's ex-wife authored an article on the high divorce rate of police. She suggested that some women are attracted to police officers because they represent the ideal "protector." When reality reveals itself, they realize they are left unprotected because he is off working nights, holidays. and weekends. That, combined with acquiring the "in control" skill, being preoccupied with "saving the world" while he gets increasingly cynical as he referees the worst of human behavior along with being a uniformed "risk taker" can become problematic for a marriage. In our case, many of these factors did not apply as Deb was very strong and we had remained faithful, yet we weren't going to make it. Excuse the tangent, back to Handler Selection.

A dog handler in the Michigan State Police is first a trooper, with the additional responsibilities of being a dog handler. Among other things, he is issued a take home patrol car and police dog. He does normal trooper duties when not training or on canine calls. He is on call 24/7 and is frequently called out. He will spend more time with his canine partner than with any other living thing. It is more than a job; it is your life, much of which is spent sleep deprived!

Around New Year's 1983, nearly a hundred troopers were scheduled to appear at the State Police Academy to compete for one of the twelve spots in the upcoming canine school. The morning was devoted to the two-mile cross country run in which an applicant was started every two minutes. It was a cold snowy morning, and the course traversed field, forest, and swamp, which was marked with surveyor tape.

We ran in our MSP fatigue uniform and combat boots, whose hard rubber soles made them little better than ice skates. If selected as dog handlers, we would be issued tracking boots with lug soles. If the runner were alert, he would see current dog handlers secluded off the trail at treacherous spots, usually where you would break through the ice. I suspect the dog handlers' role was dual purpose: safety and candidate assessment. To acknowledge them was to demonstrate situational awareness, which probably was relayed to the selection panel. The fastest twenty-five runners earned an afternoon interview for one of the twelve positions. Trooper Joe Zangaro and I tied for the fastest times.

After a shower, a change to Class "A" uniform, and lunch, the top twenty-five runners individually reported before the interview panel for the final segment of the selection process. The panel consisted of the canine unit commander, a departmental psychologist, and a command officer. After a barrage of various questions posed in a friendly fashion, we were dismissed.

Days later, I learned I had been selected to report in March, 1983 for fourteen weeks of training at Fort Custer, located just west of Battle Creek. Being over a hundred miles from Ypsilanti, I would not be commuting. I was immensely excited, yet reticent about how this change would affect my already troubled marriage. I remember when I discussed its potential impact with Deb that we decided what would be, would be, whether or not I pursued this dream.

46) Training

Meanwhile, the Canine Unit Commander, Sergeant Bill Flowers, and his assistant, Trooper Gary Shank, were preparing for fourteen weeks of training for twelve troopers and a greater number of dogs. During that era of the state police canine program, all dogs were donated. That meant the dogs had to be solicited, evaluated, and then pass a rigid physical administered by the veterinarian department of Michigan State University. In many ways, the selection of dogs was more tedious than the selection of the handler. Once the program had a stable of screened dogs, it had to match them with handlers, creating a K9 team in training.

About a week before this matching was scheduled to occur, we were invited to the canine unit kennels located at the academy to preview the dogs. Of course, this viewing had to be done on your own time with your own vehicle.

Despite our plans to separate at the onset of canine school, Deb and I decided to make it a family outing by taking the boys—Trevor, now six, and Eric, four—to the academy to preview the dogs. We drove to Lansing on one of those bright white winter days that keep you squinting. We tramped around the kennels in the melting snow, viewing and smelling the fourteen or so barking dogs. That day, nearly palpable excitement existed between man and dog.

Trooper Marv Flick, a current dog handler who would be training a new dog, would also be going through this school. He stood about 6' 2" and weighed 230 pounds; he had a shaved head and a heart of gold. He was an intimidating figure to say the least. Marv was busy checking the retriever instincts of one of the screened dogs by playing fetch.

While Trevor was ailing from car sickness, Eric was acting fearless. He was intrigued with Marv throwing the tennis ball for a dog and sauntered up to watch. After a few rounds, he got Marv's attention by tapping on his leg and saying, "How about you throw one and then I'll throw one?" Marv was okay with that.

In my naivety, I viewed the canine candidates. I was attracted to a fourteen-month-old male German Shepherd named Max. His markings were the traditional black and tan saddle, with the stature of the American bred shepherd, and erect ears. He reminded me of the legendary World War II army dog, Rin-Tin-Tin. He appeared intelligent and confident, or maybe a bit aloof. For these reasons, I hoped I would be matched with him.

About a week later, all the selected handlers were ordered to report to the academy to be issued their dog wagon—a fully marked state police station wagon—dog food, and their new canine partner. Another thing we were issued which I believe worth mentioning is a strong side holster. Until the late 1980s when the MSP transitioned to pistols in strong side holsters, officers carried revolvers in cross draw flapped holsters on their left side. Having your weapon on changing sides depending on whether you were clad in a dog handler uniform or Class 'A' trooper uniform was a real lesson in muscle memory. Many times when I reached for my radio, I found my revolver and vice versus. A warrior is wise not to confuse muscle memory.

Some of us had never met before, so after a meet and greet, Sergeant Flowers and Trooper Shank gave us an overview of the school with a "what to bring" list. We then walked out to the kennels for a final dog inspection before the matching. Just how would they do this?

After gathering us near the kennels, Sergeant Flowers had each of us write our name on a piece of paper and drop it into an empty water pail. He then got out a pouch of Redman tobacco and went around to each of us, having us take a pinch and place it between our lip and gum. I had never chewed before and had never planned to, but I figured I had come too far to screw this up. So, twelve wannabe dog handlers stood in the melting snow with mouths filling with tobacco juice while Sergeant Flowers explained in detail the selection process.

It seemed to take him forever to explain that the name he drew from the bucket first would get first pick, second, second pick, and so on. Meanwhile, my mouth got fuller and fuller until I had to choose between swallowing or drooling as we had been told spatters defaulted to final pick. To my double relief, my name was drawn first, meaning I got the pick of the litter, Max, and got to spit out that dreaded tobacco first. I have not chewed tobacco since.

I then walked to Max's kennel and knelt down in front of the door, holding my hand out for him to smell. With the other hand, I wiped the tobacco residue from the corner of my mouth as I softly told him, "We're going to catch a lot of bad people." I then opened the kennel door, snapped my lead on his collar, and walked him to my dog wagon, a brand new Ford LTD station wagon.

Some might say that Max had just been given a limousine and combination chauffer/care-giver along with great health insurance. This I know—if I were reincarnated as a dog, I would want to be a police dog. I then took my new partner home for a couple of weeks of bonding prior to the fourteen weeks of intense training.

My first decision as Max's new master was to change his name to "Scout." A few weeks later, I changed it to "Cisco" after listening to the song "The Cisco Kid" by War. Max, then Scout, and lastly, Cisco was a bit confused, but after some counseling with the dog whisperer, the name change didn't seem to bother him.

So, on a Sunday night in early March 1983, twelve canine teams in training reported to Fort Custer. Fort Custer had been an army recruit depot during World War II and the Korean Conflict, but it now reminded me of a ghost town. Numerous wood-framed barracks lined the crumbling streets in military order. They were all in poor repair, but the best one had been selected to be our home for the next fourteen weeks. These barracks now only periodically accommodated human life for specialized police or military training.

This class would include diversity not previously experienced in MSP canine schools since it included an Indian male, a white female, and a black male. It would also mark the first time any trooper quit canine school. After a few weeks, Joe Zangaro realized the strain of being away from his family for fourteen weeks of training—followed by a likely transfer, and then often being activated from off-duty to a dog call—was not in the best interest of his young family so he resigned.

Trooper Tim Chartrand had been selected as an alternate, so at the last minute, he got to fill an unexpected vacancy. Little did we know that some fourteen years later, on Valentine's Day 1997, I would be tasked with investigating the shooting of him and his partner, a story I'll tell in my next book, Paths Crossed II.

Our barracks was the typical long narrow structure. There was no floor plan other than "open," except for a latrine at one end. A latrine consisted of exposed toilets, sinks with clouded mirrors, and open showers. Privacy was nonexistent.

The open area consisted of refrigerators, a stove, a microwave, and picnic tables at one end, and bunk beds at the other. Fortunately, we were not stacked in our bunk beds; we slept on the bottom bed and stowed our gear on the top mattress.

So eleven troopers, most with families at home, would live together in a compressed environment for fourteen weeks, although we were allowed to go home on the weekends. Jackie, the lone female trooper, was housed in another barracks by herself.

Getting ourselves and our canine partners settled took a couple of days. We had to learn to sleep while being surrounded by the sound of radios, talking, card games, and other distractions. Probably by design, the dog kennels were placed beside the parade field, far enough away that we could hardly hear the dogs barking. I felt both excited and privileged to be there. As the end of the first week of training neared, an unusual spring snowstorm beset us and we struggled to get home to our families for the weekend.

Sergeant Flowers and Trooper Shank were master dog trainers who were training us to train our dogs. The philosophy being that our dogs would only know us as their trainers. So each day, the master trainers outlined training objectives, lectured, and demonstrated how to attain those objectives and then observed us train the dogs, assisting as problems surfaced.

A state police canine is commonly known as a tracking dog, but it would be more accurate to label it as a utility dog since it also does area searches, building searches, and article searches. These four primary functions have one common denominator, human scent.

Undoubtedly, tracking is the most challenging of the four primary tasks, the reason being that the dog is attempting to follow the scent left behind by a person who passed through an area. This area could be anything from sun-heated blacktop to tall cool damp grass. It could be zero degrees or eighty degrees and windy or calm. The scent could have been deposited minutes earlier or days ago.

When a dog follows a disturbed ground surface caused by a human foot, step-by-step, it is truly tracking. When it follows the scent that has blown off the person, which could have settled yards from where the person actually walked, the dog is trailing. Trailing is how police dogs most often follow humans. A dog is keyed to track, I mean trail, when a harness is placed on it. So, why do we commonly call them tracking dogs when that is not what they do?

Area searches, building searches, and article searches deal with free born human scent emitted directly from a person or article having human scent attached. Depending on air current, this scent may be blown to form what we call a scent cone, the point of the cone being the scent's origin. The dog is keyed to perform these three functions when the handler places a particular leather collar on its neck, just like the harness prompts the dog to track (trail).

Area searches are usually done in an environment fairly sterile from other humans, and where there is no known track to be followed or the track has been contaminated by other persons prior to the police dog's arrival. This function happened most often in the search for lost persons.

Building searches are obviously conducted for burglars secluded within the confines of a building. Again, the dog searches for the source of the human scent. At the basic level, the dog performs this task from a lead. At the advanced level, the dog is released in the building to search for the burglar, and when found, the dog alerts the handler by barking at the suspect, much like a hound does when treeing a varmint.

The fourth primary function is an article search, which is for any item having human scent attached to it. This search is most often done for lost property or evidence that a suspect has discarded, often while being pursued by police.

The most amazing article search I ever witnessed was performed by my brother's police dog. Following me in becoming a dog handler, my brother, Mark, founded the Casper, Wyoming Police Department Canine Unit. His dog was a Golden Retriever named Schultz. At a family picnic, my cousin's contact fell into the grass near a picnic table. Search as we might, we could not find it. We all cleared away from the table, allowing the area to cool of human scent while Mark got Schultz out of his kennel to do an article search. In short order, Schultz lay down with his head between his front paws and put his nose on the ground. Looking very closely, less than an inch in front of Schultz's nose, we saw the contact. I wouldn't have believed it if I hadn't witnessed it.

Scent discrimination is when the dog sniffs a clothing article of the sought person and discriminates out that odor from other human scents and follows it. This skill is observed more often on television than in real life. We did not train to this expectation, and I have never convincingly witnessed a dog perform at this level.

The support skills of obedience, agility, and handler protection are crucial to a successful team. Obedience focused on one word verbal commands: sit, down, come, stay, and heel. Once the dogs were competent at these, we advanced to silent hand signals. The preparatory verbal command is the dog's first name. For example: "Cisco, come." "Come" is often the most difficult command to teach because the dog is off lead. For hand signals, a preparatory command might be a hand clap or whistle. We were not allowed to use food rewards, and we did not waste time teaching tricks since they had no functional purpose.

Dogs are amazing athletes. In agility training, we coached them to develop skills lending to mission success. Jumping fences, crawling through tunnels, climbing ladders, and a host of other obstacles can confront a canine, and this training empowered the team to overcome them.

Essential to agility is the dog's confidence and trust in its handler. Dogs, like humans, fear the unknown, so exposing them to as many obstacles as possible is desirable. But just simple exposure is not adequate because the K9 team must possess skills to overcome the challenges that await it.

Playgrounds are great training arenas. Getting your dog to climb the ladder and slide down, crawl through tunnels, jump through swings, and ride a merry-go-round directly correlate to climbing into an attic or into a cramped crawl space, jumping fences, or being transported by a helicopter. As handlers, we were encouraged to let our imaginations safely run wild in agility training since it was difficult to predict the next mission's obstacles.

Looking back to the future, we would have been denied our first catch if Cisco had not trusted me to have him lie on his side while I pushed him under a fence too tall for him to jump. Another time, we were searching a church for a burglar when Cisco froze where the confining hallway was blocked by a baptismal tank. He reminded me of the cartoon dog Scooby Doo when he looked back at me and seemed to say, "RotRo." I had neglected to expose Cisco to such a challenge, so I had to play the "Trust me" card as I coaxed him into tip-toeing on the narrow edge around it. When he slipped and had an unexpected baptism, he found out it wasn't so bad. I laughed to myself when I thought of the pastor finding floating dog hair at the next baptism.

Handler protection is the politically correct title for attack training. Usually it is not hard to teach a German Shepherd to attack, and Cisco was no exception. The hard part was to have the dog immediately disengage on the command of "Out." The objective was to train the dog to attack on the command of "Stop him" or when the handler or dog was assaulted and immediately to cease and desist on the handler's command of "Out."

A collateral duty of a dog handler is presenting public relations programs on the canine unit. The department did not provide a boiler plate program so each handler created his or her own. So during the fourteen weeks of training, we also composed our presentations to be used when we returned to our posts.

Allow me to jump ahead a few years for a couple of paragraphs. Cisco and I partnered with Trooper Warren Miller and K9 Radar in presenting a program to the Kiwanis Law Enforcement Camp. In one of the demonstrations, I posed as the bad guy, wearing a padded arm and firing a blank gun toward Trooper Miller. Radar wasted no time in engaging me, leaping the final six feet in mid-air with teeth bared. Standard operating procedure is to fill the dog's mouth with the padded arm to avoid being mauled, but Radar knew my trick and had other ideas. Keeping his mouth nearly shut, he slid around the padded arm. As his mouth collided with my right calf, he only had time to open his mouth a bit and take a small chunk of me. Was I lucky? My wife had brought my boys to watch the program, so they witnessed the injury. Seeing the bite, Trooper Miller shouted "Out" and Radar immediately obeyed.

Trooper Miller finished the program while my wife rushed me to the hospital in Howell. On the way, she got stopped for speeding, but the Pinckney Police Officer was sympathetic to the bleeding dog handler in uniform and did not ticket her. Several stitches held the gapping avulsion together while it healed. Twenty-five plus years later, I still bear the scar, which I often display when I tell the story.

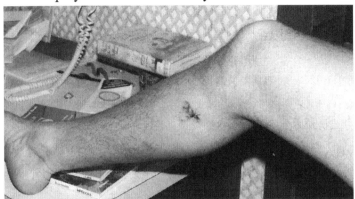

Radar's bite after stitches.

While I did not fear dogs, from that day forward, Radar made me nervous. A couple of months later, I was unable to avoid laying a training track for Radar at our weekly training sessions. As I waited apprehensively behind a car in a parking lot for Radar, I had a bright idea: Wait inside the car. Feeling much better, I waited with the window down. Out of the misty predawn darkness came Radar, promptly jumping through the window onto my lap—not at all what I had envisioned. He did not bite me, but I was never sure how my pants got wet.

Back to canine school. So the days became weeks and winter melted to spring mosquitoes, which evolved into summer heat. The building block training strategy was taking effect as scenarios became more difficult. It was imperative that the dog succeed so he could be rewarded since failures confused a dog. For success to happen, the handler needed to know where the trail was, so we marked it. This process enabled the handler to learn to read his dog, so he would be able to detect when the dog had become distracted and get him back on track—not a pun. And while training tracks were marked, the test tracks for certification were not.

My peers elected me class orator for our June graduation, where I spoke on our journey so far and what we anticipated to be the trials and tribulations that awaited us. When we returned from living at Fort Custer, Cisco and I moved into a duplex on the east side of Ypsilanti. Deb remained in the house we were buying while the divorce unfolded. When Cisco and I went into service at the Ypsilanti Post, our call sign was K926.

L to R: Lt. Schraeder, me, Sgt. Flowers, & Tpr. Shank

As a dog handler, I did normal trooper duties except when there was a dog call. Every Thursday was a training day. I was on call twenty-four hours a day and frequently called out. This situation posed a problem when I had the boys. At that time, my sister was a college student at Eastern Michigan University and lived in Ypsilanti, about six blocks away from my duplex. Like all college students, she was short on money. So we came up with a win-win. When I had the boys and got called out, I immediately called her. She raced over to babysit while I responded to the dog call. We split my overtime pay.

I remember two times that she wasn't available. On one, I took the boys to the post where Sergeant Sandy Miller agreed to watch them while I went on the call. The other was a deep dark secret until my retirement party. At the retirement party, a lot of brass was present, including the director. My oldest son, Trevor, chose to address the audience, speaking on what it was like to be a state police brat. And there he disclosed that one time I had awakened him and his brother in the night to ride to a dog call in their pajamas where they waited in the dog wagon while I ran the track. I did not leave them alone; the troopers who requested Cisco waited with them. Good thing I was retiring! As Captain Charles Bush said, "Kids can say the darnedest things."

It's the Cisco ... dog

Local state police canine sniffs with a sense of purpose

By PETER SEIDMAN
Press Staff Writer

Trooper Clifton Edward's partner Cisco is sleek and supple with a rib cage that barely protrudes from a blue-black silver streaked coat of hair.

His nose is like a vacuum cleaner and, when he sniffs, (something he does his every waking moment) it is with a sense of purpose that is instinctual rather than sublime. Like most 2-year-olds, he is playful. When somebody steps on his toe, he looks more puzzled than angry.

With a single spoken word, however, Edwards can turn Cisco into rage itself escaping in vicious snarls from 80 pounds of fur-coated muscle. With that word — the one that only Edwards can speak effectively — he becomes a terrifying beast whose sole purpose in life is to close his teeth, like a nail-studded vice, on the throat of anybody foolish enough to mess with Edwards while Cisco is around.

"He's friendly, but he's tough when he has to be tough. He's mean on command," Edwards said of the German Shepherd with whom he spends about 10 hours a day.

Cisco, who lives with Edwards and his three children in his Ypsilanti Township home, is one of 32 Michigan State Police tracking dogs located strategically throughout the state. Edwards is one of the 13 troopers chosen from a field of 60 applicants to undergo a recent training program and become a dog handler.

The job is a big responsibility. He and Cisco are on call 24 hours a day, and Edwards said he spends eight hours a week teaching Cisco new tricks and practicing old ones.

It is a dirty job as well, requiring both dog and trooper to slog, sometimes in pouring rain, through hundreds of miles of mud, much of which inevitably winds up in Edward's car.

And then there are the other innumerable ways in which Cisco can make Edward's life miserable. He can, for example, get sick and vomit in his car, snarl at his post commander, chew up his gloves or fight with another dog — and lose.

"We don't claim that they're obedience champions, because we want them to be independent and to be able to think, so the can lead the handler in the field," Edwards said.

A letter from Michigan State Police to prospective dog handlers reads:

(See CISCO, Page 8A)

Trooper Clifton Edward and Cisco, left photo. Right, Edward's children Eric, 2, left, and Trevor, 6

Compliments of the *Ypsilanti Press*

47) Frustration

Reality Check: a good canine team catches the bad guy one out of ten times! Pavlov's dog would not have been adequately reinforced with this ratio. When you come out of canine school, you may be certified, but that doesn't mean you're good—at least I wasn't. It was not uncommon to have three calls in one day, and I was beginning to wonder whether I would ever catch anyone. Dog handlers were said to be moody, and I now knew why; they live in a world dominated by sleep deprivation and a 10 percent success rate. And with each failed call, you critique yourself in hopes of discovering your error, but like a Zen koan, the lesson is not always apparent.

Cisco was now about eighteen months old, the equivalent of a teenage male in late puberty. He certainly was attracted to the scent of a bitch—a female dog. In fact, given the choice, Cisco would choose to follow a bitch's scent over that of a bad guy. After consultation with Sergeant Flowers, it was decided to have Cisco neutered. That certainly helped, but we still had work to do.

We trained hard on my Thursday training days and began training on one of my two days off. This was frustrating, yet I was determined to succeed.

**Michigan State Police Trooper Cliff Edwards
and his partner Cisco.**

"It is not the critic who counts; not the man who points out how the strong man stumbles, or where the doer of deeds could have done them better. The credit belongs to the man who is actually in the arena, whose face is marred by dust and sweat and blood, who strives valiantly; who errs and comes short again and again; but who does actually strive to do the deed; who knows the great enthusiasm, the great devotion, who spends himself in a worthy cause, who at the best knows in the end the triumph of high achievement and who at the worst, if he fails, at least he fails while daring greatly. So that his place shall never be with those cold and timid souls who know neither victory nor defeat."
— Theodore Roosevelt

48) Success

Finally the ice breaker came. The Romulus Police had a young man escape from their jail. In fairness to the Romulus Police, you should know their station and jail had previously been an elementary school, making it less than ideal for security. I heard the call go out on the police scanner and volunteered our canine services.

Romulus is a suburb of Detroit and surrounds Metro airport. Tracking in residential and city environments is the most difficult. Fortunately, this track quickly led to a sparsely wooded area. About a quarter mile later, we were confronted with a ten foot high security fence, too high for Cisco to go over. After we found a gap at the bottom, I had Cisco lie on his side with his head down. With him playing dead dog with purpose, I pushed him under the fence's jagged edge. Once Cisco was on the other side, I climbed over the fence and we continued tracking, I mean trailing.

In short order, we met the scofflaw, who was in the process of back tracking. We were all surprised to see each other. When the young man's eyes met Cisco's, there was a pause, followed by a rising of his hands in submission. Finally, we had caught one!

With darkness approaching, I headed back to the Ypsilanti Post with a big smile on my face. I was no longer a virgin dog handler. Upon arrival, I doubled with my other good partner, Joe Payne, for the second half of our afternoon shift.

That same evening, the other patrol out was Troopers Jack Edwards (no relation) and Wayne Kiser. They were in Sumpter Township, investigating a shooting. A fifty-four year old career criminal had gotten into an argument with his adult nephew and shot him. The shotgun blast nearly severed his leg.

Having cleared the scene, Troopers Jack Edwards and Wayne Kiser prowled the back roads in search of the vehicle in which the suspect had fled. Late in the shift, they met a vehicle matching the description, and as they spun the patrol car around, it darted into a farmer's driveway. When they caught up to it, they found the vehicle empty.

Jack and Wayne did all the right stuff by not contaminating the scene, setting a perimeter, and requesting a police dog. Having a protected fresh track in an ideal environment left me no excuses for failure. The pressure was on.

Upon our arrival, Jack and Wayne briefed us on the suspect, providing a description and that we should consider him armed and dangerous because of his background and that the shotgun used in the crime had not been recovered.

It would be safer to have Joe tag along as backup, but that would reduce the chance of success since Cisco had not yet evolved to the level of not being distracted by another person accompanying us on a track. I decided to go alone, with Joe paralleling downwind and trying to keep us in sight.

As expected, the track led away from the shadowy comfort of the farm's mercury light and soon the darkness became real. While your instinct is to turn the flashlight on, training taught "Darkness is your friend." We tracked without illumination as much as possible, reducing the suspect's ability to know our whereabouts. And when I had to peek, I extended my arm so the flashlight was away from my torso since the light would likely be a target for an armed suspect.

I hoped the tension of the twenty-five foot lead would pull me to my quarry. Soon it was too dark to see Cisco at the far end of the lead. When he paused to sort out scent complications, I stopped, keeping a slight tension on the lead so he knew I was there but that he was free to continue.

On we went into the darkness, becoming more and more alone. When Cisco did not clear a pause in the normal amount of time, I flashed my light to see what he was doing. The beam revealed the fugitive, who was lying prone with his arms beneath him. Was this a dream come true or a nightmare beginning?

This night, the suspect had demonstrated all the survival instincts: first fight, then flight, and now freeze. Undoubtedly, he hoped Cisco would continue on his way while I hoped he would not recycle to the first of the three basic survival instincts.

In the building block framework of training, we were still at the point where now would be the time I rewarded Cisco with praise and playing tug of war. But this wasn't training so Cisco was probably surprised to hear me shouting to the suspect, "State Police. Freeze!" as I drew my revolver.

From a distance, Joe saw my flashlight come on and heard the shouting. Armed with a shotgun, Joe charged through the corn stubble field to the woods to assist me in handcuffing the suspect. In doing so, we discovered that the suspect was lying atop the shotgun he had used in the shooting.

Once the outlaw was secured, Cisco and I went about our business of playing tug of war. Goals for Cisco's next level of training were that he bark at his quarry and not be distracted by backup accompanying us. Now that we were catching bad guys, there was a real need for it.

This catch had confirmed my belief that there is no better high than going into the darkness with your dog after an armed felon and bringing the criminal out in cuffs.

Man charged in murder try

SUMPTER TWP. — A 24-year-old township man was reported in good condition today at St. Joseph Mercy Hospital after his uncle allegedly wounded him with a shotgun over the weekend.

Richmond D. Smith of 20630 Wilmot suffered shotgun wounds in the groin and leg, said Michigan State Police.

His uncle, Dewey Combs, 54, of Belleville is being held on a charge of assault with intent to murder in Wayne County Jail.

Combs was arrested by troopers early Sunday morning in a cornfield behind the home of one of his relatives. Police used a tracking dog to find the suspect.

He was arraigned in 34th District Court Sunday and is being held in leiu of $75,000 bond. Combs is accused of shooting his nephew early Saturday morning in the 19000 block of Wilmot.

Police said a family feud that had been going on for some time led to the incident. Smith, who was wounded in the left leg, originally was taken to Beyer Memorial Hospital, then transferred to St. Joseph's.

Compliments of the *Ypsilanti Press*

49) Best

As is often the case with brothers, Mark and I fought endlessly growing up, but we had become best of friends as adults. Two years my junior, in 1980, Mark decided to follow in my footsteps to become a police officer.

While Mark would have chosen the Michigan State Police, they were not hiring and the Houston Police Department was. So he applied, was hired, and moved to Texas, where he completed the Houston Police Department's eighteen week police academy with his wife helping him with homework. However, he was unable to complete its field training program because of grammar deficiencies; while police dramas never show it, writing is an essential skill of the effective police officer. Mark was a talented wrestler and brilliant in many applications, but he had always struggled academically.

After getting a divorce and unable to complete his field training, Mark returned to Michigan, defeated, but not beaten. Enrolling in adult education classes while working in loss prevention at Meijer Thrifty Acres, he applied himself to strengthening the academic link of his chain.

In time, Mark felt ready to give it another go, applying to and being hired by the Casper, Wyoming Police Department. Just before moving, he became involved in a relationship with Jo, a divorced mother of two small children, Phyllis and Brad.

Of the seven rookies the Casper Police Department hired that year, Mark won the "Rookie of the Year" award and subsequently created its first canine unit. Mark's stubbornness proved an asset as he evolved from victim to victor.

Clif   Cisco   Schultz   Mark

Jo followed Mark to Casper and they married, but they postponed a wedding reception until Mark had accumulated enough vacation time to come home to Michigan where they could celebrate their marriage with family and longtime friends.

The day of celebration would be Sunday, August 14, 1983. The reception was held at Jo's parents' place, a most beautiful home surrounded by a large green lawn that would easily accommodate the various festivities.

While Deb and I were no longer a couple, we took our two boys there together since we were both friends with the attendees. We had vowed always to put the boys' best interests first, agreeing not to burden them with our differences. I had not seen my brother in several months, and many friends had arrived at the outdoor reception prior to us.

I found Mark playing volleyball, so I joined the opposing team, rekindling our sibling rivalry. On this sunny summer day, pockets of festivities were bursting everywhere as friends and family gathered in celebration of Mark and Jo's union. But this day, curse and miracle would spar while Mark and I would become teammates on a life and death mission.

Meanwhile, Brad, Mark's three-year old stepson, was preparing to make mud pies with his cousins. They lacked one ingredient, water. Carrying a pail, he ventured into what was thought to be locked—the structure for the indoor pool. Leaning over to dip his pail, he toppled in.

How many minutes passed until his cousin, Greg, went to check on Brad is unknown. Seeing the floating plastic pail in the pool, Greg looked further. He was shocked to see Brad unconscious underwater. By the second time Greg shouted, "Brad has drown," dead silence reigned. Mark and I broke from the herd and sprinted to the pool to find Brad appearing dead, his face, particularly around the lips, blue in color. We were told his older cousin had pulled him from the pool unconscious.

In checking Brad, we discovered he was not breathing and had no detectable pulse. I feared our lifesaving efforts would be in vain, but we felt no hesitation to try. While I delivered rescue breaths, Mark provided compressions. Our C.P.R. training had been in different states, but it was the same, and we worked together well—like brothers. With Mark counting "1 & 2 & 3 & 4 & 5—breath," I wondered whether we might not know our own strength and I had burst his lungs or Mark had crushed his sternum. My eyes met Mark's and I whispered, "Easy."

Jo, Brad's mother, had not heard the alarm cried as she was on the other side of the house bidding friends farewell. She thought it odd to see her father running to her and in a panting voice say, "There has been an accident. Brad fell in the pool. You need to get down there."

She sprinted to the pool house to have her cousin block her entrance, saying "Jo, you don't want to go in there" as she pushed around him. Hearing Jo cry, "Brad!" Mark looked up from doing compressions and their misty eyes met.

You become hyper-alert in these situations, so while busy performing C.P.R., you are thinking ahead to the next step. In times like this, your professional status has personal fringe benefits. Within the past month, I had received instruction on the availability of Survival Flight, an emergency medical helicopter based out of the University of Michigan Hospital in Ann Arbor. Between ventilations, I instructed Deb to telephone the Ypsilanti Post and tell the sergeant that Trooper Edwards needed Survival Flight sent to this location for a drowning victim. Sergeant Earl Raczkowski received her call and had Survival Flight launched. Unknown to me, my dad had climbed on the roof of the house with a white bed sheet to signal the helicopter when it neared.

And while our efforts seemed in vain, Brad suddenly gasped and vomited. Pete Mitchell, my brother's best friend, later told me that he looked at his watch at that moment and noted we had been doing C.P.R. for three minutes. I was rushed by a flood of emotion that I had to suppress, as Brad again quit breathing and we had to resume C.P.R.

While minutes seemed hours, the rescue unit from the fire department arrived and tried to relieve me with a B.V.M. (bag valve mask), but there was no chest rise, so I resumed mouth-to-mouth ventilations.

And then an ambulance, based out of Jackson, arrived. I told them I had Survival Flight summoned and we would wait for them to transport. The ambulance personnel told me they had cancelled Survival Flight and that they would transport the patient to Foote Hospital in Jackson. I was furious, but I was in a forced choice situation, relinquishing care and custody of Brad to them with Jo riding along. The ambulance had not been gone five minutes when Survival Flight was hovering overhead. Rolling with the punches, we sent them on to Foote Hospital where they waited for the ambulance to arrive.

We raced the twenty some miles to Foote Hospital in Jackson, just in time to witness Brad being loaded into Survival Flight to be flown to Mott Children's Hospital in Ann Arbor. There was no room in the helicopter for

Jo, so Mark and Jo chased it the thirty some miles to the hospital.

It was touch-and-go for Brad because his trauma was complicated with the onset of pneumonia, often the case in a near drowning. He was placed in a paralytic state (drug induced coma) and incubated for about four days. When he resumed consciousness, the first thing he said in his hoarse little voice was, "Why was Uncle Clif kissing me and dad pushing on my chest?" Brad would remain in Mott's Children Hospital until Labor Day weekend with Mark and Jo living in the waiting room.

ANN ARBOR NEWS

Ypsilanti state trooper *8-23-74* helps save life of nephew

YPSILANTI – A Michigan State Police trooper from the Ypsilanti Post and his brother are credited with saving the life of a three-year-old boy who fell into a swimming pool in Lenawee County last weekend.

Brad Lee Bolenbaugh remained in serious condition today at Mott Children's Hospital in Ann Arbor. The youth, the son of Mark and Betty Joe Edwards of Casper, Wyo., was flown by helicopter to Ann Arbor from Foote Memorial Hospital in Jackson last Saturday. Doctors at the Jackson hospital credited the efforts of State Police Trooper Clifton Edwards and his brother, who is the boy's father, with saving the youth's life.

The near-drowning occurred at the home of an Edwards' relative in Onsted in southwestern Lenawee County. Officers said the Bolen-baugh boy wandered away from members of the family and fell unobserved into a small swimming pool. He apparentLy was under water for several minutes before he was discovered and pulled out, officers said. The youth was not breathing when he was taken from the water.

Trooper Edwards and his brother, Mark, who is a police officer in Wyoming, immediately began cardiopulmonary resuscitation and moments later obtained a pulse. However, the faint pulse stopped and it took additional resuscitation to start the boy breathing again. He was taken by ambulance to Foote Hospital in Jackson where doctors advised he be transferred to the Mott Hospital in Ann Arbor. Physicians said the tot survived only because of the rescue efforts by his father and uncle.

Compliments of *Ann Arbor News*

Legal action against the ambulance was considered but because Brad made a full recovery and there was no physical harm, none was initiated. Brad put himself through Eastern Michigan University and today, he lives in Hawaii. His cousin, Greg Goings, earned a lifesaving award from his Boy Scout troop.

I consider helping to save my nephew's life to be the best thing I have ever done, and I am glad to have shared it with my brother. Months later, I again would save a life by providing mouth-to-mouth resuscitation. In contrast, it turned out to be the worst thing I ever did.

50) Mule

One night, many dog handlers spent the evening training at Fort Custer near Battle Creek, including Washtenaw County Sheriff Deputy Bill Moffett and me. It was after midnight on that bitterly cold winter night in 1984 when we headed back to Ypsilanti, travelling in tandem on the I-94 freeway.

At that time, the speed limit was 55 mph, yet we were speeding, travelling faster than traffic since you can more effectively patrol the freeways in that fashion. This tactic has you creeping upon traffic, which allows you to see and pace many more cars rather than travelling alongside the same cars. It also prevents bunching up traffic. While we were not assigned to patrol, we were hunters and we always hunted. While the Michigan vehicle code allows police legally to speed in the performance of their duties without emergency equipment activated, this practice can have poor public perception and prompt citizens to complain of speeding police cars.

As I led us back home, I noticed taillights ahead of me that I was not catching up to, so I paced the car at 75 mph. I then closed the gap, observing that the vehicle had Illinois license plates and was occupied by two persons. I radioed Bill that I was going to stop them; he responded by saying he would back me up. We had just reentered Washtenaw County.

I approached the driver's side of the vehicle while Bill provided cover from the passenger side. The driver was unable to produce a license, but he provided me with a traffic citation he had received in Illinois, which indicated that his driver's license had been taken as bond.

A citation can serve as a driver's license for the period of time the defendant has to contact the court, but that time had expired. He had no other identification, so I placed him under arrest for no driver's license, a custodial offense at the time. He complied with my request to exit the vehicle, so I frisked and handcuffed him while Bill monitored the passenger. Using the standard line, I asked him whether he had any drugs, guns, bombs, or anything else illegal in the car, to which he replied, "No." When I asked whether he minded us looking in the car, he granted me permission to do so. I secured him in a patrol car and returned to have the passenger step-out.

At that time, ten exceptions existed to the search warrant rule. If an officer could meet the criteria of at least one exception, he could search for contraband without a search warrant, which could take hours to obtain.

While Bill monitored the two men, I searched the vehicle on the authority of two exceptions to the search warrant rule—search incident to an arrest and consent.

In the backseat, I found a stuffed sock concealed within a man's cap. Curious, I looked inside the sock and found it lined with a plastic bag containing a white powder. Based upon my training, I suspected it was cocaine, so we placed the two suspects under arrest for it.

The sock turned out to contain approximately 12½ ounces of cocaine, and depending on purity, could have a street value of nearly $170,000. With one of the suspects from Detroit and the other from Chicago, I surmised they intended to make a delivery to the greater Detroit area.

We had their car towed to the Ypsilanti Post for a drug detector dog to check more thoroughly, and we transported the sixty-six year old and the forty-six year old man to the post for an interview and processing.

Despite believing myself a practitioner of "always looking for the big arrest in the sky," I dropped the ball here. I thought we had the "big arrest in the sky" because it never occurred to me to attempt a police controlled facilitated delivery of the cocaine to its intended recipient until Trooper Wayne Kiser came into work early that morning and suggested it. By then both arrestees had made phone calls, alerting recipients of their predicament.

Apparently, the guy from Chicago was a big fish because the next day we were getting calls from police departments in the Chicago area and the state of Alaska who had been somehow notified of our bust. I learned the older suspect was considered a major dealer of heroin and cocaine in Alaska, so Alaska police were pleased we had a case on him.

Within a few days, his Alaskan attorney arrived in Ann Arbor. The preliminary examination was postponed while the attorney arranged to be temporarily licensed to practice law in Michigan for this one case. During his wait, he studied Michigan law in the University of Michigan law library.

The preliminary examination was held in the quaint village of Chelsea before District Court Judge Karl Fink. I testified for quite a while. The attorney argued that the arrest for "No Operator's License" was not valid. Because the arrest was not valid, the consent his client had granted to search the car while being handcuffed was under duress, making it coerced and also not valid. The cocaine would then be considered "fruits of the poisonous tree" and not admissible. The cocaine was the corpus delecti (Latin for the body of the crime) and without it, we obviously had no case. If the judge sided with the defense attorney's argument, the case would be dismissed.

Judge Fink took the attorney's argument under advisement to rule on the examination in a week. I thought it a bad sign, which was confirmed when the judge dismissed the charges and the suspect was released.

This case was not the first I had lost; nor would it be the last. Again, I reminded myself that defense attorneys are the guardians of the U.S. Constitution, and that at least we had gotten the dope off the street.

Speeding car leads to seizure of 12 ounces of cocaine

POLICE BEAT

Two police tracking-dog handlers who were on their way home from a training session stopped a speeding car early today and seized more than 12 ounces of suspected cocaine worth nearly $170,000. Michigan State Police Trooper Clifton Edwards of the Ypsilanti post and Deputy William Moffett of the Washtenaw County Sheriff's Department found the suspected cocaine wrapped in a hat sitting on the back seat of a car they stopped for speeding on I-94 near Baker Road, according to reports. Edwards and Moffett said they were returning to Washtenaw County with their tracking dogs after a training seminar in Battle Creek. About 2:30 a.m., they noticed a car with Illinois license plates travelling an estimated 75 mph and made a traffic stop. "The officers became suspicious of the way the guys in the vehicle were acting," said Sgt. Greg Aho of the Ypsilanti post. "So they obtained permission to search the vehicle. Inside a hat that was sitting on the back seat, they found 12½ ounces of cocaine." Depending on its purity, 12½ ounces of cocaine could have a street value as high as $169,700, officers estimated. The car's occupants, a 66-year-old Detroit man and a 46-year-old Chicago man, were arrested and held on preliminary charges of possession of cocaine with intent to deliver. Both were to be arraigned later today in 14th District Court on the felony drug-possession charges.

Compliments of *Ann Arbor News*

51) Escape

It was February, 1984 when I attended Trooper Tom Hundt's transfer party at George's Bar in Ypsilanti. Deb and I had been apart for nearly a year, so I went alone. Tom Hundt was a trooper's trooper, and there are endless stories of his escapades; I'll share but two.

One time in the wee morning hours, Trooper Wayne Kiser and he had responded to a burglary alarm at a Ma & Pa restaurant on Michigan Avenue in Ypsilanti Township. Upon arrival, they surrounded the building by positioning themselves at opposite corners. Tom could see a burglar inside, so using the patrol car's public address system, he announced "State police. Come out with your hands up and you will not be hurt." The suspect replied, "Come in and get me!" Tom immediately replied, "Prepare to die," which probably wasn't politically correct. Tom and Wayne entered the restaurant and took custody of the burglar. No injuries suffered on either side.

Another time, the troopers at the Ypsilanti Post were quite upset with a command decision and held an off-duty meeting to vent. Someone suggested they acquire the blue flu, meaning quit writing tickets. Tom had been his normal quiet self until then, and while not a big ticket writer, he had a very strong work ethic. When Tom stood to speak, everyone got quiet. Tom calmly explained that we did not work for command; that we worked for the good citizens of the State of Michigan, and to them we owed a day's work for a day's pay. The blue flu had found its cure.

Tom trooped for a full twenty-five years before being promoted to sergeant and then lieutenant before retiring. He died of brain cancer in the spring of 2009.

At Tom's transfer party, I was introduced to an attractive woman named Pam. She was single, a runner, and lived and worked in the greater Ann Arbor area, which adjoined Ypsilanti. We visited at the party and then went our separate ways.

After a couple of days, Pam called me at work, which was a pleasant surprise. My investigative training recognized this as a "clue," so I asked her out. We began dating and our relationship developed, only to be accelerated, perhaps too quickly; one night we had fallen asleep on her couch when my pager began beeping. It was 1:00 a.m. on May 14, 1984.

I answered the page by telephoning the Ypsilanti Post. I learned an escape had occurred from the Huron Valley Men's Facility, one of Michigan's maximum security prisons and located in the Ypsilanti Post area. A tracking dog was requested.

In the damp chilled night, I raced my motorcycle the twenty some miles home to where Cisco and my patrol car waited. Once changed into uniform and in the patrol car, I sped Cisco to the prison with red light oscillating.

Upon arrival, I was briefed on the escapee, Charles Macklin. The prison official provided a wanted bulletin and explained that Macklin was a convicted murderer who, in retrospect, had been in physical training for this escape since incarcerated at this prison.

The prison official went on to explain some of the circumstances around Macklin's murder convictions—plural. While Macklin had been awaiting trial on a murder charge in the county jail, he complained of a toothache, so arrangements were made to take him to the dentist for treatment. While at the dentist office, he overpowered the deputy who had transported him. While he did not have to kill the deputy to make good his escape, he did anyway. Macklin was later recaptured, convicted, and sentenced to life in prison without parole. In closing the briefing, the prison official warned that, given the opportunity, Macklin would kill again.

Deputy Bob Marsh, one of two dog handlers with the Washtenaw County Sheriff's Department, was on-duty when the escape had been reported, so he had arrived on scene prior to me. Baron, his tracking dog, had run a short track, from where Macklin had dropped down to freedom, after scaling the fence and crawling through razor wire. The track led to a clump of bushes located on the mowed prison lawn about forty yards from Bemis Road. A fresh set of tire tracks led up to the bushes, so Deputy Marsh deduced that the escapee had been picked up by an accomplice.

Shortly after my arrival, it was determined that the tire tracks leading up to the bushes had actually been made by correction officers who, after the escape, had driven across the lawn to check whether Macklin might be hiding in the bushes.

Now, with no evidence that Macklin had left the immediate area, it was decided to check the area surrounding the prison more closely. Cisco and I, with Deputy Marsh acting as our backup, would search the barns and out-buildings of two nearby homesteads.

As we began to enter an L-shaped single story barn, we heard a noise from the far side. Investigating the noise, we discovered a chained dog that didn't bark; we believed it responsible for the noise.

We then began walking toward Sergeant Ritter of the Washtenaw County Sheriff's Department; he was sitting in a patrol car on Bemis Road. As we approached him, with our backs to the barn, he shouted that he had just seen someone run behind the barn we had checked.

Marsh and I spun around and began sprinting toward the barn with Cisco off leash and running beside me, under the command of "Heel." At the barn, Marsh and I split, with Cisco and I going around the west end. As I came around the north end of the barn, I observed a shadowy figure in the distance running toward the freeway. With the aid of my flashlight, I began pursuing on foot.

In the darkness, Cisco had not keyed on the suspect since he was pre-occupied with staying at a heel beside his sprinting master. During this time, I began yelling, "State Police! Halt!" and heard other officers on the perimeter yelling similarly.

Law and policy made it "open season" on Charles Macklin since he was a dangerous fleeing felon from a walled prison. However, at that time, I could not be certain it was Charles Macklin as I was mindful of a mental hospital situated nearby that often had walkaways. As I began to close on the fleeing shadow, my flashlight illuminated a person matching Macklin's description. Furthermore, his hands were wrapped in bloody cloths which probably had been sliced as he crawled over the razor wire. Now I was certain it was Charles Macklin.

About the time I came to this conclusion, an officer on the perimeter began shooting. I supposed he was firing at Macklin. Fearing I would be shot in the back by friendly fire, I began shouting, "Don't shoot." I heard no more gunfire.

When those shots were fired, Cisco broke away to do what he was trained to do—attack what he believed to be hostile gunfire. However, in this case, some unsuspecting police officer was about to be attacked out of the darkness by an eighty-five pound police dog—kind of like friendly fire, but with fangs. Realizing Cisco was gone and what his likely mission was, I yelled into the darkness, "Cisco, no! Leave it! Come!" Not missing a step in my pursuit and crossing a barbwire fence, I hoped he heard and obeyed me.

The foot chase was now nearing the fence for access to the US-23 freeway. Macklin was not the only person who had been training for this day as I continued to close the distance between us, leaving behind my backup.

With my flashlight in my left hand and my revolver in my right, I crossed the freeway. I had to break stride for southbound freeway traffic, which Macklin had cleared, but I then was able to make up the lost ground.

As Macklin climbed the fence leaving the limited access freeway, I seemed to escalate to the next level of hyper-perception. As he fell to all fours on the far side of the fence, he appeared to be lying in wait, knowing I would be vulnerable to attack as I climbed the fence. And when he heard me at the fence, Macklin suddenly pivoted left toward me while he reached into his clothing and yelled a sentence, of which I only heard the word "Kill!"

For a split second, he was undoubtedly disappointed not to find me entangled in the fence. Then I shot him. It seems apropos that the last word of a convicted killer would be "Kill." He appeared to drop dead, making no sound or movement, just like on television, but we had been told in training that such was rarely the case in real shootings.

While seconds seemed to take hours to pass, Cisco came to my side. Having heard and obeyed my command, he had returned to where I had been, only to find my scent. Following that scent, he had jumped two fences and crossed a freeway to be my first police backup at the scene of the shooting.

Had the departmental issued .38 caliber 125 grain jacketed soft pound + P bullet been immediately effective? Or was Charles Macklin playing possum, waiting for me to cross the fence so he could overtake me?

As Deputy Bob Marsh arrived, to my relief, he said, "Take care of Cisco and I'll check the suspect." It is an odd changing of gears, when a police officer's duty suddenly switches to trying to save the person you just tried to kill.

I provided cover for Bob as he crossed the fence and checked the suspect, finding no signs of life. Shortly thereafter, the perimeter of police officers collapsed upon us. Cisco and I moved to the side, our duty done. For the second time in my life, I was nearly incapacitated by severe lower back pain. I bent over to relieve the spasms as real time returned; it was 2:35 a.m.

Like a spectator, Cisco and I sat on the sidelines, witnessing a frenzy of activity surrounding the shooting scene. With the arrival of the post commander and Detective Sergeant Skip Ward, I was relieved of my service revolver, to be held as evidence while the legality of the shooting was investigated. Eventually, Cisco and I made it back to our patrol car and drove to the post to deal with the initial paperwork.

I knew Pam would be up at 6:00 a.m. to get ready for work and that she would be curious about the outcome of the dog call. Not wanting her to learn of the shooting on the radio news, I telephoned her and briefly filled her in. She insisted on taking the day off, telling me she would be at my duplex when I got home.

Per departmental policy, I was placed on administrative leave pending completion of the investigation and ruling of the prosecutor. It would be 10:00 a.m. before I arrived home, too tired to sleep, and thankful not to be alone. Pam said all the right things and mostly listened. And like a broken record, the events of the night kept running through my head. Again and again I would tell her the story, and each time she listened like it was the first.

She was there when exhaustion turned the lights off and when some sleep turned them back on. She was the salve to my recovery from this significant event, helping me eventually to put it in a box and then put the box in the closet.

I do not remember how many days I was on administrative leave, but it does not seem like it was many. Washtenaw County Prosecutor William Delhey ruled the shooting "justifiable homicide." The service revolver I earned for marksmanship was returned to me, now discreetly bearing the evidential markings of two shootings, and I returned to duty. Pam and I married that September.

The department had not yet adopted a mandatory professional counseling for officer-involved shootings, and I did not seek any. Actually, I found this shooting less burdensome than the first. This time I was not haunted with the question of whether I could do it again. I guess this incident had affirmed that I could. The police officer's nightmare of a malfunctioning or ineffective service weapon remained at bay, having disappeared after the first shooting.

In my view, mandatory professional counseling for officer involved shootings is GOOD policy.

"People sleep peaceably in their beds at night only because rough men stand ready to do violence on their behalf."
— George Orwell

MICHIGAN STATE POLICE
Interoffice Correspondence

Date   : June 12, 1984

Subject: Use of Firearms Complaint 26-3007-84, 4900-1

To   : F/Lt. Robert Pifer, Ypsilanti Post Commander

From   : Captain James A. Kneale, Second District Commander

> I have reviewed the investigative reports and associated reports regarding the
> fatal shooting of Charles Macklin by Trooper Clifton Edwards. This correspondence
> is to advise you I support the actions taken as being necessary and in accordance
> with established policies/procedures. Advise Trooper Edwards of this determination
> inasmuch as I want him reassured regarding the correctness of his actions while
> considering the circumstances existing at the time of the shooting.
>
> This concludes our review of this incident.

JAK:jw

Fast forward to the present—

Over twenty-five years have passed since the day Charles Macklin and my paths crossed. While I seldom talk about it, I am proud of what I did that day. Reading that comment, some may be troubled. Am I disturbed? I read the article "On Sheep, Wolves and Sheepdogs" by Lieutenant Colonel David Grossman to find solace.

To write this story, I had to go to the closet, get the memory box out and then open it. Reliving it was exciting and intense! And when I lay the pen down, I wonder about the deputy that Charles Macklin killed. Macklin lived thirteen years after he killed that deputy. I wonder whether he talked about it? I realize I know nothing about the slain deputy the prison official had mentioned in the briefing prior to our search.

I do some research and learn the sheriff deputy's name was Ben Ray Walker and he was thirty-five years old when Charles Macklin killed him on April 6, 1971. Doing the math, I would have been fifteen years old when this happened. Walker was married and had three daughters. He and another deputy had taken three inmates to the dentist's office. Two of the inmates were handcuffed together, one being Charles Macklin. As Deputy Walker removed their handcuffs in preparation for medical treatment, they overpowered him; Macklin took his service revolver and shot both deputies. The other deputy recovered from his wounds. I wonder whether he is still alive.

I wonder what happened to Deputy Walker's wife, daughters, and his surviving partner on that fateful day? I have heard that Macklin was awaiting trial on murder charges when he killed Deputy Walker. I wonder whether that is true and what were the circumstances of those murders? I wonder and I wonder and I wonder, and I realize it is time to close the memory box and put it back in the closet. I do not want to become a victim.

52) Worst

May 23, 1985 was one of those damp chilly mornings when the glow of streetlights reveals the moisture in the atmosphere. Being a Thursday, it was a canine training day. At about 3:00 a.m., I was walking across the parking lot of the Washtenaw County Jail when I heard a car crash from nearby Hogback Road.

I raced the short distance to the area of the crash and discovered an overturned van off the road. No one was in it so, using my flashlight, I searched the immediate area for any ejected occupants. In the brush, I found a man who was unconscious and not breathing. In the darkness, I cleared his airway and initiated mouth-to-mouth resuscitation, as rescue breathing had not yet evolved to mouth-to-mask. I recall the foul beer breath and disgust of touching lips with a man. One, maybe two ventilations stimulated the person to gasp. Having been the recipient of vomit before, I quickly turned my head and paused. I was relieved when he started breathing.

His name was Paul Byars, a person I knew of from the investigation I had conducted in the chapter titled "Knight in Shining Armor." Apparently, Byars had been paroled from prison.

The ambulance and Pittsfield Township Police arrived shortly thereafter so I turned the incident over to them. I returned to canine training, while the ambulance transported Byars to St. Joseph Hospital in Ann Arbor where he was treated and released. I do not know whether any legal action was initiated for drunk driving.

During my career I had provided rescue breathing to a handful of persons, but had only saved the lives of two. I consider the first save as one of the "Best Things" I ever did. The other—well, as it turns out, it was the "Worst Thing" I ever did.

A sexual predator had become infatuated with a married woman who lived in the same neighborhood. He surreptitiously watched and waited, coming to believe that when the pickup truck was away so was her husband.

The predator waited for the fateful night the pickup truck was gone. Armed with a knife, in the wee hours of the morning, he quietly broke into the home. Little did he know that the husband had loaned his pickup to a friend and was home, along with his young nephews, who were sleeping on the floor of the family room.

In the twilight, he stalked across the family room, stumbling across a sleeping boy on the floor. Quickly, he knelt down and slit the throat of the young lad. As he continued on, he stumbled across his sleeping brother, to whom he dealt the same fate. The youngest of the three had been awakened by the noise and cowered in the corner, witnessing the horror. The first, not yet dead but unable to speak, ran into his aunt and uncle's bedroom, having to use his hands to hold his head up as his neck muscles had been severed.

From the stupor of sleep, the boys' uncle awakened to a nightmare. As he entered the hall to investigate, he confronted a demon. As they did battle in the hallway, the uncle was slashed. Anticipating his own death, he was determined at least to mark the man he believed would be his killer for the police. And the predator—like most criminals a coward, unwilling to fight anything close to equal—fled into the night. The police were called.

First on the scene were Troopers Ernest Bucks and Jamie Dakin. Their memories would be forever imprinted with the horror of that scene. As they sorted through the massacre, they were torn between rendering aid and protecting the crime scene.

For me, that date of July 19, 1985 was but a couple of hours old and yet it had already been one of those exhausting nights of being called-out on back-to-back dog calls that had followed a normal eight-hour shift. I was some thirty miles away, struggling home from the third dog call of the night when the post radioed me.

The radio operator advised that troopers were at the scene of a double homicide in West Willow, where it appeared the perpetrator's motive had been rape. The scene had been totally contaminated by first responders who were checking the victims for life and treating the survivors.

As much as I wanted to help, the reality was that my police dog, Cisco, could offer nothing of value in the contaminated scene. However, their briefing caused me immediately to think of Paul Byars, whose life I had saved seven weeks earlier, as a suspect. I knew that he now lived with his mother in the same neighborhood as the crime, had been branded a sexual predator, and that his previous method of operation matched this incident. Being on a scannable radio frequency, I didn't dare broadcast his name, but I did share his initials. The dispatcher told me he knew who I was talking about.

Troopers found blood on the sidewalk, steps, and porch of Paul Byars' mother's house, where he was living. This evidence coupled with other information prompted a search warrant that produced Paul's blood-soaked clothing in the washing machine and him in the house, which led to his arrest.

When I came on duty that next day, I was tasked to assist Detective Sergeant Skip Ward with transporting the arrested Paul Byars from the state police post to the Washtenaw County Jail.

Teens' suspected killer jailed

By WILLIAM B. TREML
NEWS STAFF REPORTER

YPSILANTI – Paul Byars, 27, was arraigned under tight security Friday afternoon in the Washtenaw County Jail, charged with the stabbing deaths of two teenagers and the wounding of an Ypsilanti Township homeowner in his own neighborhood.

He demanded examination on the three felonies two counts of murder and one charge of assault with intent to commit murder. A Public Defender was expected to be appointed to represent him on Monday.

BYARS

Fourteen-B District Court Judge John B. Collins set July 31 for the examination, and ordered Byars held without bond.

Byars is charged with the Friday morning knife slaying of two York Township cousins, J. Bruce Harrison, 14, and his cousin, Steven D Harrison, 13, and the attempted murder of 25-year-old Dale Scott Dolinger, owner of the home where the attacks occurred. Bruce Harrison is the brother of Dolinger's wife, Debra.

At the time of the attack, both

L to R - D/Sgt. Ward, author, Paul Byars - Compliments of *Ann Arbor News*

The state police provided a police escort at the funeral procession for the two slain brothers, a service usually only provided for slain officers. The youngest brother who had witnessed the carnage battled through the psychological trauma to become a firefighter, only later to have his life snuffed out by a drunk driver.

There was one heinous villain and many primary and secondary victims that night. I doubt the uncle feels like a victor, but he was certainly a hero. Paul Byars was convicted and sentenced to life in prison without parole. If only I had not saved Paul Byars!

Trooper revived suspect

One of the more bizarre ironies surrounding Paul R. Byars' arrest involves his injury in a May 23 traffic accident and his revival at the scene by a State Police trooper who took part in the Friday's murder investigation.

Trooper Clifford Edwards was training his search dog at Hogback Road near Clark Road in Pittsfield Township when he responded to a call of a traffic accident.

At the scene, Edwards found Byars lying face down, not breathing, and with only a faint pulse.

Edwards administered mouth-to-mouth resuscitation and finally restored Byars' breathing. He was taken to St. Joseph Mercy Hospital and was released after several days of treatment.

"He had been driving west on Clark Road near Hogback and his car went off the road and hit a shed," Edwards said. "He was thrown out of the vehicle and landed face down. There was evidence he had been drinking before the accident."

The follow-up investigation of the crash was handled by the Pittsfield Township Police Department.

Edwards was part of the police detail which investigated the murders with which Byars is charged.

Compliments of *Ypsilanti Press*

Go to **www.michigan.gov/otis** *and enter offender number 143174 to view Paul Byars' photograph.*

53) PTSD

One night when troopers from the Brighton Post attempted to stop a vehicle for a minor traffic violation, a short chase ended with the driver disappearing on foot. Left behind in the vehicle were firearms and pharmaceutical narcotics. Contacting the dealership where the car had originated, troopers eventually learned the mystery driver's identity.

The man was an ex-Army Special Forces Green Beret and a combat veteran of the Vietnam Conflict—a warrior who had struggled with adapting back to civilian life and had lapsed into drug abuse. The dog handler out of the Brighton Post was not available that night, and for whatever reason, the desk sergeant had not reached out to us at the Ypsilanti Post, where I was still stationed. The suspect made good his escape.

A couple of weeks later at 9:10 p.m., my telephone rang—it was another dog call. Pam and I had settled down to watch a television show after cleaning up the dinner dishes and getting the boys off to bed. I was dispatched to track the former Green Beret combat veteran who had escaped police a couple of weeks earlier.

I grew up in awe of the Army Green Beret. As a boy, one of the first songs I ever memorized was Barry Sadler's "The Ballad of the Green Berets." Movie characters like Billy Jack and Rambo depicted their martial art expertise and invincibility. This mystique, combined with the location of the track being less than a mile from home, was intimidating. As I rushed from the house with Cisco, I told Pam to make sure she kept the doors locked.

Upon arrival at the scene, I learned that, this time, Ohio authorities had contacted the Brighton Post and told them that the suspect had failed to return from a test drive of a brand new Pontiac Firebird, so they were deeming it stolen. Further, they thought he might be headed for his estranged wife's house in the Brighton Post area, and they considered him armed and dangerous. They requested officers BOL ("Be On Lookout") for it.

A while later when officers spotted the stolen car, a short chase ensued with the suspect losing control and crashing. When officers caught up to the overturned car, they found only a sawed-off shotgun in it. The .45 caliber pistol he was also reported to have was not in the car, leading us to believe he had probably fled with it.

While responding to the scene, I recognized the voice of my first cub, Jerry Ellsworth, on the radio. Jerry had since transferred to the Brighton Post and become a member of the Emergency Services Team of the Michigan State Police. I hoped Jerry could run as my backup.

The rain had just ended and the terrain was enveloped in a hazy dark when Cisco and I arrived at the scene. A chill ran down my spine when the on-scene briefing was complete and it was time to begin the track. Jerry was unavailable to be my backup since he had been dispatched to another emergency. As I scanned the available officers, a young trooper by the name of Tom Dunneback volunteered.

All I knew about Tom was that he was a cub and obviously eager. I told him to follow me from about six feet and match me step-for-step or he would fall behind. Also, that while I would be primarily watching the dog, he was to be looking up, down, and all around. Looking me in the eye, he said, "Got it." With him carrying the issued H&K .223 patrol rifle, we began the track.

As the track unfolded, the environment transitioned from farming to residential because of its close proximity to a chain of lakes along the Huron River. Many of the houses were cabins. The track went back and forth between dirt road, woods, field, and yard—sometimes under the illumination of a mercury light, sometimes not. I thought of the suspect's background and repeated to myself a line from the movie Rocky III where Apollo reassures Rocky about his opponent, Clubber Lang, "He's just a man."

From a distance, we heard noise approaching us. We crouched in the shadows to see a figure traipsing our way. With rifle pointed, Trooper Dunneback shouted, "State Police! Put your hands on your head!" while Cisco growled. Surprised at our presence, the ex-Green Beret hesitantly complied. We handcuffed and searched him, finding no pistol.

Standing him up to escort him to a patrol car, he turned to us and said with all sincerity, "Congratulations; that was some good work." He told us that he had been laying a series of backtracks in hopes of confusing any tracking dog, and he had removed his shoes in preparation to swim across the lake. The troubled veteran was lodged in jail by the officers who had initiated the chase.

Concerned that Pam might be afraid, I had the post telephone and advise her that the suspect had been caught. When I got home that night to tell Pam my story, she didn't seem too interested. It reminded me of how Deb was indifferent the night of my first shooting. Perhaps the burden of being married to a dog handler was tarnishing the glamour.

The next morning, Cisco and I returned to the area of the track and did an article search for the missing .45 caliber pistol, but we were unable to find it. I do not know what the court outcome was for this case.

As the years passed, I lost track of Trooper Tom Dunneback. Sometime after the fact, I learned of his death from brain cancer, which was long before he was eligible for retirement. Looking back, it seems many of my colleagues suffered that fate, making a suspicious mind wonder about the radar units used in our patrol cars.

Weeks later, I would again be summoned to Hamburg Township in Livingston County to track another ex-Army Green Beret who was also a Vietnam combat veteran. He too was struggling with some personal issues that resulted in the township police arresting him for spouse abuse.

Having handcuffed him behind his back and secured him in the back-seat of their caged patrol car, the officers went back into his home to complete their investigation. Being an ex-Green Beret, guess what he did? He escaped. His wife told officers that her husband had built a series of hideouts in the woods surrounding their house, so there was no telling what he might have in store for them. Search as they might, the township police officers could not find him. Cisco and I were home when our services were requested.

Upon arrival, Sergeant Pat DeBottis of the Hamburg Township Police Department briefed me on the situation. There were now about six officers on the scene. It was apparent that the scene was too contaminated for a track.

Sergeant DeBottis suggested a somewhat unconventional response to the predicament. As a group, all of us were to hike to the confluents of trails on the property. During that hike, all the officers, except for him and me, would shine their flashlights about. At this intersection, he, Cisco, and I would peel off and hide in the darkness. The others would shine their flashlights while they returned to their patrol cars and drove away, giving the appearance that the police had given up the search. I concurred with his idea.

For the next hour, we sat quietly in the woods, feeding multitudes of bloodthirsty mosquitoes. Gradually, the environment returned to its natural sounds of night. I studied Cisco for clues in the dim moonlight. While his head rested on his front paws, he was alert. Like a radar screen, I watched Cisco's twitching ears and nose for any clue of an approaching person.

As our budgeted time was about to elapse, Cisco raised his head, staring intently into the blackness of night. Within a few minutes, we too could hear, but not smell, what Cisco had sensed.

Eventually, a shadowy figure emerged into our field of vision, creeping in our direction, and apparently, oblivious to our presence. Cisco, along with me, shivered with excitement but yet remained still and quiet. When the escapee was close, we doused him with light. While Sergeant DeBottis gave him orders to surrender, I told Cisco to "Watch him," a command to bark and intimidate. The fugitive was ours. If this ex-Green Beret were impressed, he didn't mention it.

54) Defendant

Civil rights suit filed against trooper

8-2584 Ypsilanti Press

ANN ARBOR — An Ann Arbor man who claims he was unjustly beaten during a drunken driving arrest in May is suing a Michigan State Police trooper for violating his civil rights.

Kyle Freeman is seeking damages of more than $10,000 in his lawsuit, filed Tuesday in U.S. District Court.

Freeman said Trooper Clifton Edwards of the state police Ypsilanti post stopped him about 3:30 a.m. on U.S.-12 in Ypsilanti Township and arrested him for operating under the influence of liquor.

Freeman said he was handcuffed by Edwards and taken to Edwards' patrol car. He contends he tried talking to Edwards while stepping into the patrol car and was "hit in the mouth, kicked, choked and jumped on" by Edwards.

Freeman, who is black, claims the alleged attack by Edwards, who is white, was unprovoked and racially motivated.

Compliments of *Ypsilanti Press*

My day in court came on my thirtieth birthday. It is much different being the defendant, and this case was my first exposure to Federal Court.

Over a year earlier, Joe Payne and I had arrested an African-American for drunk driving. Once handcuffed, I escorted him to the backseat of the patrol car while Joe tended to the arrestee's vehicle. As I protected the back of the suspect's head as I seated him, he suddenly kicked me in the chest. Instinctively, I pressed into him, causing us to lie face-to-face in the backseat of the patrol car. As I did so, I fisted my right hand and cocked my arm to strike him, but then I caught myself and did not follow through with the hit because he was handcuffed and no longer a threat.

I disengaged from the suspect and summoned Joe to monitor him while I cooled off. While I was not hurt, it aggravated me to have his shoeprint on the front of my dark blue uniform shirt. Nevertheless, I did not retaliate and we lodged him in the county jail.

Within a month or so, the prosecutor told us that the defendant's attorney was threatening to file a lawsuit in federal court for civil rights violations if we did not dismiss the charges. I had done nothing wrong, and this threat would not compromise our position on prosecution. As I recall, the drunk driving case was disposed of with a guilty plea.

Months passed until I was served with a lawsuit, naming me as a defendant in federal court on an alleged civil rights violation. I notified my superiors, who contacted the Attorney General's (AG) Office. A review of the incident deemed my actions to be appropriate and an assistant AG was assigned to defend me.

When the Attorney General's Office is on your side, it's always a good sign. Then you have no attorney expenses, and if you lose, most likely the state will pay the settlement. So the months passed with the AG holding firm and refusing any out of court settlement.

As coincidence would have it, on the morning of my thirtieth birthday, I was at the Federal Court in Ann Arbor seated in the defendant's chair while we chose a jury to try me on charges of violating his Civil Rights. I had never celebrated a birthday this way before. By late morning, a jury was seated.

Being the defendant meant the other side got to make its case first. I was not surprised by how they submitted their case, but I might be biased. At the conclusion of their presentation, the assistant attorney general stood and made a motion for a directed verdict, a request that the judge dismiss the lawsuit because the plaintiff's case was too weak to continue. As a part of the prosecution team, I had witnessed many a defense attorney make this motion in criminal matters, but I had never seen the judge grant it.

I am glad there are first times, and I was relieved this time was one of them. The dismissal of the charges was unlike any birthday gift I had ever received.

55) Bite

During the wee hours of a September night, I was jolted awake by the ringing telephone. Pam had learned to sleep through this frequent disturbance. As I hastened to the hallway to answer it, I glanced out the window to see the moon reflecting off a calm lake and felt the warm breeze of an Indian summer night. I could hear Cisco in the background, whining with excitement in his kennel; he too had heard the ringing and knew what it meant.

Over the telephone, the sergeant told me that the Washtenaw County Sheriff's department was requesting our services in Ypsilanti Township, providing me directions to rendezvous with them. Like a fireman, my gear was staged in the lower bedroom, and I rushed to meet my own set standard to be en route within ten minutes of receiving the call. Cisco and

I raced the twenty-five miles to the scene under an oscillating red light.

As I neared the location, I could see the police helicopter scanning the ground with its beacon. The throbbing of the helicopter rotors was reminiscent of a Vietnam War movie. While Cisco and I had previously been inserted and extracted from search areas by helicopters and had worked under them in daylight, this would be our first experience in darkness. Helicopters were rare and expensive to operate, and its presence was a clue this was not a routine call. Supporting the eye in the sky were the patrol cars, parked along the road with their spotlights shining into the darkness. It seemed the stage had been set and now awaited Cisco's appearance. I hoped he would have a star performance.

Upon arrival, the scene supervisor from the Washtenaw County Sheriff's Department briefed me on the situation. Alan Lumsden, on parole for second degree murder, was now wanted for three recent execution style murders. It seemed he targeted drug dealers so he could quench his own drug habit with their products and proceeds.

In the Washtenaw County homicide, he put the victim's young daughters in a closet while he robbed and killed their father. In the Wayne County incident, he got the wrong apartment, killing a young, recently married couple who were not involved in the drug trade.

Sheriff's detectives had developed Lumsden as a suspect and staked-out a Ypsilanti apartment he was known to frequent in hopes of arresting him. When they observed him leave in a red pickup truck, they radioed for a Ypsilanti patrol car to stop and arrest him.

When the Ypsilanti Police went to make the stop, a wild chase ensued with Lumsden losing control of his pick-up truck and rolling off the south side of US-12, east of I-94. In the moments it took officers to get to the crash site, Lumsden had vanished, undoubtedly fleeing on foot into the nearby stubble fields and wood lots. Further, he was believed to be armed with a pistol and sawed-off shotgun.

The sheriff's department had quickly established a triangle-shaped perimeter, using I-94 and US-12 for two of the sides and a gravel road for its third. Their helicopter, equipped with a searchlight, along with the patrol cars, hoped to keep Lumsden confined in that perimeter.

Our counterparts from the Washtenaw County Sheriff's Department, Deputy Bob Marsh and K9 Baron, and Deputy Bill Moffett and K9 Champ were on the scene. They had already searched to no avail and wanted to try a fresh dog. Frequently training together, we shared both friendship and mutual respect.

Following the briefing, Bob, Bill, and I then huddled while they briefed me on their earlier efforts. We decided that Cisco and I would attempt to initiate a track for Lumsden with Bill acting as my backup since K9 Champ was fatigued from his earlier efforts. Meanwhile, Bob and K9 Baron would go to the downwind perimeter line and free search into the wind, hoping to pick up an airborne scent from Lumsden.

As I harnessed Cisco and attached the lead in preparation for the track, I was glad for the bright moon. Its eerie light would reduce both my need and want to shine my flashlight, which made me an easier target. Again I reminded myself, darkness is my friend.

Our first challenge would be to get on the right track, not the one Bill had laid in his failed attempt to track Lumsden with K9 Champ. On television, this is the part where the dog sniffs an article of the suspect's clothing and then flawlessly sorts that scent from other human scents and tracks the suspect down. This wasn't TV.

To have the chopper overhead with noise, light, and rotor wash would diminish Cisco's keen senses of sound, sight, and smell. So while we hunted Lumsden, it would patrol the perimeter boundaries in hopes of keeping the quarry contained.

As Cisco cast for a track, I coaxed him with "Track...track." Suddenly, Cisco bolted into the darkness with me in tow. I held him to a fast walk so he would be less likely to miss a turn, while I remained busy keeping his lead from becoming tangled in the brush. I hoped he had pick-up on the scent of Lumsden.

Having crossed a stubble field, we entered the bare earth of a mature cornfield awaiting harvest. I decided to risk using my flashlight to check for a shoeprint that might corroborate being on the right track. In the bare dirt, I observed a fresh heeled shoeprint which I knew from numerous training tracks was not the Vibram sole of Bill's boot. This finding gave me both confidence and fear that we were on the right track.

Mature cornfields, especially in the darkness of night, dull all your senses and it is easy to become lost or separated. While Cisco was teth-ered to me by a leash, Bill was not, and when we emerged from the cornfield, I realized I had somehow lost my backup in the maze. We were now caught-up in the chase and to stop now was to risk failure. We continued on alone.

From the eight foot tall cornstalks, we entered a field of thigh-high weeds as we headed toward an island of tree saplings. Suddenly, Cisco began leaping into the air, reminding me of a bird dog attempting to flush a pheasant. I recalled a track earlier in Cisco's career where he had flushed and caught a pheasant in midair. I trusted we were past that.

Cisco pulled me into the saplings where the tree canopy would have obstructed the view of spotters in the helicopter had they flown over. Once in this microcosm jungle, my lead went slack, followed by a low menacing growl. I fed up the lead to within a few feet of Cisco, and holding my flashlight away from my body, shined my light ahead. I saw the bare back of a crouching man whose hands were concealed in front of him. Believing it Lumsden, I dropped the leash and drew my revolver, yelling "State police! Put your hands on top of your head!" When he made no response, I repeated myself, again to no avail.

What I did not know was that Lumsden had lost his guns when his pickup rolled and he fled into the bush. What he did have was a large folding knife which he had opened and now clasped, concealed from my view. Undoubtedly, he hoped his unresponsiveness would prompt me to move within range of his edged weapon.

Cisco was trained to attack on command and in self-defense, and neither of these scenarios existed. Yet, Cisco sensed imminent danger and made a peremptory attack, biting Lumsden in the back. In the academy, troopers are taught to use just enough force to affect the arrest. Cisco somehow knew that. Lumsden reacted by raising his hands as he dropped the knife. With that, I commanded Cisco "Out" followed by "Watch him," a guard command. Cisco had seized this opportunity to excel with a star performance.

The spotters in the helicopter had sighted my now illuminated flashlight and zoomed to our location, turning night into day with its spotlight, and showing Deputies Marsh and Moffett where I had vanished. Within a minute, they were at my side, taking custody of Lumsden.

Cisco and I celebrated with a good old game of tug of war. Far away, I thought I could hear the song "Going the Distance" from the *Rocky* movie soundtrack. Forever more, that instrumental will remind me of that victorious moment.

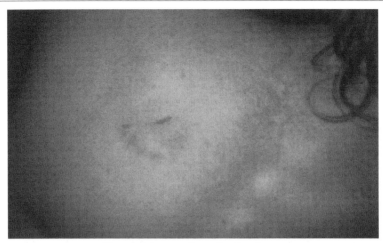

Cisco's bite mark on back of suspect.

On our way home, I stopped at a 24-hour drive-thru restaurant and violated Cisco's strict diet by purchasing him a pastrami on rye sandwich. He obviously liked it, and I was confident he wouldn't tell anybody.

In the upcoming trials, I would make appearances in Wayne County Circuit Court and Washtenaw County Circuit Court. Lumsden was subsequently convicted of First Degree Murder and sentenced to natural life in prison, no possibility of parole.

Go to www.michigan.gov/otis and enter offender number 147753 to view Alan Lumsden's photograph.

THE ANN ARBOR NEWS • THURSDAY, OCTOBER 3, 1985

■ A3

Slaying suspect visited jail

By CHONG W. PYEN
NEWS STAFF REPORTER

YPSILANTI — A fugitive suspect in last month's robbery slayings of an Ypsilanti Township man and a Dearborn couple had walked into Washtenaw County Jail to visit an alleged accomplice and walked away before police learned of his implication, according to court testimony Wednesday.

Rodney Warren Crawford, 35, being sought by police in Washtenaw and Wayne counties, walked by investigators at the Washtenaw County Sheriff's Department on the morning of Sept. 23 to see Alan Wilson Lumsden, 28, a suspect in the triple slayings.

At the time, Lumsden had just been picked up for carrying concealed weapons and had not been charged with murder, testified Sheriff's Detective Lloyd Stamper.

"No, I didn't speak to Rodney," Stamper said. Crawford, who was not then a suspect in the murders, was accompanied by two women acquaintances of both men, Stamper added.

After Wednesday's preliminary hearing, Lumsden and one of those women, Robin Denise Feldmann, 26, were bound over to Circuit Court by 14B District Judge John B. Collins on first degree murder and armed robbery charges. They are accused in the execution-style murder of James E. Visel, 53, at his home at 1232 Pageant St. on the morning of Sept. 22. They are being held in County Jail with no bond. Their arraignments are scheduled for Oct. 8 before Circuit Judge Edward D. Deake.

Lumsden also faces two counts of weapons charges.

Lumsden, Feldmann and Crawford are also suspects in the slaying of a Dearborn couple, James Hoos and Sally Tuck, both 35, about three hours before the Visel murder. The Dearborn couple were shot in what appeared to be a random robbery, according to court testimony.

The other woman who visited Lumsden at the jail on Sept. 23 was a 17-year-old girlfriend of Crawford's, who took the stand Wednesday. She was identified only as "Deborah" because she is in protective custody, said Assistant Prosecutor Kirk Tabbey.

Stamper said a stakeout team near an apartment building at 701 Pearl St. spotted Lumsden driving off in a pickup truck less than 24 hours after the Visel murder, driving in an erratic manner. A chase ensued, and the driver fled on foot after the truck rolled over several times off Michigan Avenue near Hewitt Road.

Lumsden was arrested in a cornfield, Stamper said, after a search aided by tracking dogs and a helicopter. Found in his truck were a .22 caliber semi-automatic pistol and a .12 gauge sawed-off shotgun.

When Lumsden was brought to the main station, his friends were waiting to meet him, Stamper said. It was hours later that police learned that Feldmann, Lumsden's girlfriend, and Crawford, with a long criminal record including armed robbery and assault convictions, may also have been part of the Visel murder.

A search of a dumpster near the Pearl Street apartment turned up Visel's personal belongings and two wallets with identification papers for the Dearborn couple. Police also found Visel's jewelry in the apartment.

Both Lumsden and Feldmann attributed the Visel killing to Crawford in separate interviews with investigators, officers Stamper and Joe Hall testified.

Dr. Lila Blaibas of the University of Michigan Medical Center, who performed an autopsy on Visel, said his face was "extremely deformed and the nose bridge was sunken." He was shot twice on the back of his head, she said.

Kellie Visel, 18, the victim's daughter, and her friend Lisa Preston, 18, recounted the ordeal from the witness stand. Both said they were tied up with electric cords, with

See SUSPECT, A4

SUSPECT

CONTINUED FROM A3

faces covered with sheets throughout the robbery and murder and did not see any of the assailants.

The intruders demanded money and drugs. "Where is that? Where is that?" one of them asked Visel, Kellie Visel said. "My dad said, 'It's all I got.' " And someone hit Visel, she said. Police describe Visel as a small-time drug dealer.

Preston said one man said to Visel, "You are too flashy, Jimmy. We know you have more than what you are telling us." Visel also gave the men a name and address, drawing a map for them, according to testimony.

After the intruders left the room with Visel, the women heard two gunshots. Kellie Visel freed herself, ran across the street and called police.

Lumsden was represented by Robert West from the Public Defender's Office, but Feldmann was assigned a private attorney, Jane Thurston, because court rules do not allow co-defendants to be represented by lawyers from the same office for possible conflict of interest.

"Deborah" said she saw the three leave her apartment to rob Visel on the night of Sept. 21. "I told Rodney not to go. I knew they were going over to Jimmy's to rob him. He had lot of money. I asked him not to go, telling him it wouldn't be worth it. Rodney said it would be all right. He said nothing will happen."

After the three returned, no one told her what had happened, she said, but the two men became angry at each other for some reason. "From what I heard from Robin (Feldmann), Rodney and Lum had been shooting at each other."

Detectives began watching the Pearl Street house after receiving a tip on the Visel murder from a caller who feared "there would be another homicide," according to Stamper. Investigators theorize that the two men got in an argument over the share of the loot which Detective Hall said could be "lot of money" taken from the safe in Visel's basement.

Compliments of *Ann Arbor News*

NEWS PHOTO • JACK STUBBS

Washtenaw County's three K-9 teams (from left): State Trooper Clif Edwards and Cisco; Washtenaw County Sheriff's Deputy Robert Marsh and Barron; Sheriff's Deputy William Moffett and Champ.

Compliments of *Ann Arbor News* - picture of 3 K9 Teams.

56) Potential

On June 19, 1982, prior to becoming a dog handler, I took the sergeant promotional test. Preparing for that examination truly tested my self-discipline since, at the time, I had no desire to be promoted. Being on the road was where it was, not coaching from a desk. Seeking counsel from wise sergeants, they convinced me to study for and take the test just to keep open my future options.

The written test comprised 75 percent of the final score while the remaining 25 percent is called "potential" and assigned by your post commander. Competition was keen, and if you didn't score in the 90s, called the first band, you had little chance of being promoted.

My dad had always preached, "Anything worth doing, is worth doing right, or it isn't worth doing at all," a tenet I did not adopt until after high school. So, I studied for the examination. While I scored well on the written portion, the post commander awarded me potentials of twenty, rather than the maximum twenty-five. My written score combined with my twenty potential would not get me into the first band. I was appalled!

In my mind, I suspected this low potential was a lingering byproduct of the one and only grievance I ever filed, which was against this post commander. It arose out of an incident that occurred during the Republican National Convention when I was working from 6:00 p.m. to 6:00 a.m. and for no good reason, he decided to telephone me at home during the day and interrupt precious sleep time before the next twelve hour night shift. Adequate sleep is essential to survival and can be very scarce in the heat of the summer in a home with no air conditioning, two small boys and lots of outside noise. And while I was not currently interested in being promoted, it was now about the principle.

My options were to accept the score or appeal it. Appeal involved appearing before a panel of three high level command officers at headquarters and presenting my case for a higher potential. It would require much preparation and a convincing presentation. I submitted the following letter requesting an audience before a Promotional Potential Committee:

MICHIGAN STATE POLICE
Interoffice Correspondence

Date   :   September 14, 1982

Subject: Request to appeal promotional potential

To   :   Captain James A. Carter, Commanding Officer, Personnel Division

From   :   Trooper Clifton L. Edwards #854, Ypsilanti Post

I wish to appeal my promotional potential of 20% for Sergeant IIIB and 20% for Detective Sergeant IIIB. I do not feel it is a fair and accurate rating of my competency as a trooper or potential as a Sergeant or Detective Sergeant. The examination was administered on June 19, 1982.

In brief, I don not feel these potentials are representative for the following reasons:

1. I was a graduate of the first Service Trooper Recruit School that graduated September 6, 1974. I was elected class orator by my fellow classmates.
2. I graduated academically sixth from the 89.5 recruit school. Have continued my college education since entering the department and have earned an Associate Degree in Criminal Justice with a grade point average of 3.31.
3. When evaluated through the Achievement Development Inventory in August of 1979, was rated as the most proficient trooper at the Ypsilanti Post and among the top ten percent in the department. In the later Achievment Development Inventory, I was rated high, but no score or placement was given.
4. Have earned and maintained the distinguished expert shooting award, gold level physical fitness award, and the Oscar Olander award for eight years of safe driving.
5. Have received three awards for Professional Excellence and three Letters of Accommodation.
6. On three prior occassions, have been selected as a training officer for probationary troopers an am scheduled to begin my fourth such assignment this month.
7. Received temporary assignment with the Washtenaw Area Intelligence Team which is a combined agency concept. During this assignment I worked in a surveillance, undercover, and case builder role. I was responsible for several cases that resulted in the issuance of arrest and search warrants. This assignment also enabled me to strengthen departmental relations with area police agencies.

During my six years as a trooper I have always strived to do the best job possible for the department and the citizens of Michigan. I consider myself a motivated and enthusiastic officer which is substaniated by my consistent reporting early for my shift, hours of voluntary overtime, and activity generated. I feel dissappointed in receiving anthing less then a full 25% promotional potential in both sergeant levels.

I do appreciate the opportunity to express myself on this issue.

The preparation was intense and the presentation exciting. I awaited the board's decision. On October 20, 1982, I received a memorandum from Captain James A. Carter, Commanding Officer of the Personnel Division, advising that Civil Service would notify me of a change in my potential rating. That change was to a full potential rating of twenty-five. I was now in the first band for promotion, whether or not I wanted to be promoted.

At the time, I resented the post commander, First Lieutenant Robert Pifer, for giving me only a potential rating of twenty. In hindsight, however, it was a gift! Just how often does a lowly trooper have the undivided attention of three high level command officers at headquarters?

Three years would pass before I received word on the results of that change. In the fall of 1985, Cisco and I had just celebrated our most successful month yet as a team. We were on our way home in hopes of a couple of days off when I received a radio message to telephone the assistant post commander, Lieutenant Douglas Swix.

I called him once I reached home. His first words were "Congratulations; you have just been promoted to sergeant, to report to the Detroit Post in two weeks." He was stunned when I waivered by asking how long I had to think about it. Troopers don't turn down promotions. I asked whether it was okay for me to deliver my decision when I returned to duty in two days. He told me that was highly unusual but he was okay with it.

During those two days, I felt flattered to receive a call from the new post commander, First Lieutenant Al Byam, telling me why I should not reject this opportunity. When I returned to duty, I submitted the following letter.

State of Michigan

DEPARTMENT OF STATE POLICE

TO   : Major Michael J. Anderson, Uniform Division Commander   DATE : 10/17/85

FROM   : Trooper Clifton L. Edwards #854, Ypsilanti Post

SUBJECT : Promotion and Transfer to Detroit Freeway Post.

During the afternoon hours of 10/16/85 I was advised by F/Lt. A. Byam and Lt. D. Swix that I had been promoted to sergeant and transferred to the Detroit Freeway Post, effective 10/20/85. After considerable thought, I wish to decline same and remain in my current assignment.

Since entering the department in 1974 it has been my goal to be a trooper - dog handler. In 1983 I realized that goal. Since that time I have been striving to be the best trooper - dog handler possible. Hours of training, both on and off duty, have recently allowed me to attain the level of profiency I had set for myself. I enjoy much self satisfaction in my current position and feel it would be an injustice to the department and myself to abandon this goal at this point in time.

Many hours of contemplation have gone into this decision. I hope it is not one I will regret. I thank you for the opportunity to make it.

APPROVED

Douglas D. Swix

Operation Lieutenant

Cisco and I were not done yet.

57) Challenger

It was January 28, 1986, and Cisco and I were savoring that intrinsic reward that comes from a job well done. Cisco had just tracked down an armed robber in what is considered a challenging environment—from storefront to residential sidewalk to where we found the suspect lying in the weeds near the I-94 freeway. The robber was probably waiting for his getaway car that was late—it's hard to get good help. On top of that, Cisco had also located the revolver the suspect had tossed some fifteen feet from where he was hiding.

When we returned to the post to refuel, one of my colleagues took a picture of us at the gas pump, glowing with big smiles from our success. When we walked into the post, however, Sergeant Manuel Reyes ignored us as he watched the television screen.

I could not imagine what was more important than him congratulating us on a job well done. I looked to the screen to learn that the Space Shuttle *Challenger* had broken apart seventy-three seconds into its flight, leading to the deaths of its seven crew members. It was no longer a good day. Like most, I remember what I was doing when I heard about this tragedy.

Police dog tracks down armed suspect

YPSILANTI — "Cisco," the Michigan State Police tracking dog, accounted for another apprehension over the weekend when he led troopers to a 21-year-old armed robbery suspect.

Clifford Edwards, a trooper at the Ypsilanti Township post where Cisco is assigned, brought the dog to an area along I-94 near Ecorse Road shortly after an attempted armed robbery Sunday night at the Stop-N-Go store, 1390 Ecorse Road.

In that incident, a young man confronted a store clerk with a nickel-plated handgun and demanded that she open the cash register. The clerk began backing away and the robber unsuccessfully tried to open the register. When several customers entered the store, the bandit put the gun back in his pocket, muttered he "should have shot her" and fled.

Cisco picked up the suspect's scent along I-94 near the robbery scene and led Edwards into a wooded area. There the dog went directly to a spot where Delano L. Lynch of Lansing was lying face down in underbrush. Edwards took Lynch into custody at gunpoint, and moments later Cisco led the trooper to a spot 15 feet away where a nickel-plated handgun was found. Lynch was booked on an armed robbery charge.

Article compliments of the *Ypsilanti Press*

58) Pursuit

When we think of exciting police action, we list shoot-outs, car chases, fights, and foot pursuits. Of these, my favorite is the foot pursuit because it offers little risk to innocent bystanders and tests an officer's fitness and tactics. Yes, they are dangerous, but that is part of the job. Perhaps this interest in foot pursuits was first imbedded in my mind as a result of my first chase of the shoplifter while in college, when I vowed never to be out of shape again.

I had developed my fitness around control tactic success. I would start my runs at a sprint, holding it as long as I could, and still be able to settle into a mile-eating pace. I also developed strategies for foot pursuits, such as: keep the quarry in sight, try to catch a lean man as fast as possible since he may have the endurance edge, follow a big man until he collapses, so he will be unable to fight. When I look back decades later, I now can only remember ten foot pursuits. Of them, this one was the toughest.

It was a Sunday morning when a silent burglary alarm came in for the George Elementary School located on Ecorse Road in Ypsilanti Township. The sheriff's patrol arrived moments ahead of me, radioing that he could see a lone male in the school. We assumed positions at opposite corners of the building to establish a perimeter.

Cisco and I were anxious to conduct a building search for the burglar, but we needed first to be relieved of our perimeter point. While I waited for the arrival of Trooper Wayne McAlpine, I put the back window of the dog wagon down just in case the burglar decided to make a run for it. About a block away, I could see the blue goose approaching to take our point.

Suddenly, the school's side door burst open and out sprinted a lean, nineteen-year-old male in what we called felony shoes (athletic) in full flight. Cisco barked with excitement, as if begging me to give him the green light to stop the suspect. I shouted toward the fleeing suspect, "Halt or I'll send the dog!" but I received no response. Fearing mayhem, I repeated my command, giving the suspect time to create more distance. Like spectators at a track meet, my warning only seemed to motivate him to run faster.

My command of "Stop him!" was like pushing the launch button on a heat-seeking missile. Out of the back window leaped eighty-five pounds of hell-bent German Shepherd. When his paws hit pavement, you could hear the scraping sound of toenails breaking traction. I chased after Cisco.

By now, I could see the suspect's plan to get onto an eight foot high fence before Cisco got to him. With Cisco not more than two steps behind, the suspect jumped high to the top bar of the chain length fence, followed by a furry missile crashing into it at full speed. When Cisco looked back at me, I could see swear words in his eyes. He was not the only one angry with my hesitancy to send him. It was now up to me.

As I neared the fence, Trooper McAlpine pulled up, yelling out the window to go ahead while he would secure Cisco. The obstacle course I would have to take was in a densely populated postage stamp lot subdivision where everybody had his little yard fenced.

Wearing the twenty-five pounds of gear of a modern day police officer, I leaped to the upper fence bar. Using those muscles earned in palm away pull-ups, I heaved myself over the first obstacle. As I landed, I got a flitting glimpse of my quarry jumping the four-foot fence at the back of the yard. I raced to that spot. I prayed someone would have a big mean dog in his backyard for my prey to feed, but that was not how it would evolve. So across that block, another street, and into more backyards we scrambled.

As my lungs gasped for air and I wondered whether I could continue, I remembered to assure myself that I was in better condition than the suspect, and if I were thinking of quitting, he was about to collapse. I could only hope!

As I rounded an unattached garage, there on the narrow path that separated it from the chain length fence, lay my quarry gasping. I, too, was in near respiratory arrest and was barely able to handcuff him. Once done, we both laid there like a couple of beached carp gasping for breath. This race had been won.

Trooper outruns burglary suspect

YPSILANTI — A state trooper won a half-mile footrace with a burglary suspect Sunday after an early-morning break-in at George School, 1076 Ecorse Road in Ypsilanti Township. Troopers from the Ypsilanti post of the Michigan State Police and deputies from the Washtenaw County Sheriff's went to the school after a burglar alarm was tripped at 7:30 a.m. As officers surrounded the school, Trooper Cliff Edwards saw someone run from the building. Edwards chased the suspect for nearly a half-mile through backyards and over fences before catching up with him in the 600 block of Kennedy Street. The suspect, identified only as a 19-year-old Ypsilanti Township resident, was held overnight in the county jail and was to be arraigned later today on a charge of breaking and entering.

Compliments of the *Ypsilanti Press*

59) Failure

One night, the post called me at home to inform me that my past partner, Joe Payne, was handling an armed robbery at a Wendy's Restaurant and was requesting Cisco's services. We raced to the scene. Joe had done a good job protecting the area where the suspect had last been seen and where we would try to begin our track—the door of the Wendy's restaurant. A lone robber armed with a shotgun had confronted the cashier and stolen money from not only the register, but also the safe, suggesting he had some inside information. The track was about forty-five minutes stale.

Cisco tracked west from the door, across the blacktop parking lot, and onto the grass shoulder on the south side of Ellsworth Road. He continued about one hundred yards and then crossed the road to the north shoulder where the track seemed to end. I attempted to get Cisco to restart the track several times and even cast the area for any track, but with nil results. I did not know what had happened; perhaps the suspect had been picked up by a car. Like nine out of ten tracks, we went home, knowing only the frustration of not solving the case.

What I did not know, I would learn a week later. Working the case, Joe had an informant contact him with details of the robbery. Those details named the suspect and explained how he had run west on Ellsworth Road from the scene and crossed the road into the stubble field to await pickup. From this vantage point, the suspect watched the police come, followed by the canine unit and then the track.

With intermittent lighting of streetlights and cars, the suspect watched the tracking dog and handler follow his escape route. As they crossed the road toward him, he readied the shotgun for service, determined that he was not going to jail. So he lay in wait, to do what he thought he must, but for some unknown reason, the canine team did not continue into the field.

Eventually, the handler and dog returned to their patrol car and drove away, allowing his pickup driver, who was in a holding pattern in the area, to make good his end of the bargain. Joe was able to charge the suspect, but he lost the case in trial.

On that day, I was saved by the 90 percent failure rate. This incident was my third "near hit" I knew of, and I wasn't out yet. My luck was holding.

60) Dilemma

Pam and I had purchased her parents' home in Livingston County, requiring me to commute some twenty-five miles to the Ypsilanti Post. When the dog handler position opened at Brighton, the closest post to our home, I transferred there. My boys' mother, Deb, had moved to Florida, making me our sons' primary custodian. The boys would spend most of the summer, Christmas, and Easter with their mother in Florida, but they were otherwise with Pam and me full-time.

Married just over two years, my relationship with Pam was already faltering. Looking back on the strain Pam endured as both a stepmother and wife to a dog handler, it was no wonder. In autumn, 1986, in a marriage saving attempt, I resigned from the canine team.

While Cisco was owned by the State of Michigan, it had been the practice of the department to retire the dog and sell it for a dollar to his handler. However, in my case I was approached by Sergeant Steve Rankins, the canine unit commander; he asked how I would feel about reassigning Cisco to Trooper Vic Martin, the dog handler at the Lansing Post, since his dog had just been retired for health reasons.

Cisco was in his prime, and I knew that if I were reincarnated as a dog, it would be my hope to be a police dog. I agreed with the caveat that when it came time for Cisco to retire, I would get him as a pet. A deal was struck and I was back to trooping out of the Brighton Post, absent the responsibilities of a dog handler.

My most constant companion for nearly four years was gone.

> *"Nothing is lost; everything is transformed."*
> — Antoine Lavoisier, founder of modern chemistry.

Cisco would serve the state another three years out of the Lansing Post as a part of K911. The department stood by its agreement, and when he was retired, Cisco was returned to me as my pet. Cisco and I often sat in front of the fireplace and talked of our adventures. Like always, he mostly listened. Cisco lived out his remaining years with me and my family.

Part G – Brighton Troop
(November 1986 to May 1987)

61) Dopers

The summer before my resignation from the canine unit, I trained six drug detector dogs at the state police academy in Lansing. I would commute to and from my home, being available at night for dog calls in my area of primary responsibility, the Brighton Post area.

July 9, 1986 / The State News

Four-legged cops

After checking out more than 100 dogs, Michigan State Police Sgt. Steve Rankens found six that had the qualities needed to become a state police narcotics dog.

Rankens and state trooper Cliff Edwards, who commutes from the Brighton post to help Rankens, work out of the State Police Training Academy just off U.S. 127, south of Lansing.

The troopers take the canines through a nine-week training program and then evaluate them to determine if the dogs can graduate into the field.

"We're training six dogs with hopes of graduating at least four," said Rankens, who has been on the canine training team for nine years.

The trainers look for dogs between the ages of 10 months and 3 years that are aggressive retrievers. Five out of the six dogs in the current class are labradors. Rankens said labradors tend to be better retrievers than German shepherds, which are primarily used for tracking and general purpose duties.

The dogs that pass the training then work with handlers who are troopers from various Michigan posts. The dogs that graduate from the current class will go to posts in Brighton, Flint, Grand Haven and St. Clair Shores.

With more emphasis being placed on stopping drug use and trafficking, the demand for narcotics dogs is on the rise, Rankens said.

The dogs are trained to sniff out marijuana, hashish, cocaine and heroin.

The towels are wrapped around a packet of marijuana dogs search out by scent when training.

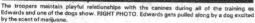
The troopers maintain playful relationships with the canines during all of the training as Edwards and one of the dogs show. RIGHT PHOTO. Edwards gets pulled along by a dog excited by the scent of marijuana.

Compliments of *The State News*

Back then, a patrol car was always refueled at a state police facility. That meant that when I drove home from Lansing, my dog wagon was not full of gas. One night, I responded to a couple of distant dog calls. Exhausted, I cheated and went home for a couple of hours of sleep instead of driving to the post to refuel. That morning, I woke with that rubber hammer look of sleep deprivation and began my hour drive to Lansing.

As I drove, my gas gauge fell to empty; I feared I would run out before making the next post.

I decided to buy gas with my own money, thinking five dollars worth should get me there. Still in a stupor, I pulled up to crowded gas pumps and got out, shutting my door. Did I just lock my keys in the patrol car? Yes, I had. My second pair, which I always carried in my pocket, still hung from the driver's sun visor.

Now I was wide awake! As I pumped my five dollars of gas, I brainstormed how I would get back into my patrol car. By now, a long line of cars were waiting their turns. As usual, the tailgate window of the dog wagon was down about two inches to provide Cisco with fresh air. I thought, "If I had a long light pole, I might be able to reach to the visor and hook the hanging keys." What I needed was a fishing rod!

As I scanned the parking lot, I noticed a man fueling his boat on a trailer. I hoped he was going fishing and would have the pole I needed. After paying my five dollars, I sauntered over to the man, who was preoccupied with the gas nozzle.

In an effort to paint this picture more vividly, I should share an affliction I then had. When I was sleep deprived, I suffered from dripping head sweats, and this day was no exception. Years later, I would learn they were compounded by a food allergy I had developed to donuts—a cop mainstay.

When I walked over to the boat owner, I startled him as I asked, "Sir, are you going fishing?" Turning his head, he saw a sweating state trooper with a barking dog in the background and responded, "Yes, do you need to see my fishing license?" "No, I need to borrow your longest fishing rod." I was glad he didn't dare question why as he quickly climbed aboard his boat and handed me one.

To add more attention to the situation, Cisco was being Cisco, barking at everyone who got near my car in this congested filling station. With all eyes on me, and almost able to hear the spectators saying, "Oh dear, what is he doing?" I walked to the rear of the dog wagon and began fishing the long pole through the two-inch window gap. After a few minutes, I was able to reach and hook the keys; now if I could only pull out the rod without dropping them. As I grasped the keys, I thought, "Yes!" Then I returned the rod, thanking the man without explanation, and quickly I looked away to avoid witnessing a smirk from him. I was glad to get out of there.

Training a drug detector dog is a much easier task than training a utility dog. First, start with a dog who is an obsessive retriever. Then reward him for finding the desired scent—drugs—by playing fetch. Certainly, there is more to it than that, but that's it in a nutshell.

During that summer, I realized I needed more human stimuli than what six obsessive retrievers could offer, so I decided not to pursue the full-time position of departmental dog trainer, which would be an assistant to the canine unit commander. At the completion of the training, I got the "pick of the litter." While all six dogs were very competent, I chose Goldie, a female yellow Labrador Retriever.

My resignation from the canine unit came before I had an opportunity to deploy Goldie on a real call. However, for a time after my resignation, Goldie remained kenneled at my home until it was decided to what handler she would be reassigned. During that time, opportunity came knocking.

Through an informant I had developed from a traffic violation, I learned of a person retailing marijuana—spelled m-a-r-i-h-u-a-n-a in Michigan's Compiled Law book—out of his house in the Lake Chemung area of Livingston County. Research indicated that I was not the first officer to uncover this information.

Using an informant for the umpteenth time, I did what Detective Sergeant John Flis had taught me in 1977—I arranged a controlled purchase of marijuana. Having made this play countless times while posted at Ypsilanti, it was my first at the Brighton Post.

The plan went like clockwork, which led to a search warrant being issued that resulted in a raid. The raid yielded an arrest of an adult repeat offender, along with seizure of cash, dope, and property.

Hopefully, the objective of all drug investigations is to identify and prosecute the highest level dealer possible. In debriefing the person arrested, we learned the name of his supplier, a new name in the "Who's Who among Livingston County Dope Dealers." The person arrested was willing to cooperate if we could accomplish a bust without him being directly involved since he hoped to avoid having to testify in court.

Gambling that word had not yet got out on the street, we had him telephone his supplier and order ten pounds of marijuana to be delivered that evening. Knowing the delivery vehicle description and predicting the route to the delivery point, we schemed to conduct what would appear to be a random highway drug interdiction.

Our information indicated that the contraband would be concealed in a plastic garbage bag in the pickup truck. Assuming we could articulate a bona fide violation for a traffic stop, we then would need to apply one of the ten exceptions to the search warrant rule to search for the contraband.

Having a drug detector dog along could be helpful, and while I was no longer officially a dog handler, I just happened to have one at home.

We laid in wait for the pickup truck to make its trek. My dog wagon had been turned in when I resigned from the canine unit, so my partner and I, along with K9 Goldie, utilized a conventional four door sedan patrol car. With slobber and hair mounting on our pressed uniforms, we waited patiently to be rewarded with the passing of the described vehicle. Fortunately, it was after dark and the pickup had a defective license plate light, which provided us with a bonafide reason to stop the vehicle—so far, so good.

With driver's license in hand and having explained the reason for the stop—a defective license plate light—we conducted a check of the required safety equipment on the vehicle. What I had done routinely as a service trooper on the Vehicle-Driver Check Lanes remained a valuable ploy for spending more time with a vehicle and occupants in hopes of detecting indicators of criminality afoot. Walking around a vehicle to check tires, lights, and wipers affords the officer a chance to peer into the vehicle from different angles. Contraband that might be concealed from the driver's side of a vehicle may be in plain view from a different angle, and "plain view" is one of the ten exceptions to the search warrant rule.

During this inspection, I observed the garbage bag in the pickup bed, which among other things, corroborated my informant's information. But this was information I preferred not to reveal to the suspect at that time.

Another exception to the search warrant rule is a "consent" search, as long as it is not coerced. While this exception is probably the most frequently used, I chose not to request it in this case.

So while my partner, via radio, checked the license and warrant status of the driver, I had Goldie sniff around the outside of the pickup truck. As hoped, she indicated the presence of drugs in the bed area of the pickup.

Drug detector dogs are trained to indicate drugs primarily one of two ways: either by sitting, termed a passive indication, or trying to get to the scent's source, called an aggressive indication. At that time, MSP was training the latter.

This method tends to excite the dog more, but the handler must prevent the dog from causing damage to property, evidence, or exposing itself to a dangerous substance. Explosive dogs are trained to sit for obvious reasons.

Another exception to the search warrant rule is "probable cause and exigent circumstances." Case law says that the mobility of vehicles usually makes them exigent, and our information, corroborated by Goldie's indication of drugs, arguably met the threshold of probable cause. So we legally searched, and BINGO!—we found ten pounds of marijuana in the garbage bag.

We had made the second rung of the ladder, but this guy did not cooperate, so we could not make the third. I do not remember whether we followed-up by applying for a search warrant for his house. We should have, and I think I would remember if a seizure were made.

We will never win the war on illegal drugs or crime for that matter. Many people argue that drugs are a victimless crime so they should be legalized, but I know of few families that have not been, at least indirectly, victimized by them. I know my extended family has. Some think we should only target the high level dealers, but no one wants a retail drug house in the neighborhood because they tend to draw trouble. I anticipate that we will continue to wage war on the illegal drug trade, but we should have no illusions of winning. This war is waged on many fronts, and aggressive uniform patrol is an important one. Like a padlock on a door, our efforts keep the honest person honest.

While a drug, marihuana is not a narcotic. Undoubtedly, society would be better without marihuana. The same can be said for alcohol and tobacco, but getting rid of them just isn't going to happen. Today, it appears we are on the path of decriminalizing marijuana, but we need to figure out a way to regulate and tax it.

The canine unit commander was not pleased with my initiative, thinking I should have requested a drug detector dog and handler through channels. As the saying goes, it's better to beg for forgiveness than ask for permission.

Goldie was reassigned to Trooper Jack Peet. Jack and I had graduated from the same trooper school and canine school. As you can see from the article titled *Dog sniffs airline's baggage*, Goldie was a great service to the state.

Dog sniffs airline's baggage, finds $11 million in cocaine

By Scott Faust
News Staff Writer

Goldie, the drug-sniffing police dog, and a nosy United Airlines ticket agent teamed up Wednesday for an $11 million cocaine bust at Capital City Airport in Lansing.

Officers arrested three suspects after the state police narcotics dog discovered about 30 pounds of cocaine in two suitcases arriving from Los Angeles through Chicago at 8:45 a.m.

The cocaine arrests followed an early morning tip to Los Angeles police from a United ticket agent, who reportedly became suspicious of a man who paid cash for a round-trip flight between Los Angeles and Lansing with only a three-hour layover in Michigan.

Los Angeles police contacted the tri-county metro narcotics squad in Lansing, and Goldie went into action. The bust was the drug unit's biggest ever, a squad member said, but only one of dozens for Goldie in her first year on the job.

"I'M PRETTY pleased for her," said Jackson state police Trooper Jack Peet, who handles the 3-year-old golden retriever. "It's a good knock-off for everybody as far as I'm concerned. It feels good to get something like that."

Goldie's reward: praise, play and two McDonald's hamburgers.

"She gets praised as much if she finds a single joint of marijuana or finds as much drugs as she did today," Peet said.

Plainclothes officers arrested the cocaine suspects outside the Lansing airport, as the suspicious passenger — a Los Angeles man — began to drive away in a 1984 Cadillac with a Bridgetown woman and a Saginaw man.

The three are held in the Clinton County Jail pending arraignment today in 65th District Court, said Detective Lt. Gene Wriggelsworth, field supervisor of the tri-county drug squad.

Please see **Bust/4B**

Compliments of *Lansing News*

62) Burglars

The transition to trooping without a dog was seamless. In fact, Pam commented to the post commander at the Christmas party that I seemed as busy without a dog as with a dog. Being in Livingston County, the fastest growing county in Michigan at the time, Brighton was a busy post. However, it did not suffer from the violent crime prevalent in the Ypsilanti Post area.

As I mentioned before, the ability to cultivate and utilize informants effectively should be an objective of all officers, along with the skills to draft search warrants. The majority of my informants were generated from mere traffic violations or shoplifting cases. I did not enjoy shoplifter calls until I learned their potential for providing valuable intelligence.

During this time, an informant told me of the burglary of an electronics store in the Alpena area and that the perpetrators were Brighton residents. I telephoned the Alpena Post and contacted Trooper Sam Boyer who confirmed the occurrence of the burglary and sent me a list of the stolen property. In checking one of the suspects' backgrounds, I learned the description of the vehicle he drove and that his driver's license was suspended. When time permitted, I patrolled the vicinity of his residence to watch for him.

It wasn't long before I observed him driving the described vehicle with a visual obstruction, i.e. a dangling object from the mirror, which is a violation of the Michigan vehicle code. When I made a patrol stop, I saw that he had a radar detector and stereo speakers matching some of the items on the list of stolen property provided by Trooper Boyer. When I asked him where he got the radar detector, he said that Mary, his girlfriend, had given it to him. I arrested him for driving while his license was suspended; then I searched and handcuffed him and placed him in my patrol car.

State police cars do not have prisoner cages. Supposedly, the reason is that during mobilizations, three troopers are assigned to a car, and a cage would lock the third trooper in the backseat. Personally, I suspect it has something to do with budget.

While I searched the suspect's car and tried to keep an eye on him in the patrol car, his girlfriend showed up. When I asked her where her boyfriend got the radar detector, she said she didn't know. As I continued searching his car, a passing motorist stopped alongside and honked her horn. I thought, *"Can't she see I'm busy?"* as I turned to her and said, "May I help you?" She said, "No, but you might be interested to know that a handcuffed person has just run from the patrol car." Things were getting embarrassing.

I locked the suspect's car and my patrol car, so things didn't go from bad to worse. Then I ran in the direction the citizen had pointed. Behind a business under construction, I came across several laborers who confirmed a handcuffed male had just run by. I asked them to watch the adjacent field and rushed back to my patrol car, prematurely I might add, to radio for assistance.

I say prematurely because when I returned to the construction workers, I found they had captured the suspect for me. My radio broadcast made it too late to conceal my goof-up. For days to come, my colleagues would enjoy reminding me of it, but I was glad it didn't make the newspaper.

After taking the suspect to the post, I got a confession that incriminated him and his partners and led to the recovery of nearly all the stolen property. Trooper Boyer obtained burglary warrants in Alpena and picked up the suspects in the Livingston County Jail.

Robbery trial slated

By NICOLE ROBERTSON

Three Brighton residents were recently arrested and charged in Alpena for breaking into an electronics store and cleaning it out one night in October.

The men, 21-year-old Robert Thomas Sloan of 1049 Hillcrest Drive, David Jonathon Price, 20, of 7727 Price Drive and Jeffrey Allen Carpenter, 17, of 2081 Euler Road, were transported to Alpena for trial on charges of breaking and entering a business. Sloan and Price were also charged with probation violation.

They were taken to Alpena by state police troopers and arraigned Nov. 1. Bond was set at $10,000 or 10 percent.

State police of the Brighton post received a confidential telephone call advising them of a burglary at the Energy and Electronics Store, 1402 State St., Alpena. Numerous pieces of stereo, television and video equipment were taken as well as $500 cash and a rifle.

Police followed a trail of electronic equipment which matched the descriptions of items taken in the theft. Some had been sold by the suspects to area residents, other pieces were installed in the suspects' vehicles. Suspects were interviewed one by one until all corroborated the story police used as evidence against them.

Five Brighton residents said they had gone to Alpena to stay in a cabin on Lake Huron for four days, and had been driving around Alpena while high on drugs prior to the burglary.

One broke his radio, they said, and when the others complained they had no music, he suggested they get a new one. They said they found the electronics store, and the three suspects broke the windows, went inside and took several items.

Compliments of *Livingston Daily*

Informants are frustrating. My experience is that only about one in ten produces information that leads to anything tangible. But that 10 percent will probably yield 10 percent of all the felony arrests an officer makes, and it often solve crimes that otherwise wouldn't be. The article titled "Court hears of break-ins" is yet another example from the same time period where an informant provided the spark to solving a case.

Court hears of break-ins

3/4/87

By NICOLE ROBERTSON

One of four men charged with breaking into four Brighton Township businesses a year ago has pleaded guilty to one count of breaking and entering in exchange for the dismissal of the other three charges.

The other three have waived circuit court arraignments, but trial dates have not been set.

Two of the suspects, 18-year-old Duane Delbert Moffatt, 6274 Shady Lane, and Thaddeus Louis Bickman, 23, 6185 Coventry, are from Brighton. The other men are Trenton residents Sean Robert Matich, 18, 24110 Crescent, and Casimir Zane Rhinehart, 22, of 19612 S. Grand Blvd.

The men were charged with four counts each of breaking and entering for allegedly burglarizing four stores adjoined in a strip mall on Grand River Avenue at the corner of Old US. 23, across from the old state police post.

Michigan State Police said the four broke into Evie's Dog Depot, Front Row Video, Faletti's Pizzeria and American Home Satellite on Feb. 13, 1986.

Rhinehart, incarcerated at Scott Correctional Facility in Plymouth, pleaded guilty to breaking into Faletti's Pizzeria in exchange for dismissal of the other three pending matters. His sentencing is set for April 6.

State trooper Cliff Edwards of the Brighton post said thieves broke into the Dog Depot to gain access to the adjoining video shop, but after tearing through wall covering discovered the two businesses were separated by a cement wall and another entry point was sought.

More than $4,750 worth of video equipment was taken from Faletti's Pizza and the video shop, police said. More VCR equipment and video tapes were taken from American Home Satellite, located next door.

Police were unable to recover the stolen property. Edwards said he believes the equipment has been sold through to a stolen goods trafficker operating downriver.

The four were arrested in February.

Edwards said he first received information about the crime in September, but wasn't able to build a case against the four suspects until November.

Interviews with the two Brighton residents incriminated the other two, leading to the arrests, Edwards said.

Bonds were set at a total of $40,000 personal recognizance for Moffatt and Bickman, but for Matich, bond was set at $5,000 cash or surety for each of the four counts of breaking and entering.

Police requested a high bond because animal control had to be called in to assist in Matich's arrest when he used a German shepherd guard dog to threaten arresting officers, police said.

Police said Bickman and Rhinehart met while they were cellmates in the Wayne County Jail. They told troopers that when they were released, they agreed to get together socially, and after a night of drinking with the other two friends, they allegedly decided to break into the businesses.

Compliments of *Livingston Daily*

63) Debtor

No longer having dog handler status, I now had to bid by seniority for my shift of preference. I found myself on midnights by default. During this time, I was competing in triathlons and had purchased a wind trainer to enable me to maintain bicycle fitness during the winter months. I was dissatisfied with the wind trainer and was preparing to mail it back for a refund when my midnight shift partner said he would like it. He agreed to have me paid by the time my credit card bill came due at the end of the month.

During our partnership, we responded to an armed robbery of a Domino Pizza employee. The incident occurred when the employee was making a 2:00 a.m. deposit of cash at the bank drop box. The pistol brandishing suspect was described as a white male, concealing facial features with a red bandanna, and fleeing the scene on foot. It had been a long time since I'd had to request a tracking dog.

Two men charged in robbery

2/16/87

Two Livingston County men were charged last week with holding up a Domino's employee making a night deposit by intimidating her with a BB gun.

State police said 22-year-old Kenneth Denbraven of 1562 Hughes Road, Brighton, and 17-year-old George William Davies were identified as suspects in the late-night armed robbery in Brighton Township Feb. 16.

They were arraigned in District Court before Judge Frank Del Vero and bond was set at $50,000 cash for each. Preliminary examinations were set for today.

The robbery occurred at about 2 a.m. Monday while the pizzeria manager was depositing money at the Citizens Trust bank, near Domino's. The victim said the man who took the money was wearing a red bandana.

A state police canine tracking unit followed a scent from the scene of the holdup to the parking lot of Alpine Heating in Brighton Township, where the scent disappeared. Police assumed the suspect had gotten into a car at that point.

Trooper Cliff Edwards of the Brighton post said a security guard at Cars & Concepts had observed a car parked with the motor running at Alpine Heating.

"I guess I was in the right place at the right time," said 26-year-old Brighton resident Robert Triffo, security sergeant for Cars & Concepts. He said he became suspicious when he saw the car driving out of the parking lot with its lights off, so he got the license-plate number of the car and notified police.

Police spent the day staked out at a place informants had said the suspects might be found, but had no luck until the next morning, when the car was finally stopped with both suspects inside. They were taken to the Livingston County Jail and arraigned the same day.

Police said they had confiscated a BB pistol, a sum of money and a tennis shoe which appeared to match footprints at the scene. Brighton city police assisted in the arrest, according to Chief Jack Taylor.

Prosecutors said there is no difference under the law whether a holdup is committed with a toy pistol or a real gun.

Compliments of *Livingston Daily*

The canine team tracked the suspect to the parking lot of a nearby business where the track ended. We surmised the suspect probably got in a car with a getaway driver. Fortunately, an alert security guard from a nearby manufacturer had earlier seen what he thought was a suspicious vehicle parked where the track had ended, so he had jotted down the license plate number.

Information from the license plate, again combined with informant intelligence, provided us with the suspects' names and where we might find them. We staked out that location, and when they left the next morning, we stopped and arrested them. The pistol, which turned out to be a BB gun, money, and other evidence was recovered.

When my credit card bill arrived for the wind trainer, I was no longer working with that trooper. He remained on the midnight shift while I had moved to the dayshift. The way our shifts were, I would not actually see him, so I left him notes to pay me for the wind trainer. While he said he did not have the money to pay me, I noticed he had purchased a new rechargeable flashlight that cost about the same amount of money as he owed me. When he was not working, the flashlight sat in its charger at the Brighton Post. It occurred to me that his new flashlight could serve as a hostage!

One day when I went off duty at 4:00 p.m., I took his flashlight, leaving in the charger a note that said when he paid me the money owed, I would return the flashlight. When he came on duty at midnight, he undoubtedly found my note in place of his flashlight.

That night, I dreamed the state police came banging on my door with this trooper threatening to get a search warrant for his flashlight if I didn't return it. When I reported for work the next day, Lieutenant William Pertner, the post commander, called me into his office and presented me with a personal check from the trooper in question and said, "Now give him his dang flashlight." Having occasionally to play dad for troopers is probably why we referred to post commanders as the "old man."

64) Crashes

```
1st/Lt. William J. Pertner                    March 9, 1987
Brighton State Police Post
4803 Old US-23
Brighton, MI 48116

Dear Lt. Pertner:

Please accept this letter on behalf of the outstanding performance of Officer
Clifton Edwards (Badge No. 854) for his assistance at an auto accident on November
11, 1986 at approximately 12:50 p.m. on US-23.

I suffered severe injuries from the accident.  Officer Edwards was extremely
skilled in handling the accident and in administering first aid at the scene.
I want to commend him for his services.  Because of the type of work police
officers are required to perform, they very seldom hear praise for the many
good deeds they do.  They are taken for granted.

Thanks again for a job well done above the call of duty!

Sincerely,
```

Thank-you letters are the best rewards.

In the twentieth century, we called them accidents, but now in the twenty-first century, we more appropriately refer to accidents as crashes. The word "accident" suggests something unavoidable while the word "crash" is more neutral.

Perhaps I have not proportionately described the number of personal injuries and fatal crashes that are part of an officer's career. Undoubtedly, my predecessors were exposed to more when cars were less safe, use of seatbelts was uncommon, drinking and driving was more prevalent, and speed limits were higher.

Crashes are the venue where you most often practice your first aid skills, and during this era, many personal protective gear items were unheard of, such as latex gloves, rescue breathing masks, and hepatitis B vaccinations. As troubling as the mayhem can be, so are the circumstances leading to the tragedy—especially when they involve the innocent victim. Crashes often stain the prism from which the officer witnesses the fragility of life.

If you plan to become a police officer, take pause and listen to what I have to say. It seems more and more police officers are getting maimed or killed in patrol car crashes. And what is worse than that is when the officer's actions result in an innocent person getting maimed or killed. I ask myself why this is happening? Training has gotten better and cars are safer, but cars have also gotten faster and there are more distractions, like onboard computers and cell phones. What hasn't changed is the heart of the risk-taker, which law enforcement attracts and needs. I truly wish I knew where the fulcrum point was for how fast to go. But as time goes by, you learn that bad things happen to good people. To live with being the catalyst to the bad thing—well, by luck, that is a burden I have been able to dodge. Whenever possible, try not to rely on luck.

My time being a trooper at the Brighton Post would be short because again I was offered, and this time accepted, promotion to sergeant at the Detroit Post. While not superstitious, over the past eleven years, Trooper Badge 854 had shielded me from harm. I felt some trepidation when I exchanged it for Sergeant Badge 400.

Part H – Sergeant

(May 1987 to May 1989)

65) Promotion

It was May 1987 when I accepted the second offer of promotion to sergeant at the Detroit Post. While I had long aspired to be a detective sergeant, I had come to recognize that "without an uncle in the furniture business," I would first have to serve as a desk sergeant. I vowed to myself only to do so for two years. If by then I had not obtained a detective sergeant position, I would demote back to a trooper. Little did I know the valuable experiences of supervision and post operations I would gain while a desk sergeant.

It was about an hour commute from our home to the Detroit Post, which was located on the bottom floor of the state plaza building on Howard Street, just off the Lodge Freeway. This promotion would mark the beginning of what, to date, would be the darkest days of my life.

My resignation from the canine team had not remedied the marital problems Pam and I were struggling with. Pam had tried to embrace being a step-parent, but it simply was not in her heart. With Deb living in Florida, Pam had little relief during the school year. When Deb notified us that she would soon be moving back from Florida, I was hopeful. I knew

Deb's move back to the area would offer Pam relief from the 24/7 step-mother role she had assumed. But it turned out to "be a bridge too far," so we separated prior to Deb's return. Perhaps a case of too little too late, or maybe it was never meant to be. The pain of this separation was immense, but I was committed to my tenet that I may have ex-wives but not ex-kids.

The Detroit Post was the largest post in Michigan with over one hundred personnel and the only post where the state police served only as a highway patrol. I was one of two sergeants assigned to day shift.

The day shift troopers entered the ditches (trooper slang for freeways) in two waves; one at 6:00 a.m. and the other at 7:00 a.m. One sergeant started at 5:45 a.m., to prepare for and provide a formal briefing to each wave of troopers before they went on patrol. Working eight-hour shifts, the later sergeant would oversee the troopers to the end of their shift, with the baton being passed to the afternoon crew at 3:00 p.m.

Both sergeants were primarily assigned to the office, rarely getting out on patrol. They supervised the freeway patrol, dispatch center, desk operations, report/citation review and a myriad of other duties. We were very busy. Soon after promotion, I was cycled through the training academy for a variety of sergeant training.

In my view, the Detroit experience had a negative impact on the troopers. Here, I would first experience what Sergeant Lyle Schroeder had once told me, "You don't know what kind of an asshole a trooper can be until you become a sergeant." I am sure he wasn't referring to me when he shared that.

When I perused the arrest book at the Detroit Post, I was shocked by how few felony arrests had been made in such a high crime environment with so many troopers. Perhaps the Detroit trooper adage of being "AAA with a gun" was heartfelt, meaning Detroit troopers tended only to assist motorists (like a AAA wrecker does) while overlooking crime. This was not the nature of any trooper I had ever known, and I wondered how a trooper's appetite to hunt criminals could have been curbed. The pattern of a newly assigned trooper making several felony arrests and then tapering off to near none seemed common.

Eventually, I began to recognize the catalyst to this low productivity among my troopers. Not only did a trooper have to do an MSP report on a felony arrest, but he also had to do a Detroit Police Department (DPD) report and then turn the case over to a DPD detective for prosecution. Many of the DPD officers resented MSP taking over their freeways so attitudes were terse and DPD detectives often did not pursue prosecution on MSP cases.

Rumors existed that troopers regularly dumped the contraband they seized in the sewer and gave felony warnings, something I had never known troopers to do. The hours of paperwork that would follow any arrest or "official" seizure of contraband kept them off the street, and these efforts were too often for naught.

By now, the Detroit Freeway Post had been in existence for over ten years, and yet command had failed to create an efficient and effective work environment. In fairness to command, I must add that much of this was out of their control because of the strained relations between D.P.D. and M.S.P. and the system we had entered.

66) Depression

By June, it became apparent that divorce was imminent for Pam and me. I would be the one to move out since the land contract was held by Pam's parents, and they did not want to lose what previously was their lakefront home. After some dickering, they paid me my fair share for my financial interest in the house.

It was during this time that my parents, after thirty-some years of marriage, also divorced. They had succeeded in not only raising their three kids but creating a very successful business. I rented the basement of my mother's house that summer while I tried to find direction. When Deb returned to Michigan and I told her of my situation, she shed tears. I needed to decide where I was going to settle with the boys, but I couldn't.

With the new job, moving, and the boys, I was very busy and very sad. The only time to mourn was during my now ninety-minute one-way commute and in my dreams.

On July 10, 1987, I sadly drove to court to file for divorce. I turned on the radio to divert my attention, only to learn that three Inkster police officers had been murdered that morning while serving a minor arrest warrant. Inkster was part of the Ypsilanti Post's area where I had served for eight years, and while I did not personally know these officers, I knew of them. Detective Lieutenant Thomas Finco and his team of detectives from the Ypsilanti Post were conducting the murder investigation. I wept.

67) Catastrophe

Eric, my youngest son, celebrated his eighth birthday on August 16, 1987 during my long weekend. That morning, my sister Zonya, my brother Mark, and I competed in a team triathlon in Sylvania, Ohio. Zonya swam, Mark biked, and I ran, and we were proud to be awarded medals. I picked the boys up from their mother's that afternoon and celebrated Eric's birthday with my family at Mom's.

While I was having a great day, that evening Northwest Airlines flight 255 crashed just after take-off from Detroit Metropolitan airport, killing one hundred fifty-six souls. Miraculously, an infant was the sole survivor.

This catastrophe was unknown to me when I went to bed that evening. About 2:00 a.m., I answered a ringing phone. It was the Detroit Post, briefing me on the plane crash and ordering me to work ASAP. I raced the normal ninety-minute drive, but found I-94 blocked at I-275 because of the plane crash, so I took an alternate route.

Upon arrival, I was assigned a squad of troopers to relieve the first wave of troopers providing scene security on I-94, where debris and bodies were spread on and across both sides of the freeway. Our task was to bar all persons—press, curiosity seekers, and thieves alike.

We arrived in the melting darkness to see the ground littered with yellow emergency blankets covering over a hundred bodies. It reminded me of, as a boy, dumping a cardboard shoebox full of plastic toy army men on the floor. It was both eerie and surreal.

We guarded these fallen souls from both human and animal scavengers while teams were being assembled to process and then remove each of them to a temporary morgue for autopsies, followed by release of their remains to family. A few intruders attempted to penetrate the perimeter but none were successful. That afternoon, my squad was relieved by night shift troopers. Following them came the mass casualty teams, and in my absence, the gruesome task of recovery was completed. I felt so fortunate not to have been part of the team that recovered those bodies, one by one. In many ways, the people on those teams are unsung heroes who will be haunted by this deed for the remainder of their time on this earth.

Later in my career when I became a detective sergeant, I received mass casualty training. I am glad I never had to use it.

68) Epiphany

As the end of the summer approached, I needed to establish residency within the Dexter Community Schools District since that is where the boys had been attending school. So, I rented a small cottage on Pierce Lake, southwest of Dexter.

Because I left for work so early, I hired the neighbor lady to come over to the house and get the boys up and off to school when I left. Years later, I would have contact with her and her husband in the Norvell area while investigating information that they were harboring a fugitive. I learned that her husband had pending charges for drug trafficking. Close call!

My boys were now in second and fourth grades. As the cool nights of autumn arrived and the smelly furnace strained to keep the small cottage warm, I realized that this place wasn't going to work.

Then I had an epiphany—I decided to move back to the Irish Hills and build a house. There I would have the assistance of the boys' maternal and paternal grandparents. This lure of home had also brought my brother and his family back to Michigan where he was now a successful contractor. I bought a lakefront lot and contracted my brother's company, Irish Hills Construction, to build our new home.

A widow friend of my mom's lived in a large house nearby, so I rented living space from her while our new home was built. I transferred the boys to Onsted Community Schools, the same school their mother and I had graduated from.

During this chapter of my life, I started work at the Detroit Post at 5:45 a.m. That meant I woke at 3:30 a.m., to leave the house by 4:00 a.m., in order to arrive at the post and change into uniform by 5:30 a.m. I hired a high school senior to overnight at the house and get the boys up and on the bus in the morning.

I departed work at 1:45 p.m. and drove home to greet the boys when they got off the bus. We played, did homework, fixed dinner, and then it was off to bed by 8:30 p.m.—me too, for sleep always seemed short. The next day, we would start it all over again. On my days off or when the boys were with Deb, I worked on our new home, playing carpenter alongside my brother.

One day, I had just finished the 7:00 a.m. briefing at the Detroit Post when I received a telephone call from the babysitter; she said Eric was sick and could not go to school. Fortunately, my dad was able to relieve the babysitter, so she could go to school, while I drove the hour-and-a-half back home.

After getting home, I sat rocking my sick son while looking out over the lake. It was one of those warm, fuzzy moments cherished by parents. As I gazed outside, a large hawk entered my field of vision, hovering over the water. Suddenly, it dove into the lake, nearly submerging itself; then it flapped its wings, struggling to get airborne with a fish in its talons. It landed in a nearby tree, where I witnessed the fish being devoured, piece-by-piece.

I learned that the hawk was an Osprey. In that moment, I felt a kinship to this raptor and adopted it as my totem. When our new home was done, I christened it Osprey Point.

I now had a working plan, but I was struggling with the long commute to Detroit. While it is rare to get out of a Detroit Post assignment in less than two years, I was able to pull off a transfer to the Jonesville Post within six months. Jonesville, in contrast to Detroit, is a small rural post. I was assigned to the midnight shift there, which allowed me to help my brother more with building my house during the day and still be a father to my boys in the evening. My commute was reduced by over half. The only thing still missing was sleep time.

69) Transfer

Local Notes
Edwards joins post

JONESVILLE — The Jonesville post of the Michigan State Police had a new sergeant on board effective Nov. 1.

Sgt. Cliff Edwards comes to Jonesville from the Detroit post of the state police. He was promoted May 17.

Edwards joined the state police Aug. 12, 1974, as a service trooper in Jackson. He became a trooper Sept. 17, 1976, and has since served at posts in Brighton, Ypsilanti and Romeo. During his tenure as a trooper, Edwards was a dog handler for four years.

Sgt. Cliff Edwards

Originally from the Onsted area, Edwards has returned there with his two sons, ages 8 and 10.

Compliments of *Hillsdale Daily News*

The Jonesville Post consisted of a post commander, three sergeants, and if I remember correctly, eight troopers. The post area entails Hillsdale County with a population estimated at less than 50,000. While the post was open 24/7 and manned by an officer, this staffing level sometimes created a gap in the schedule when there was no patrol.

I reported to the Jonesville Post in early November 1987, and after a few days of orientation, I assumed responsibility for the midnight shift. With few exceptions, it would be a long slow night with administrative duties being completed within a couple of hours. I suppose I was being paid for what I could do, not what I was doing.

70) Smugglers

When I reported for duty on November 14, 1987, the afternoon shift sergeant, Bill Hendrick, briefed me on a suspicious situation that Troopers Stuck and Colson had handled. The manager at the Hillsdale County Airport had reported that a chartered Piper airplane from Virginia, piloted by a female, had landed with two passengers, both white males in their twenties. The airport manager had been told by her attendant, a sixteen-year-old boy, that he had observed one of the male passengers with a pistol beneath his jacket. He described it as looking like a .45 and in a shoulder holster. The manager overheard the passengers invite the pilot to a party, but she declined and asked to be taken to a motel in Hillsdale since she would be flying them back to Virginia the next day. The pilot and her two passengers were transported from the airport by a Hillsdale resident.

The totality of these circumstances was very suspicious. During that time, permits to carry a concealed pistol were very rare and were usually state specific. Were these men assassins, law enforcement, drug dealers, or what? It reminded me of the lyrics from the song "Smuggler's Blues" by Glenn Frey. I spent much of that midnight shift developing information on the pilot, the aircraft, and the person who had picked them up. The identity of the two passengers remained a mystery. Checks at the address of the Hillsdale resident were nil since the vehicle in question was not there, and no one appeared to be home.

When 8:00 a.m. came, I briefed the dayshift sergeant, Curt Robertson, and the post commander on this case. It was decided to authorize overtime for me to pursue the investigation during the day. Excitement overcame my midnight shift fatigue and I teamed up with Louis Frizzell, a senior trooper nearing retirement.

Trooper Frizzell and I went to the airport to interview the manager and check the aircraft, while Sergeant Robertson tried to locate the sixteen-year-old attendant by telephone. We confirmed that the aircraft was still tethered at the airport, and we obtained detailed descriptions of the four persons in question.

Ironically, the sixteen-year-old boy turned out to be the son of Rebecca, the ex-wife of Trooper Doug Halleck. You may remember that Doug and I had attended the academy together, and when we were service troopers, went on motorcycle trips together with our wives. Rebecca was now married to the man with whom she had been having an affair while Doug was in the academy and they shared this son. Rumor had it that Rebecca's husband was a doctor of some sort at Wayne State University.

In the aftermath of this case, I obtained a departmental citizen's award for the information her son had provided. Little did I know that in a couple of years, I would be arresting Rebecca and her husband, whose doctor status was a fiction, on a complex white collar crime which would land them in prison.

Hillsdale only had a few motels so we soon determined the pilot was registered in room #25 of the Hillsdale Motel. In the room next to her was registered a Matt Walker, who had a Virginia address. The clerk told us that Walker had not checked in until 3:15 that morning. We suspected he was one of the mystery passengers.

Not knowing whether the pilot was involved in the suspected criminality afoot, we staked-out her room in plain sight with a ruse, appearing to run radar for speeders in front of the motel. At about 10:20 a.m., a taxi stopped in front of room #25 and a person matching the pilot's description entered it. We followed the taxi away from the motel before pulling it over under the guise of a traffic stop.

When we interviewed the pilot, we found her both cooperative and seemingly credible. She informed us that one of the passengers had a pistol, but he had told her he was a police officer. She gave us her consent, one of the ten exceptions to the search warrant rule, to search her aircraft. When we did, we found no contraband. I later arranged for my former drug dog, Goldie, and her handler to check the plane. They detected no drugs.

We returned to the Hillsdale Motel just in time to see a jogger, matching the description of the person with the pistol, running toward the motel. We waited until we saw him run toward room #24. As he placed his hand on the door handle, we pulled up and honked our horn. Not knowing whether he might be armed, we ordered him to put his hands on his head and frisked him for weapons, finding none. We asked him whether he was a police officer. He replied, "No." He told us his name was Matthew Walker, which we later confirmed.

We then practiced the art of "knock & talk," a communication technique in which all officers should seek to be competent. In doing so, we told him we had information that he had a gun, and we asked whether he had a permit for it. He stated he did not. When we asked where the gun was, he said it was in his room.

In his sweatsuit pocket, we found the key for room #24, and when we requested it, he provided us written permission to search the room. Had he denied us consent, I think we could have drafted a search warrant worthy of issuance. We cautiously entered the room.

While Trooper Frizzell monitored the suspect, I first made certain no one else was in the room. When we asked the suspect where the pistol was, he nodded toward the nightstand. I checked the top drawer, a place you usually find a Gideon's Bible, and discovered a nine millimeter Taurus pistol, loaded with thirteen rounds.

I checked the pockets of a leather jacket and frosted blue jeans lying crumbled on the floor; I found them stuffed with cash and plastic baggies appearing to contain cocaine.

The suspect, glancing at the door, appeared to be getting increasingly anxious, so we blocked any flight temptations he might have had by my verbally placing him under arrest and handcuffing him.

The cash in Walker's pants totaled $4,007.00 and the quantity of cocaine was over fifty grams. The denominations of the cash in his jeans suggested they were payments from several retail level drug deals. Walker claimed the cash, but he disowned the gun and coke. When we asked where his partner was, he told us he was supposed to pick him up around noon.

Trooper Frizzell hid the patrol car around the block, and then the three of us made ourselves comfortable in his motel room. At 12:10 p.m., we heard knocks on the door, pretty punctual for a doper, but he and his associate did have a plane to catch. We instructed our host to say, "Come on in." As the visitor entered the room, he was surprised by his greeting party.

A search of this suspect yielded only a little bit of compressed marijuana and a small vial containing suspected cocaine. We learned his name was Anthony Crego and that he was originally from the Jackson, Michigan area but now living in Virginia.

While keeping the two suspects separated, we had them transported to the Jonesville Post where we interviewed the new arrival. While he agreed to be interviewed, he revealed nothing new.

Having completed our investigation, we felt the charter pilot was not knowingly involved in the drug smuggling, so no legal action was taken against her or forfeiture proceedings initiated for the airplane.

At this time, my old partner, Joe Payne, was now a detective lieutenant and running a drug team out of Lansing. This case garnered his attention so he paid me a visit, gladly taking possession of the forfeited money. Had we kept it at the Jonesville Post, the funds would have eventually gone into the state's general fund, but by turning it over to a drug specific team, it could be used directly to supplement that team's budget. Joe relayed our case information to the Virginia authorities for further investigation.

While not very much cocaine by metropolitan standards, Hillsdale is very rural and off the beaten path. Rumor was this case was the largest cocaine bust in the history of Hillsdale County, where little cocaine had ever been seized. But even then, it does seem like a lot of overhead for the amount of cocaine and money we seized. I pondered how much cocaine had actually been delivered, the payment sent by another means. We will never know. As I recall, the defendants were allowed to plead guilty to a greatly reduced charge and served only county jail time.

Two arrested, charged

11/16/87

A former Hillsdale resident and a man from Virginia were arrested Saturday by Jonesville state troopers on several charges stemming from cocaine possession, according to Michigan State Police Sgt. Curt Robertson.

Anthony W. Crego, 21, now of Pleasant Lake, Mich., was arrested for possession of marijuana and cocaine. Matthew M. Walker, 22, Sterling, Va., was charged with possession of cocaine, carrying a concealed weapon, and possession of a firearm in committing a felony.

According to Robertson, Walker had three ounces of cocaine in his possession.

The police were alerted to the arrival of the pair at the Hillsdale airport Friday evening which lead to an investigation and arrest the next morning.

Crego is being held on $22,000 bond and Walker on $50,000 cash bond and 10 percent of $40,000 bond. Neither man has been released.

Compliments of the *Hillsdale Daily*

71) Redemption

In February 1988, the big day came when my new home under construction was issued an occupancy permit. Making it even more memorable was the failure of the furnace that first night. On our first morning, my boys and I stayed warm by burning 2 x 4 stubs in the wood burner while waiting for the school bus. While many projects awaited me before I could call this house done, here is where I would raise my boys. The darkest days were now behind me.

Deb and I had stayed true to our agreement always to put the boys' best interests first and never to badmouth each other in their presence. I believe this behavior is a key ingredient for rearing children successfully in a divorce situation. In time, Deb moved to the same neighborhood as me and the boys rode the same school bus to either house.

In that same vein, Deb and I attended parent-teacher conferences together. On the way to one of the conferences, Deb told me about Kim, a single, second grade teacher, with whom Deb thought I would have a lot in common. She told me she knew Kim liked to camp and compete in triathlons. I vaguely remembered Kim as a cheerleader who had graduated from Onsted a couple of years ahead of us. As we walked down the hall to Eric's classroom, Deb introduced me to Kim, who was standing outside her classroom.

Kim and I began dating. On our first date, I remember saying to her that I had heard she liked to camp; she replied that she did, and she even had her own gear, including a 4x4 pickup and a Doberman Pincher dog. When I brought up triathlons, she listed several she had completed and one in which she had medaled. She appeared to be the real deal, not pretending, like other women I had dated.

While Kim had no children of her own, as a second grade school teacher, she liked kids. Deb was right; we did have a lot in common. As the months passed, our relationship developed, and although she had a home of her own, she came to live with us that autumn.

72) Pervert

Part of my duties as a midnight desk sergeant was to review the open cases and keep them moving forward to closure. One of those cases was an unsolved sexual assault that had occurred in June, 1986.

In that incident, a nine-year-old girl and her seven-year-old sister had been walking down a country road to a neighbor's house to play when a gray sports car drove past them. When they got to the next intersection, they saw the same car had turned and parked.

As they began to walk by the car, a naked man stepped out, wearing only shoes and socks, and fondling his penis. While the nude man allowed the seven year old to pass by, he stood in the way of the nine year old, asking, "Where does Kathy live? She is sixteen and I have sex with her."

The nine-year-old girl cried, "Don't hurt me," to which he replied, "I won't; I just want to see your cunt." The girl turned and ran away screaming, with her sister watching and screaming from afar. The pervert chased her, knocked her to the ground, and pulled her shorts down, exposing her crotch. He then touched her vagina with his fingers. As the girl struggled to get away, he threatened to hurt her worse. Suddenly, the pervert ran back to his car and drove away.

While the trooper had done the basic investigation, which had identified a strong suspect, he had been confronted with obstacles he had been unable to overcome. The primary obstacle was a legal one, surrounding an Appellate Court decision, which ruled that current law did not allow the government to force a person to stand in a corporeal (live) line-up unless he was in legal custody. The trooper had done a photographic line-up, which had resulted in a tentative identification, not positive, and the prosecutor would not charge on those merits.

The suspect, Ronald Gene Bowers, resided in the Lansing area and had a long history of sexual deviance, supposedly the longest in the MSP sex motivated crime database at that time. I was not about to allow this case to be closed without first adapting, improvising, and hopefully, overcoming these obstacles.

In December 1987, I began brainstorming with the trooper in search of an angle that might solve the case, but his attitude suggested that he believed it a lost cause. Each month during case review, I would renew the discussion, but he thought every idea I had was a bad one. Unable to get him to take the initiative, I made a list of probes for him to undertake. The next month, when the case came back up for review, no action had been logged, so I asked the trooper what he had done. He said he had tried all the probes and they hadn't worked out. When I asked why he had not documented his efforts in a supplementary report, he replied that he thought it a waste of time. When I asked for the list of probes I had given him, he said he had discarded it. In May 1988, he submitted a supplementary report to close the case.

Vince Lombardi once said, "Luck is where ability and opportunity meet." Ralph Waldo Emerson said, "Nothing great was ever achieved without enthusiasm." Of the three ingredients of ability, opportunity, and enthusiasm, it was apparent this trooper lacked enthusiasm. His lack of initiative made me sick, and yet I had learned that you can't make a trooper solve a mystery he doesn't want to.

I presented the trooper's closing supplementary report to Lieutenant Thomas Finco, now the Jonesville post commander, and I requested the case be reassigned to me. Normally, a case is investigated by a trooper or detective sergeant, but this trooper lacked case initiative, and no detective sergeant was assigned to the Jonesville Post. While not usually part of a sergeant's job description, Lieutenant Finco, formerly a detective, granted my request.

On the trooper's supplementary report, I used liquid paper to white-out where the other trooper had typed "FINAL DISPOSITON: Closed" and typed "STATUS: Open, pending further investigation by Sgt. Edwards." While I had failed to mentor the trooper into solving the case, I was enthusiastic about doing part-time what I hoped to do full-time someday—investigations.

I recreated the list of probes and then followed my own direction. It soon became apparent the trooper had not completed the list. In the end this case, like most, would echo, "When discovered, solutions are often simple. It is the perseverance to discover the simple solution that is difficult." I will spare you all the dead-end probes and the revealing of circumstantial evidence that this investigation would entail and fast forward you to the "game breaker."

I discovered that the Brighton Post of the Michigan State Police and the Jackson County Sheriff's Department held outstanding misdemeanor warrants for Ronald Bowers, who was a fugitive. I contacted the officers in charge of these cases and explained the legal dilemma. Then I asked them to attach a note to the face of their warrants, instructing the arresting officer, whoever he might be, to contact me immediately when Bowers was arrested. My goal was to conduct a corporeal line-up on my case before he was released on bond on their misdemeanor warrants.

The prosecutor endorsed this tactic. I briefed the girls' mother on our plan and explained to her what to expect when it came time for the girls to attend a corporeal line-up. I warned them that we might not have much notice. We would wait a month before we received word of the arrest of Bowers. It was August 9, 1988 when I was notified that Bowers was in the Livingston County jail.

While Trooper Scott Reinacher of the Brighton Post arranged the corporeal line-up, I arranged for an attorney to be retained to represent the legal interests of Bower at the line-up and the transportation of the witnesses from Hillsdale to Howell.

On August 11, 1988, over two-years after the crime was committed, Ronald Bowers stood in a corporeal line-up before now eleven- and nine-year-old girls. He stood alongside five similarly appearing males. The sisters viewed the line-up separately and were not aware of each other's findings until the line-up was over. The victim was unable to make identification, but her younger sister, who had witnessed the assault, made a positive identification of Ronald Bowers. Bingo!

On September 27, 1988, Ronald Bowers was arraigned in Hillsdale County on felony charges of Criminal Sexual Conduct. Michael Smith was appointed as his attorney. The matter did not go to trial until after the first of the year, by which time, Michael Smith had been elected as prosecutor. Because of this legal conflict of interest, the Branch County Prosecutor, John Livesay, was appointed to act as prosecutor in this trial.

Man charged with CSC

9/28/88

JONESVILLE — A Lansing man was arrested Tuesday for second degree criminal sexual conduct by state police of the Jonesville post following a 27-month long investigation.

Ronald G. Bowers, 47, was arrested for the 15-year felony, troopers report.

Bowers allegedly assaulted a nine-year-old girl on a rural road in Jefferson Township on June 17, 1986, according to the state police.

After being arraigned in District Court, Bowers was remanded to the Hillsdale County Jail in lieu of ~75,000 bond. *HILLSDALE NEWS*

Compliments of *Hillsdale Daily News*

The trial was before Judge Harvey Moes. During the trial, the prosecutor called his star witness, a young girl, to the stand. Looking down, she timidly described what had happened that horrific day. He then asked her whether the man who assaulted her was in the courtroom. Without looking up, she said, "No." I concealed a gasp!

Calmly, John Livesay called the victim by her first name and asked her to look up. Pointing first to the left side of the courtroom, and working to the right, he directed her to look at each and every person in the courtroom, and then he again asked her whether the man who had assaulted her was in the courtroom. Again looking down, she nodded her head, "Yes." He then asked her to point at that man. She looked up and pointed directly at Ronald Bowers. Victim turns victor!

At the end of the trial, Ronald Bowers was convicted as charged and given a long prison sentence. This case was used to illustrate to the legislature why a law was needed to empower the government to force a person to stand in a corporeal line-up short of being charged. That law was eventually passed.

> *Nothing in the world can take the place of persistence. Talent will not; nothing is more common than unsuccessful men with talent. Genius will not; unrewarded genius is almost a proverb. Education alone will not; the world is full of educated derelicts. Persistence and determination alone are omnipotent.*
>
> — Calvin Coolidge

73) Change

It seemed such a waste of manpower to have a midnight desk sergeant, whose duties were normally completed in two hours, opposed to not having a detective sergeant. In May 1988, I began to author a series of memorandums to district headquarters suggesting the midnight desk sergeant position be changed to detective sergeant. It was a time when technology was on the brink of allowing phone calls, radio traffic, and alarms to be forwarded to other venues. It was also the onset of an era of budget constraints when the department would be forced to become more operationally efficient and realize it could not be all things to all people. While I hoped to be that detective sergeant, my motives were not entirely

238 ~ PATHS CROSSED   Villains - Victims - Victors

self-serving. Traditions and institutions change slowly, and I transferred before my suggestion became a reality.

MEMORANDUM

JONESVILLE POST

DEPARTMENT OF STATE POLICE

DATE : May 23, 1988

TO   : Inspector Sherman Ampey

FROM   : Sgt. Clifton L. Edwards #400, Jonesville Post

SUBJECT : Proposed change of duties of mid-night shift commander at MSP 45

Undersigned officer has been the mid night shift commander at the Jonesville Post since November of 1987. With this experience, I feel a duty to bring to your attention what I believe is inefficent utilization of allotted personnel and suggest some ideas how that position could be used more efficently to promote MSP services.

It is my contention that the current duties of that position do not make efficient use of personnel, nor is it rewarding or challenging to the individual. As you know, the Jonesville Post is a minimally staffed Post that is currently unable to provide 24 hour coverage. Often times the Post is short personnel resources needed to properly complete the Departments mission. I believe reapplication of the duties of this position would be advantageous to the Departments objectives and make for a more challenging and rewarding position.

Normal "in house" supervisory responsibilities can be completed in less the two hours. Those responsibilities do not necessarily have to be completed during the mid-night shift. Other duties are of clerical nature and could be performed by current civilian clerical staff.

In addition to MSP 45 dispatch responsibilities, the Jonesville Post also provides those services for Jonesville P. D. and Litchfield P. D. Even with those added duties, telephone calls received requesting police services average about three calls a night and LEIN traffic is minimal. Walk in traffic to the Jonesville Post during the mid-night shift probably averages about 5 times a week with the majority of them being truck drivers asking directions. Utilization of current technology could enable us to direct telephone, radio, and LEIN traffic to MSP 43 during the midnight shift. Recent discussions with mid-night sergeants at the Coldwater Post indicate that this added telephone/radio/LEIN traffic would not overburden them.

MSP 45 is within the City of limits of Jonesville which staffs a 24 hr police department. J.P.D. officers could promptly respond to any emergencies that originated from the installed "hot-line" at the front door of the Post and could provide Post security.

I would propose that this position be utilized in one of two areas of responsibilities:

1. Serving as a road supervisor between the Coldwater Post, Jonesville Post, and Adrian Post. He could provide relief at Posts 42 & 43, enabling those sergeants to periodically go on the road to supervise, train, evaluate their personnel and promote departmental relations with the mid-night staff of police departments in their respective post areas. More prompt supervisory response could be made to major crime and accident scenes and he could fill in on sick calls, reducing overtime expenditures and maintaining MSP patrols.

   Such an action would be in line with the departments goals of sergeant role enhancement and not require the back filling of civilian staff.

2. Change it to a detective sergeant position. The Post would certainly benefit in the quality and depth of its criminal investigations.

Implementaion of such changes would require the department to overcome many obstacles, such as equipment purchases, political ramifications, and association opposition. I believe the benefits would be in enhanced MSP services at little or no additional expense.

I stand eager to further research or assist in implementaion of such a concept.

Respectfully submitted,

Sgt. Clifton L. Edwards

74) Hope

The Ypsilanti Post was nearly an equal distance from my home as the Jonesville Post and it had a desk sergeant vacancy. It also had six detective sergeants, one of whom was slated to retire within six months. In December 1988, I filled that desk sergeant vacancy at Ypsilanti in hopes of getting the retiring detective sergeant's position in the coming months. I was assigned to day shift, reminiscent of the business of the Detroit Post.

Having trooped at the Ypsilanti Post, I would now be supervising some troopers with whom I had previously partnered. This predicament is one that smaller agencies regularly deal with, but the state police usually avoid it by transferring you upon promotion. I was kind of a boomerang.

One duty of the day shift sergeant is to authorize court overtime. The department had taken a position that for a trooper to get court overtime, he must appear. One day, a trooper whom I had once partnered with presented me with his subpoena and request for two hours of court overtime. I knew he had not attended court so I questioned him on it. He said he had been on telephone standby at home. I reminded him of the policy and refused to authorize the overtime. He was not happy and vowed to get the overtime back one way or the other. I told him that was on him, but this was on me, and for me to make an exception to the rule would not be fair to his colleagues. It was a hard call—part of the fun of being a mid-level manager.

The post commander was now Lieutenant Garry Kregelka, who had been a detective sergeant at the Ypsilanti Post when I trooped there. The senior desk sergeant was Ray Beamish, whom I had trooped for at Ypsilanti and admired greatly. Like me, the other desk sergeants were young.

Soon after arriving at Ypsilanti, Lieutenant Kregelka held a staff meeting where we brainstormed how to make the Ypsilanti Post more efficient and effective. As the post commander directed a round table discussion, each new sergeant offered what he believed new ideas as Sergeant Beamish took notes. Sergeant Beamish was the last to address the group.

He opened with a phrase from the biblical book of Ecclesiastes, "There is nothing new under the sun." He then spoke to the supposed new ideas one by one, providing time and place where they had been previously tried and their outcome, which was usually abandonment. Sergeant Beamish was not a pessimist; he was a wise realist, and his expressed experience prevented us from wasting time and effort. I have witnessed this redundancy in many institutions.

75) Traffic

As a state police agency, opposed to a highway patrol, we responded to all criminal complaints outside of an incorporated city. The Ypsilanti Post area encompassed most of Washtenaw County, whose population exceeded 300,000, and some townships in Wayne County. Combined, this population was nearly equal to that of the state of Wyoming. The demand for services this population generated had caused the Ypsilanti Post to neglect its traffic safety responsibilities. We could not forget that, as state police, we still held highway patrol responsibilities, and whether a citizen was murdered or killed in a crash, dead was dead.

While the Jonesville Post had no freeways, four different freeways were in the Ypsilanti Post's area. To get our services back in balance, Lieutenant Kregelka assigned me three troopers whose primary duties would be Freeway Traffic Enforcement (FTE). As their supervisor, I was to create and implement a plan to make the freeways safer. I referred to these troopers as the FTE Team.

Once we had devised our plan, a part of implementation was Public Information & Education, known as P.I.E. While my troopers did the work, I became the PIE "talking head."

The stratagems implemented were:

- Operation Wolfpack—where an unmarked car equipped with radar will clock speeding vehicles and radio ahead to other troopers.

- Operation VASCAR (vehicle average speed computed and recorded)—which involved using a past generation speed detection device immune to radar detectors.

- Operation Big Bird—where speeders are clocked by aircraft.

- Operation Pace Car—where marked patrol cars travel the freeways at the speed limit during rush hour traffic, ticketing anyone who passed them.

- Operation Scarecrow—in which civilian volunteers parked unoccupied patrol cars on the freeway.

It was not long after we implemented Operation Pace Car that I was ordered to abandon it, being told that members of the state legislature were complaining that it was causing citizens to be late for work. I must admit this directive troubled me. Were they serious? Shouldn't people just be responsible by leaving on time so they did not have to rely on speeding to make up the difference?

This I know—just as there will always be criminals, there also will always be traffic violators. As police officers in a free society, sometimes referred to as the "thin blue line," our goal must be to keep the populace reasonably safe and secure.

These officers are Operation Wolfpack. From left to right, Steve Farrell, Darrell Dixson and Lorenzo Veal.

SLOWDOWN TEAMS: WHAT THEY ARE AND HOW THEY WORK

The Enforcement Team is operating five programs. It is being closely monitored for success by other state police posts around the state. The programs include:

■ **Operation Wolfpack,** in which an unmarked car equipped with radar parks along the expressway and targets speeders or careless drivers, then radioes ahead to marked cars, who pull the drivers over. It targets "professional speeders," who consistently travel 15 mph or more over the speed limit and use radar detectors.

■ **Operation Slowdown,** in which pairs of marked cars travel at or below posted speeds during rush hour, encouraging motorists to travel at the same speeds.

■ **Operation Vascar,** which targets truckers with a speed determination system not detectable by radar detectors.

■ **Operation Big Bird,** which utilizes a helicopter to catch "professional speeders."

■ **Operation Scarecrow,** in which a vacant marked car equipped with radar is parked at areas heavily traveled by speeders.

Ann Arbor News   4/9/89

Compliments of *Ann Arbor News.*

76) Quest

In late April 1989, Detective Sergeant Jack Beeson of the Ypsilanti Post announced his retirement. I wanted his spot so badly I could taste it. About that time, I got an offer from Detective Lieutenant Tim Ryan to serve as a district detective sergeant in Jackson, which was also a commutable distance from my home. Being within commutable distance was imperative for me since I had promised my boys they would not have to change schools again. Ironically, Ryan was one of the detectives who worked on the Howard Stoker murder back in 1972 (see Part I: Howie).

Ryan granted me a couple of days to think about it. During that time, I attempted to contact Lieutenant Kregelka, who was attending the F.B.I. academy near Washington D.C. I wanted reassurance that I would get Beeson's spot when he retired. He never returned my call. Consequently, I accepted the position offered by Ryan. It turned out to be one of the best decisions of my career. The work would prove challenging and rewarding, while it usually spared me shift and weekend work, allowing me more easily be a dad to my sons. It was two years to the month since I had been promoted, and I had adhered to my vow not to be a desk sergeant any longer than that. At the time, being a desk sergeant had seemed an eternity. In retrospect, it was a great education in a short period of time.

My brother always says, "You only know what you know." When I reported to Jackson as a detective sergeant, I thought I was an ace investigator. I soon realized I had a lot to learn.

To be continued....

The master in the art of living makes little distinction between his work and play, his labor and his leisure, his mind and his body, his information and his recreation, his love and his religion. He hardly knows which is which. He simply pursues his vision of excellence at whatever he does, leaving others to decide whether he is working or playing. To him he's always doing both. — James A. Michener

Afterword

More of an officer's time is mundane than not, especially if you allow it to be. The splendor of the job is that when you work the hardest, it is the most rewarding and time flies. I prefer being busy to the opposite.

Booker T. Washington wrote, "Excellence is to do a common thing in an uncommon way." I have often shared this quote with junior officers. It frustrates me to hear a patrol officer say there is "nothing going on." You must always believe "criminality is afoot," and if you can't find it, you need to change tactics. Another pet peeve of mine is when I hear an officer is dispatched to "take a report." I don't take reports; I conduct investigations, which I report. Attitude and perspective are so powerful in whatever we do.

In Paths Crossed, I have shared a few of the interesting incidents from the first half of my career in the MSP's uniform services division; many have lessons the general public and future police officers can learn from. During this time, I evolved from student to service officer, to trooper, to dog handler, and lastly to sergeant.

The function of patrol would be absent from the second half of my remaining MSP career, which I served in the investigative services division. In Paths Crossed II, I will share my experiences as a district detective sergeant, an undercover detective sergeant, a post detective sergeant, and as a detective lieutenant where I led a multi-jurisdictional drug team. The stage for many of my investigations was already set and patiently awaiting my arrival. Unfortunately, I too would leave behind some unsolved cases to await solution.

While not flawless, the Michigan State Police strives to uphold its motto: "A Proud Tradition of Service through Excellence, Integrity, and Courtesy." I am proud to have been one of them!

Clifton L. Edwards
www.pathscrossed.info

Copyright Permission

Many stories in *Paths Crossed* are authenticated by newspaper articles. For them to be included in the book necessitated me to contact the representatives of those newspapers to request permission. Without exception, these Ladies and Gentlemen have been most gracious in granting permission to include the works of their respective companies. I extend my appreciation to:

- President Danny Gaydou and Executive Assistant Sally Loftis of Mlive Media Group representing the *Ypsilanti Press*, *Ann Arbor News*, *Kalamazoo Gazette*, *Saginaw News*, and *Lansing Journal*.
- Associate Editor Sara Scott representing the *Jackson Citizen Patriot*.
- Executive Assistant Jody Williams of A Gannett Co. representing the *Detroit Free Press*.
- General Manager & Executive Editor Richard Perlberg representing the *Livingston Daily News*.
- Managing Editor Donald Nauss representing the *Detroit News*.
- Managing Editor Dennis A. Setter representing the *Romeo Observer*.
- General Manager Chris Troszak representing the *Advisor Newspaper*.
- Permissions Manager Omar Sofradzija representing the *The State News.*

Sincerely,
Clifton L. Edwards

Acknowledgments

THANK-YOU to the below persons who have
contributed immensely to my writing of
Paths Crossed.

To my family -
Mother & Step-Father, Sister & Brother-in-Law, Brother & Sister-
In-Law, my Sons, and Father & Step-Mother.

To these friends –
Deborah, Kay, and Nancy.

To the critical reviewers -
Craig Medon, Nicholas Meier, Ruth Weber, Cindi Agge,
Howard Swabash, Francis Ridge, Travis Fletcher,
Kaitlyn LaClear, Samone Harper, Nickolas A. Leslie,
Kevin King, George Erickson, and Mary Lois Sanders

Special mention
To these three who gave so much of their own time –

- My Mother, whose patient encouragement and candid suggestions restarted this project many times.
- My Friend, Nick, whom I happened to cross paths with on Isle Royale and for reasons unknown, but for I am immensely thankful, has provided me unending assistance in this project.
- My Friend, Craig, whom I unknowingly inspired when he was a 15-year old explorer scout, who later became an outstanding police officer and family man, and then donated so much time to this book while himself immersed in the busiest time of life.

With Gratitude, *Clifton L. Edwards*

About the Author

Clifton L. Edwards' professional life has been in law enforcement. He was recruited into the Michigan State Police at the age of eighteen. During his nearly twenty-seven year career, he thrived on the training and experiences provided by this fine department, while striving to make his mark.

The first half of Clif's career was served in the Uniform Services Division, primarily as a trooper. Serving between six posts, he was a field training officer for five rookies, assigned to an undercover team, and served as an advanced accident investigator, a dog handler, and a shift supervisor. He earned four Professional Excellence Awards and two Letters of Commendations for investigations he conducted.

The second half of Clif's career was served in the Investigative Services Division as a detective. He assisted police departments across a nine county area, managed major crime task forces, conducted both sensitive & cold-case investigations, was a street supervisor/operative for an undercover drug enforcement team, and served as a post detective. As a Detective Sergeant, Clif earned three Meritorious Awards: one for solving a serial kidnapper/rapist case, one for solving an organized crime case, and the last for solving a fifteen-year old murder case. He was twice nominated trooper of the year. Clif was then promoted to Detective Lieutenant to command a multi-jurisdictional drug enforcement team. This position is the highest rank in the MSP hierarchy where enforcement duties are part of the job description. During this period, Clif taught a variety of investigative classes in the academy. At age forty-five, he retired from the Michigan State Police.

At age forty-seven, Clif graduated from the National Park Service Seasonal Law Enforcement Ranger Academy, Wildland Fire Fighter Training, and Emergency Medical Technician Training. He now serves proudly as a Protection Ranger for the National Park Service, where the core skills he employs are law enforcement, emergency medical service, wildland firefighting, and search and rescue. He also provides training to his fellow rangers on investigations and officer survival. He has served at Isle Royale National Park, Everglades National Park, and Pictured Rocks National Lakeshore.

Clif is a proud father and grandfather.

Visit Clif at www.pathscrossed.info for speaking engagements, email him at pathscrossed@ymail.com.

PATHS CROSSED
Series
Narrative nonfiction vignettes of a peace officer as lived by Clif Edwards

Book 1
Villains-Victims-Victors
Experiences as a Michigan State Police Trooper

Book 2
A Closer Look
Challenges as a Michigan State Police Detective

Book 3
Protecting National Parks
Adventures as a National Park Service Ranger

Villains-Victims-Victors and *Protecting National Parks* are available through Amazon.
A Closer Look is currently pending publication.

For a reduced price for purchases of multiple copies, email: pathscrossed@ymail.com.